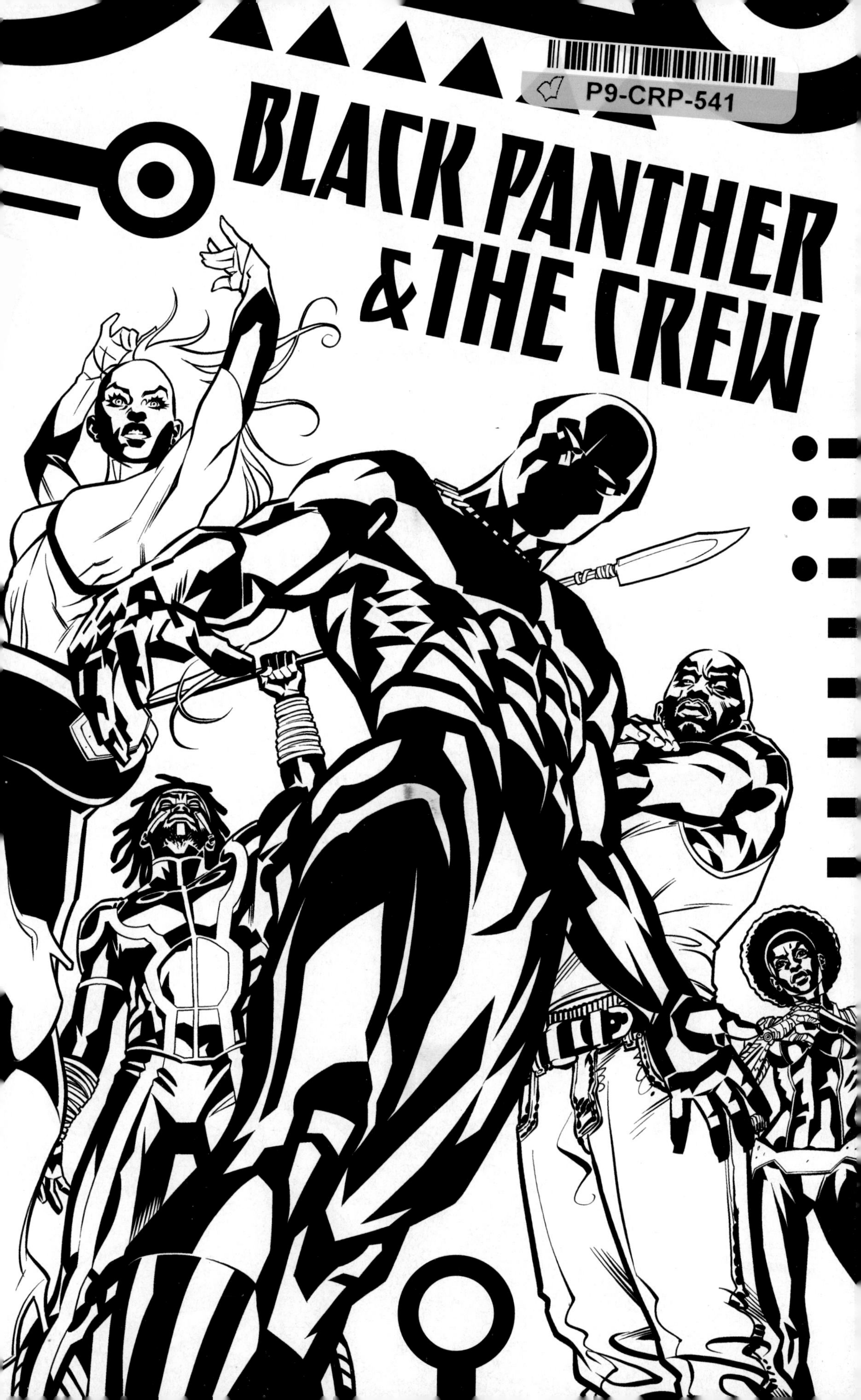
BLACK PANTHER
& THE CREW

BLACK PANTH...

WE ARE THE STREETS

Writers/**Ta-Nehisi Coates** (#1-6) and **Yona Harvey** (#2, #4, #6)

Pencilers/**Butch Guice** with **Mack Chater** (#2-3, #5-6) & **Stephen Thompson** (#5)

Inkers/**Scott Hanna** with **Mack Chater** (#2-3, #5-6) & **Stephen Thompson** (#5)

Colorists/**Dan Brown** with **Paul Mounts** (#5)

Cover Art/**John Cassaday** with **Laura Martin** (#1-2), **Dan Brown** (#3) & **Paul Mounts** (#4-6)

Letterer/**VC's Joe Sabino**

R & THE CREW

The Crew is a team of super heroes that has come together specifically to deal with problems that afflict the community they come from or have come to be allied with. Recently they helped Black Panther stop a wave of suicide bombers in Wakanda, but that wasn't the first time the team came together. The origin of the Crew begins in the streets of **Harlem...**

Special Thanks/**Brian Stelfreeze &
Rian Hughes**

Logo Design/**Rian Hughes**

Assistant Editor/**Charles Beacham**

Associate Editor/**Sarah Brunstad**

Editor/**Wil Moss**

Executive Editor/**Tom Brevoort**

COLLECTION EDITOR/**JENNIFER GRÜNWALD**

ASSISANT EDITOR/**CAITLIN O'CONNELL**

ASSOCIATE MANAGING EDITOR/**KATERI WOODY**

EDITOR, SPECIAL PROJECTS/**MARK D. BEAZLEY**

VP PRODUCTION & SPECIAL PROJECTS/**JEFF YOUNGQUIST**

SVP PRINT, SALES & MARKETING/**DAVID GABRIEL**

BOOK DESIGNERS/**ADAM DEL RE & MANNY MEDEROS**

EDITOR IN CHIEF/**AXEL ALONSO**

CHIEF CREATIVE OFFICER/**JOE QUESADA**

PRESIDENT/**DAN BUCKLEY**

EXECUTIVE PRODUCER/**ALAN FINE**

BLACK PANTHER CREATED BY **STAN LEE** & **JACK KIRBY**

BLACK PANTHER AND THE CREW: WE ARE THE STREETS. Contains material originally published in magazine form as BLACK PANTHER AND THE CREW #1-6. First printing 2017. ISBN# 978-1-302-90832-4. Published by MARVEL WORLDWIDE, INC., a subsidiary of MARVEL ENTERTAINMENT, LLC. OFFICE OF PUBLICATION: 135 West 50th Street, New York, NY 10020. Copyright © 2017 MARVEL. No similarity between any of the names, characters, persons, and/or institutions in this magazine with those of any living or dead person or institution is intended, and any such similarity which may exist is purely coincidental. **Printed in Canada.** DAN BUCKLEY, President, Marvel Entertainment; JOE QUESADA, Chief Creative Officer; TOM BREVOORT, SVP of Publishing; DAVID BOGART, SVP of Business Affairs & Operations, Publishing & Partnership; C.B. CEBULSKI, VP of Brand Management & Development, Asia; DAVID GABRIEL, SVP of Sales & Marketing, Publishing; JEFF YOUNGQUIST, VP of Production & Special Projects; DAN CARR, Executive Director of Publishing Technology; ALEX MORALES, Director of Publishing Operations; SUSAN CRESPI, Production Manager; STAN LEE, Chairman Emeritus. For information regarding advertising in Marvel Comics or on Marvel.com, please contact Vit DeBellis, Integrated Sales Manager, at vdebellis@marvel.com. For Marvel subscription inquiries, please call 888-511-5480. **Manufactured between 8/25/2017 and 9/26/2017 by SOLISCO PRINTERS, SCOTT, QC, CANADA.**

10 9 8 7 6 5 4 3 2 1

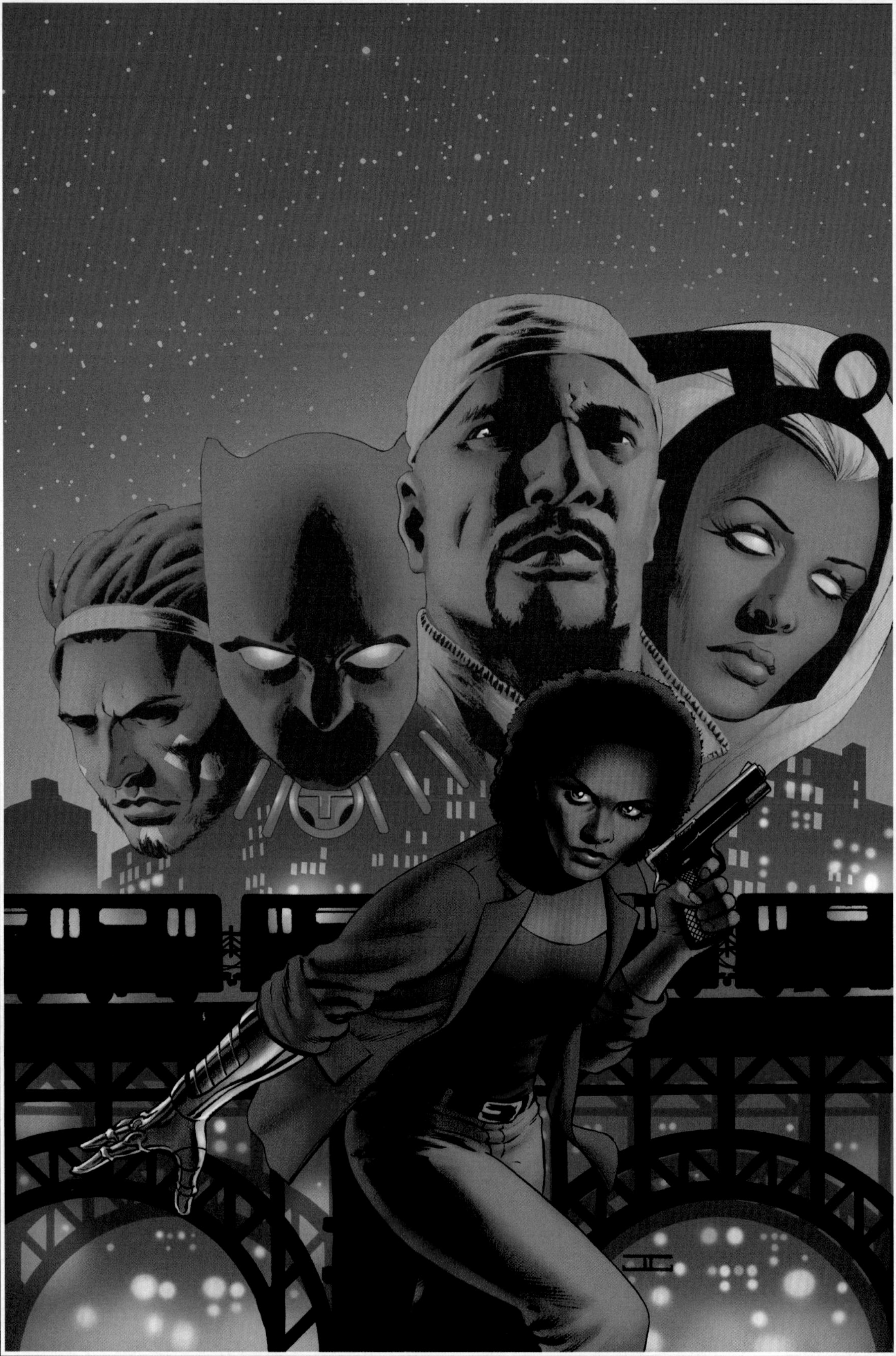

PART 1 DOUBLE CONSCIOUSNESS

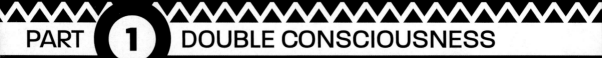

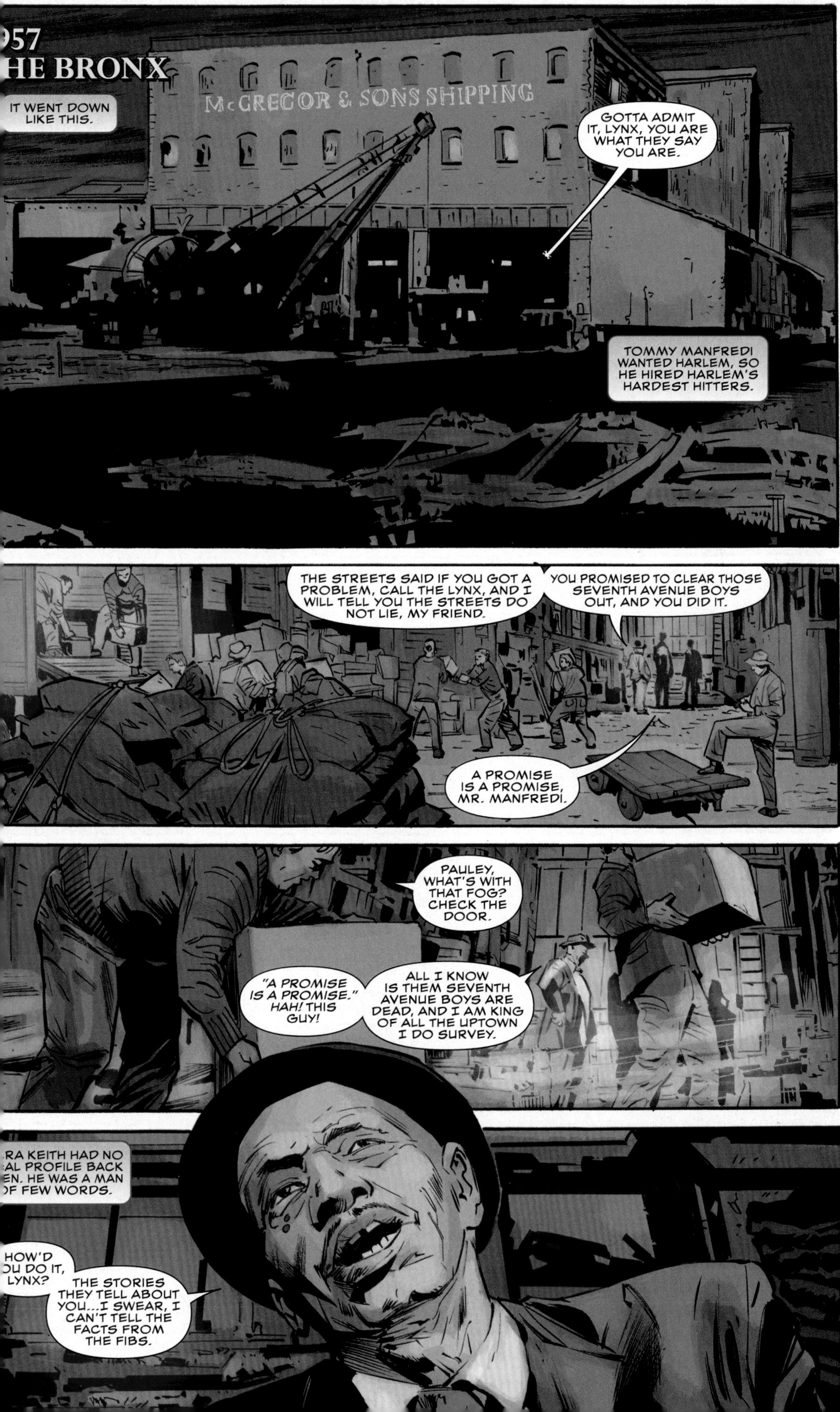

957
HE BRONX
M c GREGOR & SONS SHIPPING
IT WENT DOWN LIKE THIS.
GOTTA ADMIT IT, LYNX, YOU ARE WHAT THEY SAY YOU ARE.
TOMMY MANFREDI WANTED HARLEM, SO HE HIRED HARLEM'S HARDEST HITTERS.
THE STREETS SAID IF YOU GOT A PROBLEM, CALL THE LYNX, AND I WILL TELL YOU THE STREETS DO NOT LIE, MY FRIEND.
YOU PROMISED TO CLEAR THOSE SEVENTH AVENUE BOYS OUT, AND YOU DID IT.
A PROMISE IS A PROMISE, MR. MANFREDI.
PAULEY, WHAT'S WITH THAT FOG? CHECK THE DOOR.
"A PROMISE IS A PROMISE." HAH! THIS GUY!
ALL I KNOW IS THEM SEVENTH AVENUE BOYS ARE DEAD, AND I AM KING OF ALL THE UPTOWN I DO SURVEY.
RA KEITH HAD NO AL PROFILE BACK EN. HE WAS A MAN OF FEW WORDS.
HOW'D OU DO IT, LYNX?
THE STORIES THEY TELL ABOUT YOU...I SWEAR, I CAN'T TELL THE FACTS FROM THE FIBS.

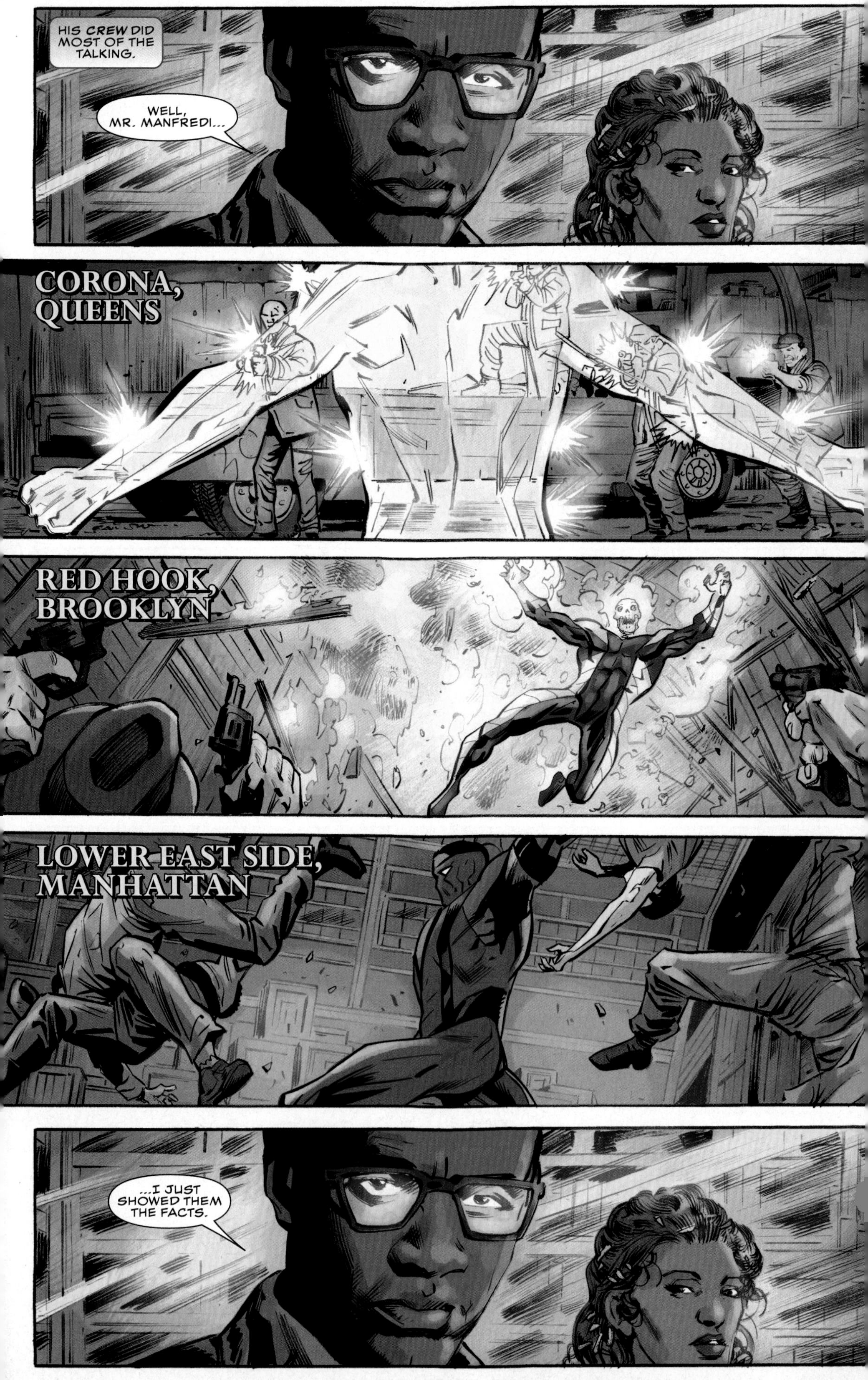
HIS CREW DID MOST OF THE TALKING.
WELL, MR. MANFREDI...
CORONA, QUEENS
RED HOOK, BROOKLYN
LOWER EAST SIDE, MANHATTAN
...I JUST SHOWED THEM THE FACTS.

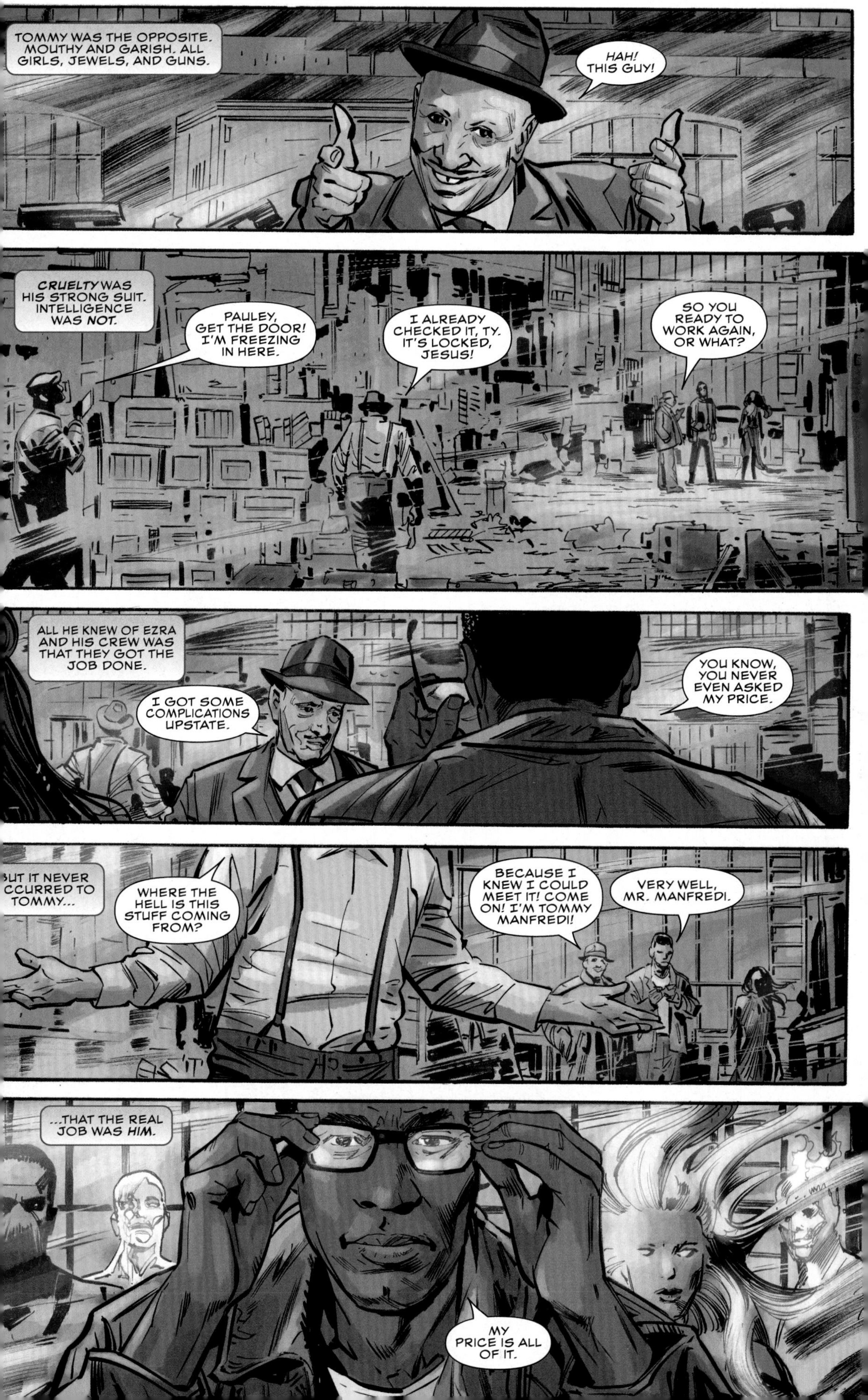
TOMMY WAS THE OPPOSITE. MOUTHY AND GARISH. ALL GIRLS, JEWELS, AND GUNS.
HAH! THIS GUY!
CRUELTY WAS HIS STRONG SUIT. INTELLIGENCE WAS NOT.
PAULEY, GET THE DOOR! I'M FREEZING IN HERE.
I ALREADY CHECKED IT, TY. IT'S LOCKED, JESUS!
SO YOU READY TO WORK AGAIN, OR WHAT?
ALL HE KNEW OF EZRA AND HIS CREW WAS THAT THEY GOT THE JOB DONE.
I GOT SOME COMPLICATIONS UPSTATE.
YOU KNOW, YOU NEVER EVEN ASKED MY PRICE.
UT IT NEVER CCURRED TO TOMMY...
WHERE THE HELL IS THIS STUFF COMING FROM?
BECAUSE I KNEW I COULD MEET IT! COME ON! I'M TOMMY MANFREDI!
VERY WELL, MR. MANFREDI.
...THAT THE REAL JOB WAS HIM.
MY PRICE IS ALL OF IT.

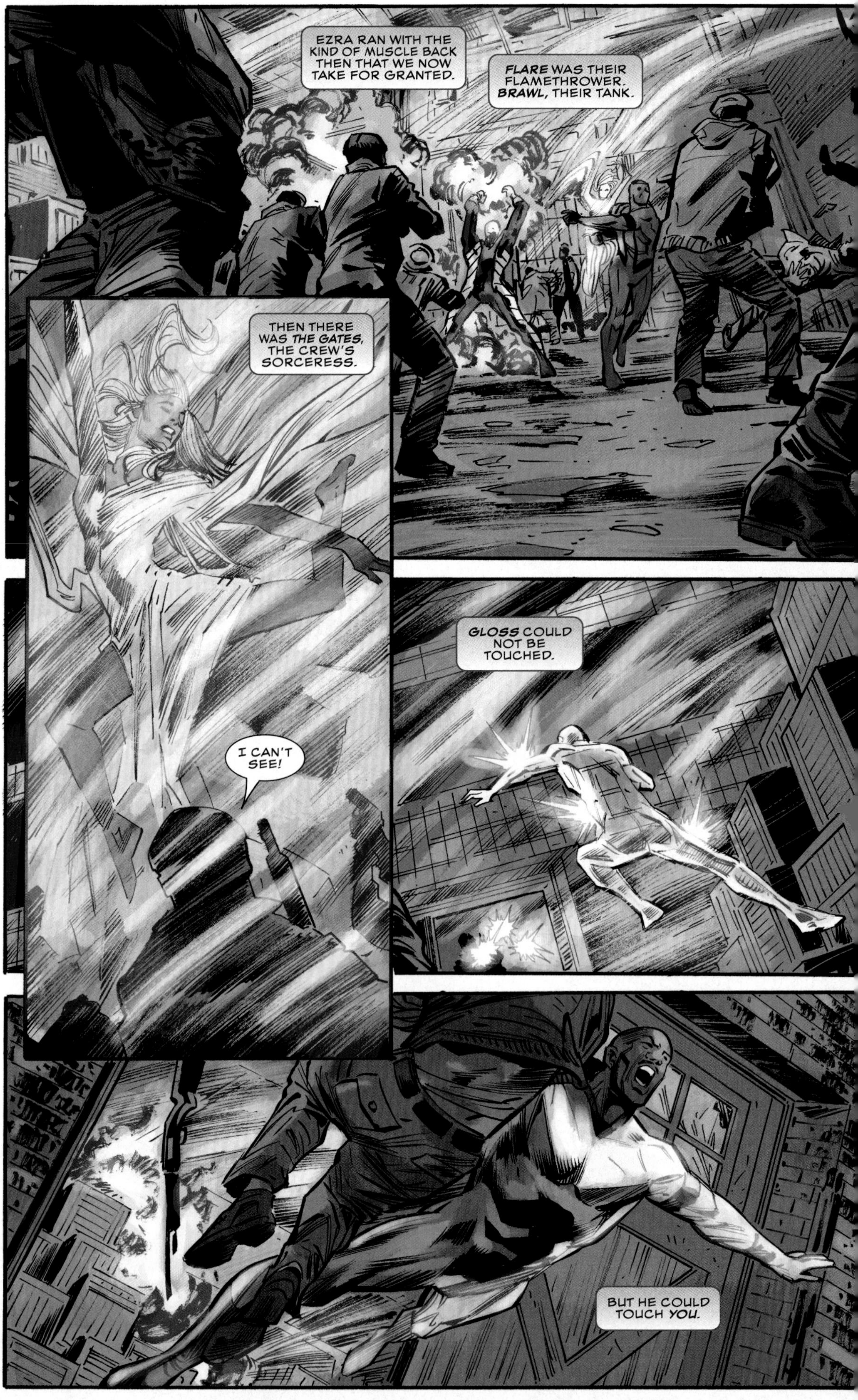
EZRA RAN WITH THE KIND OF MUSCLE BACK THEN THAT WE NOW TAKE FOR GRANTED.
FLARE WAS THEIR FLAMETHROWER. BRAWL, THEIR TANK.
THEN THERE WAS THE GATES, THE CREW'S SORCERESS.
I CAN'T SEE!
GLOSS COULD NOT BE TOUCHED.
BUT HE COULD TOUCH YOU.

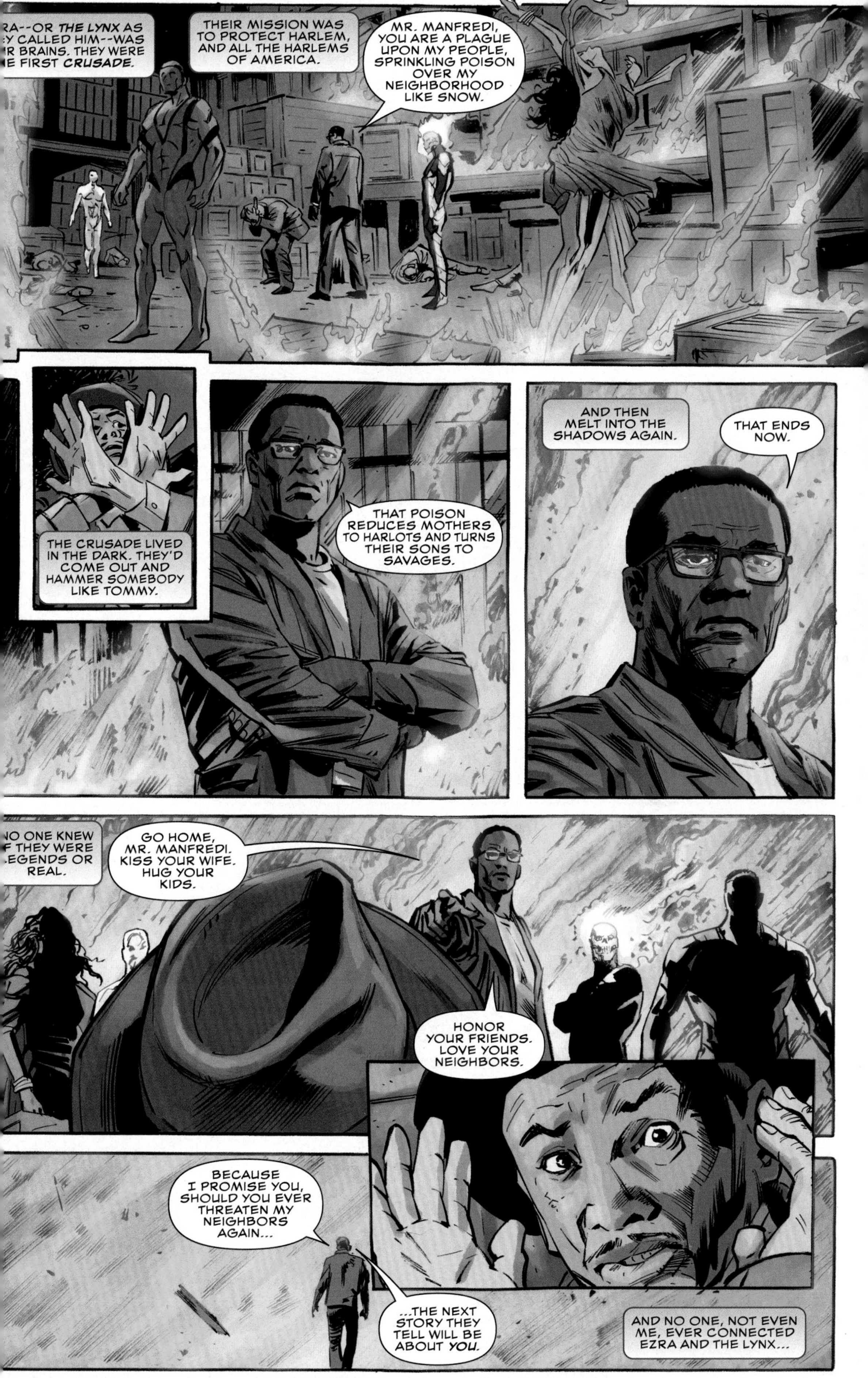

RA--OR THE LYNX AS
Y CALLED HIM--WAS
R BRAINS. THEY WERE
E FIRST CRUSADE.
THEIR MISSION WAS TO PROTECT HARLEM, AND ALL THE HARLEMS OF AMERICA.
MR. MANFREDI, YOU ARE A PLAGUE UPON MY PEOPLE, SPRINKLING POISON OVER MY NEIGHBORHOOD LIKE SNOW.
THE CRUSADE LIVED IN THE DARK. THEY'D COME OUT AND HAMMER SOMEBODY LIKE TOMMY.
THAT POISON REDUCES MOTHERS TO HARLOTS AND TURNS THEIR SONS TO SAVAGES.
AND THEN MELT INTO THE SHADOWS AGAIN.
THAT ENDS NOW.
NO ONE KNEW
F THEY WERE
EGENDS OR
REAL.
GO HOME, MR. MANFREDI. KISS YOUR WIFE. HUG YOUR KIDS.
HONOR YOUR FRIENDS. LOVE YOUR NEIGHBORS.
BECAUSE I PROMISE YOU, SHOULD YOU EVER THREATEN MY NEIGHBORS AGAIN...
...THE NEXT STORY THEY TELL WILL BE ABOUT YOU.
AND NO ONE, NOT EVEN ME, EVER CONNECTED EZRA AND THE LYNX...

...UNTIL LONG AFTER HE WAS DEAD.

JUSTICE FOR EZRA

JUSTICE

NO

BLACK LIVES

FOR EZRA

NO MORE KILLING

NO!

NO MORE...

NO POLICE

CAN'T REPAIR

I SHOULD HAVE MADE THE CONNECT.

BEFORE I WAS MISTY KNIGHT, BEFORE I WAS ANYTHING, I WAS POLICE.

POLICE

I KNEW EZRA, LIKE ANY OTHER POLICE, AS A COP-HATER WHO LIKED TO GET HIMSELF ARRESTED.

WE WERE BLIND TO HIS TRUE MOTIVATIONS, TO THE GHOSTS HE WAS CHASING.

KILLER COPS! WE KNOW Y'ALL MURKED EZRA!

GET A JOB, TYRONE.

POLICE

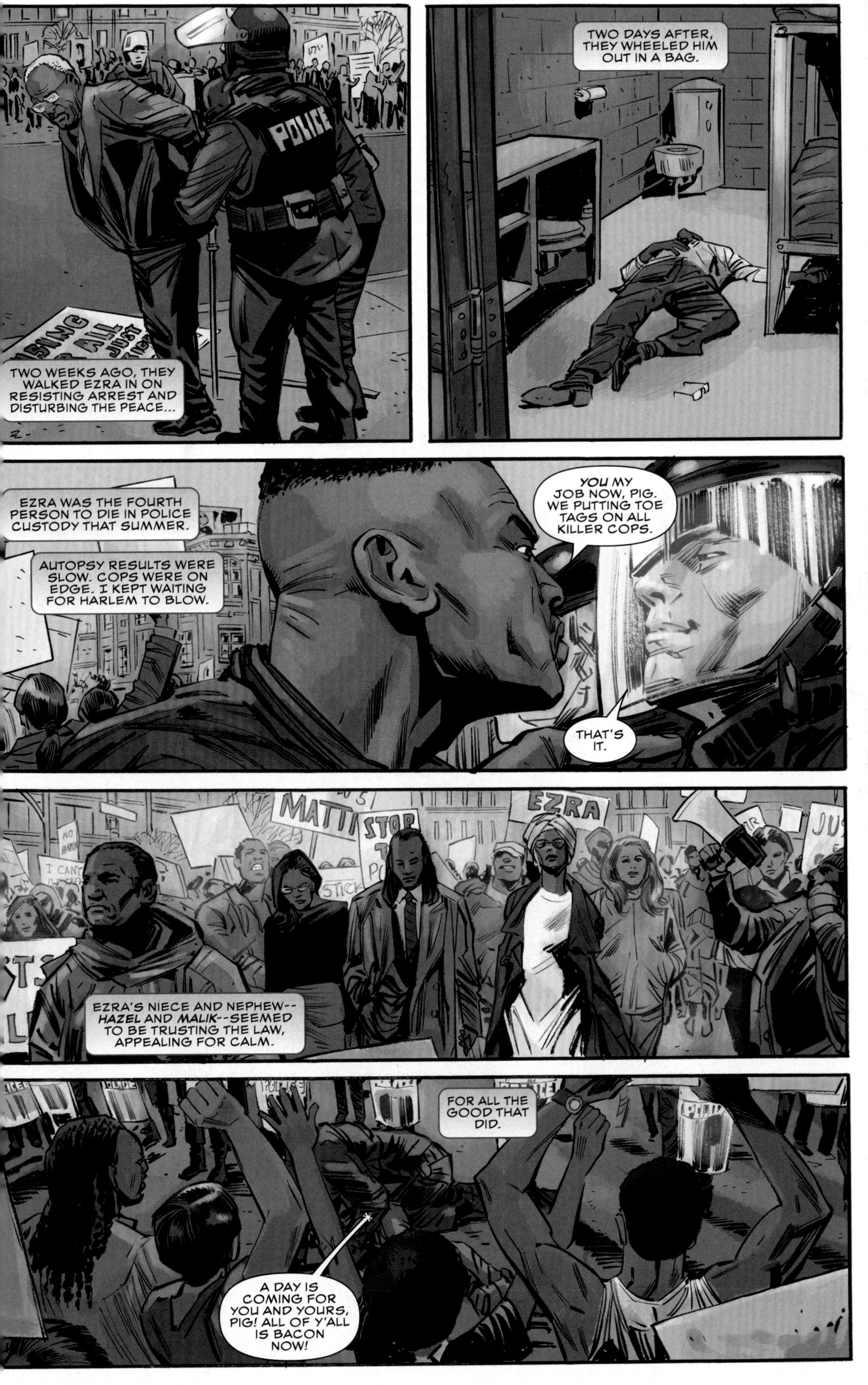
POLICE
TWO WEEKS AGO, THEY WALKED EZRA IN ON RESISTING ARREST AND DISTURBING THE PEACE...
TWO DAYS AFTER, THEY WHEELED HIM OUT IN A BAG.
EZRA WAS THE FOURTH PERSON TO DIE IN POLICE CUSTODY THAT SUMMER.
AUTOPSY RESULTS WERE SLOW. COPS WERE ON EDGE. I KEPT WAITING FOR HARLEM TO BLOW.
YOU MY JOB NOW, PIG. WE PUTTING TOE TAGS ON ALL KILLER COPS.
THAT'S IT.
EZRA
EZRA'S NIECE AND NEPHEW-- *HAZEL* AND *MALIK*--SEEMED TO BE TRUSTING THE LAW, APPEALING FOR CALM.
FOR ALL THE GOOD THAT DID.
A DAY IS COMING FOR YOU AND YOURS, PIG! ALL OF Y'ALL IS BACON NOW!

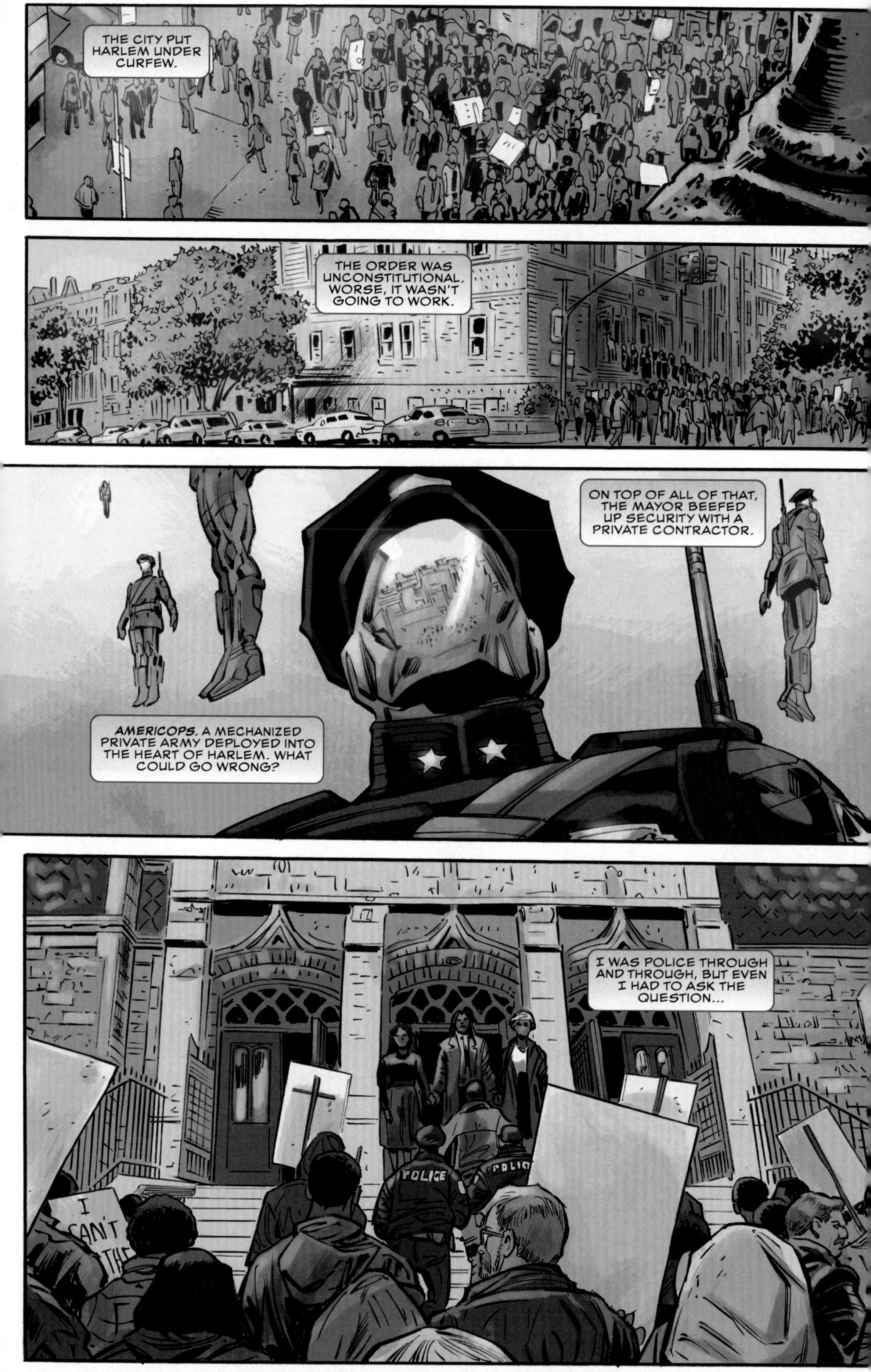
THE CITY PUT HARLEM UNDER CURFEW.
THE ORDER WAS UNCONSTITUTIONAL. WORSE, IT WASN'T GOING TO WORK.
ON TOP OF ALL OF THAT, THE MAYOR BEEFED UP SECURITY WITH A PRIVATE CONTRACTOR.
AMERICOPS. A MECHANIZED PRIVATE ARMY DEPLOYED INTO THE HEART OF HARLEM. WHAT COULD GO WRONG?
I WAS POLICE THROUGH AND THROUGH, BUT EVEN I HAD TO ASK THE QUESTION...
POLICE

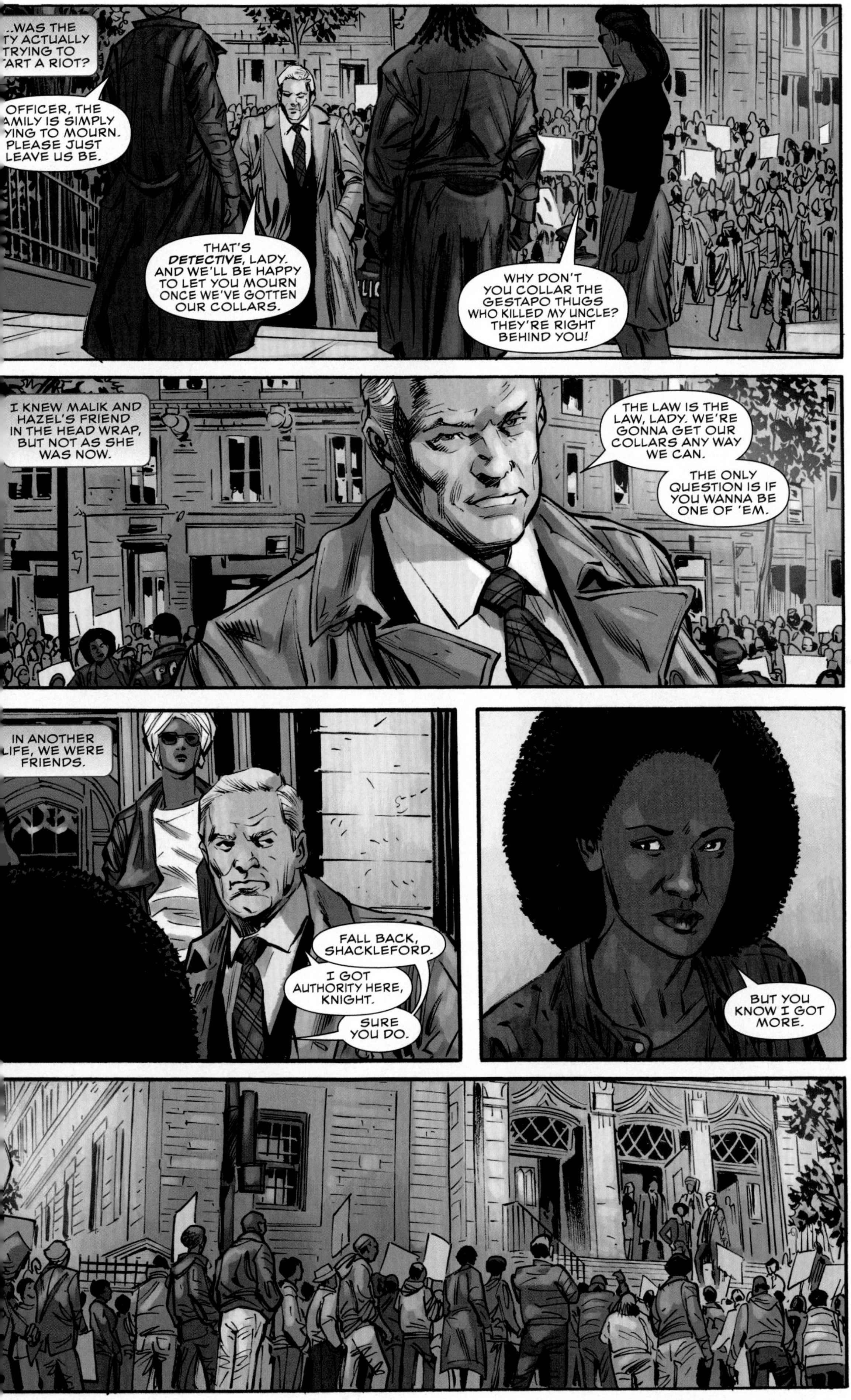
..WAS THE TY ACTUALLY TRYING TO ART A RIOT?
OFFICER, THE AMILY IS SIMPLY YING TO MOURN. PLEASE JUST LEAVE US BE.
THAT'S *DETECTIVE*, LADY. AND WE'LL BE HAPPY TO LET YOU MOURN ONCE WE'VE GOTTEN OUR COLLARS.
WHY DON'T YOU COLLAR THE GESTAPO THUGS WHO KILLED MY UNCLE? THEY'RE RIGHT BEHIND YOU!
I KNEW MALIK AND HAZEL'S FRIEND IN THE HEAD WRAP, BUT NOT AS SHE WAS NOW.
THE LAW IS THE LAW, LADY. WE'RE GONNA GET OUR COLLARS ANY WAY WE CAN.
THE ONLY QUESTION IS IF YOU WANNA BE ONE OF 'EM.
IN ANOTHER LIFE, WE WERE FRIENDS.
FALL BACK, SHACKLEFORD.
I GOT AUTHORITY HERE, KNIGHT.
SURE YOU DO.
BUT YOU KNOW I GOT MORE.

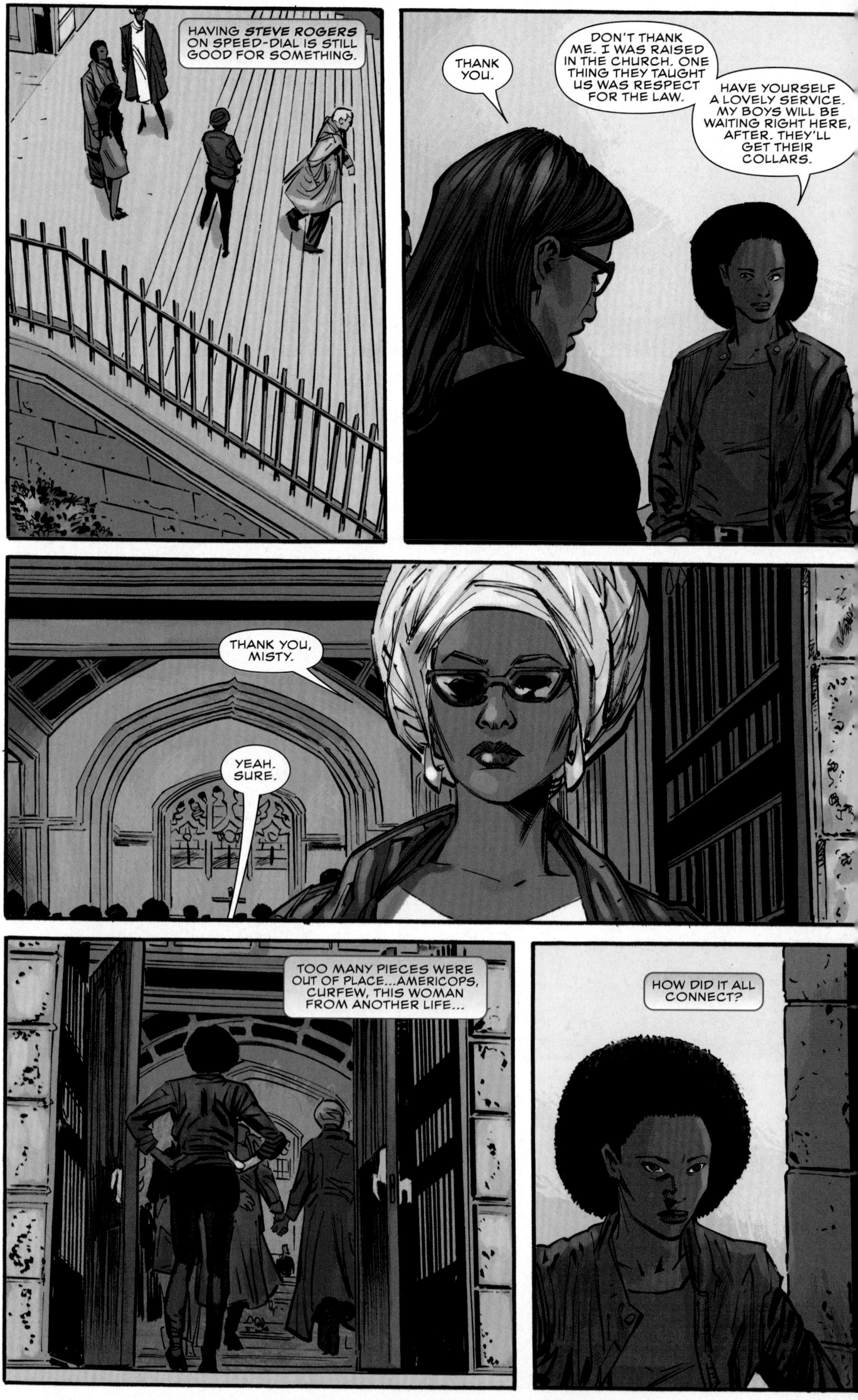
HAVING STEVE ROGERS ON SPEED-DIAL IS STILL GOOD FOR SOMETHING.
THANK YOU.
DON'T THANK ME. I WAS RAISED IN THE CHURCH. ONE THING THEY TAUGHT US WAS RESPECT FOR THE LAW.
HAVE YOURSELF A LOVELY SERVICE. MY BOYS WILL BE WAITING RIGHT HERE, AFTER. THEY'LL GET THEIR COLLARS.
THANK YOU, MISTY.
YEAH. SURE.
TOO MANY PIECES WERE OUT OF PLACE...AMERICOPS, CURFEW, THIS WOMAN FROM ANOTHER LIFE...
HOW DID IT ALL CONNECT?

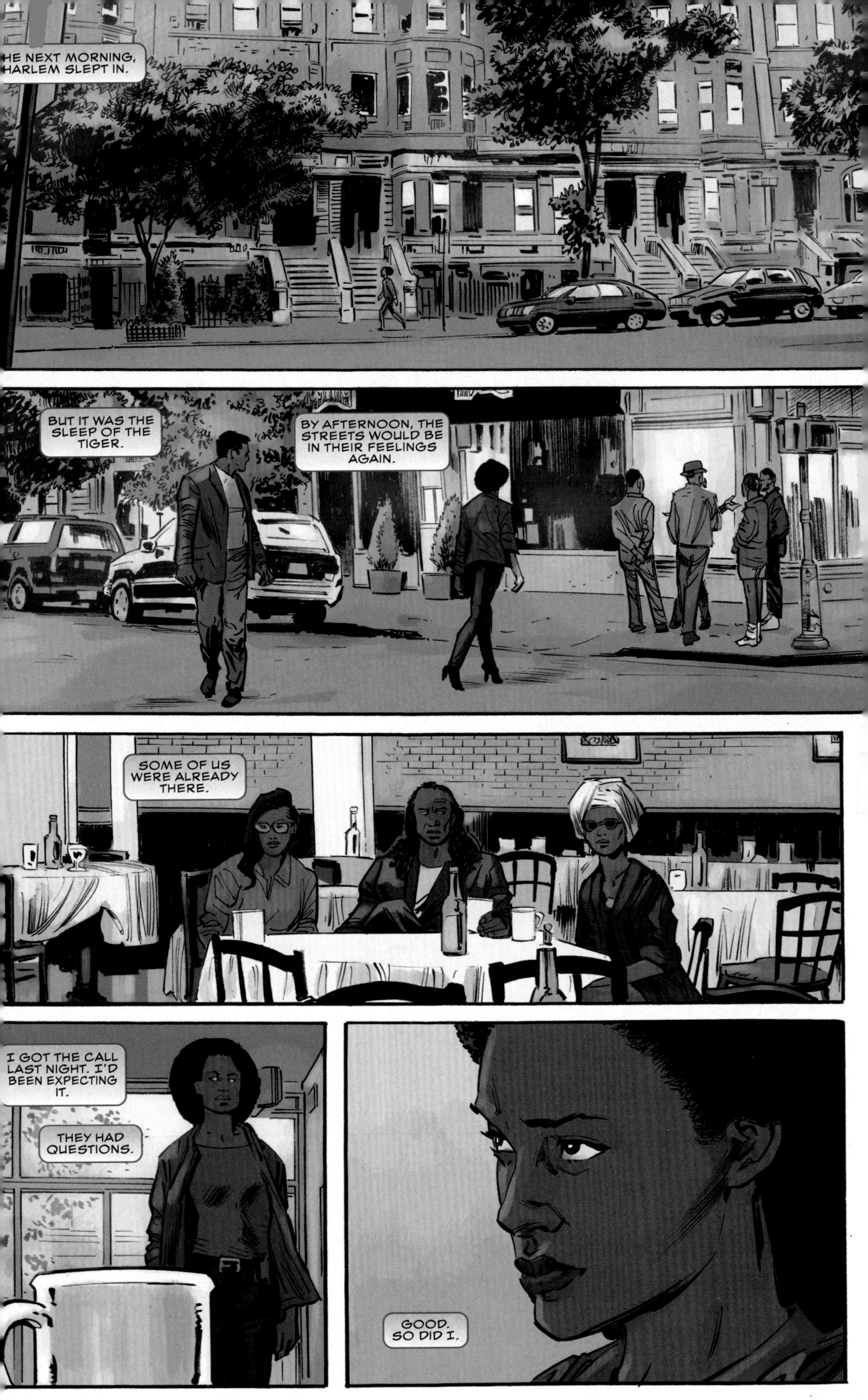
HE NEXT MORNING, HARLEM SLEPT IN.
BUT IT WAS THE SLEEP OF THE TIGER.
BY AFTERNOON, THE STREETS WOULD BE IN THEIR FEELINGS AGAIN.
SOME OF US WERE ALREADY THERE.
I GOT THE CALL LAST NIGHT. I'D BEEN EXPECTING IT.
THEY HAD QUESTIONS.
GOOD. SO DID I.

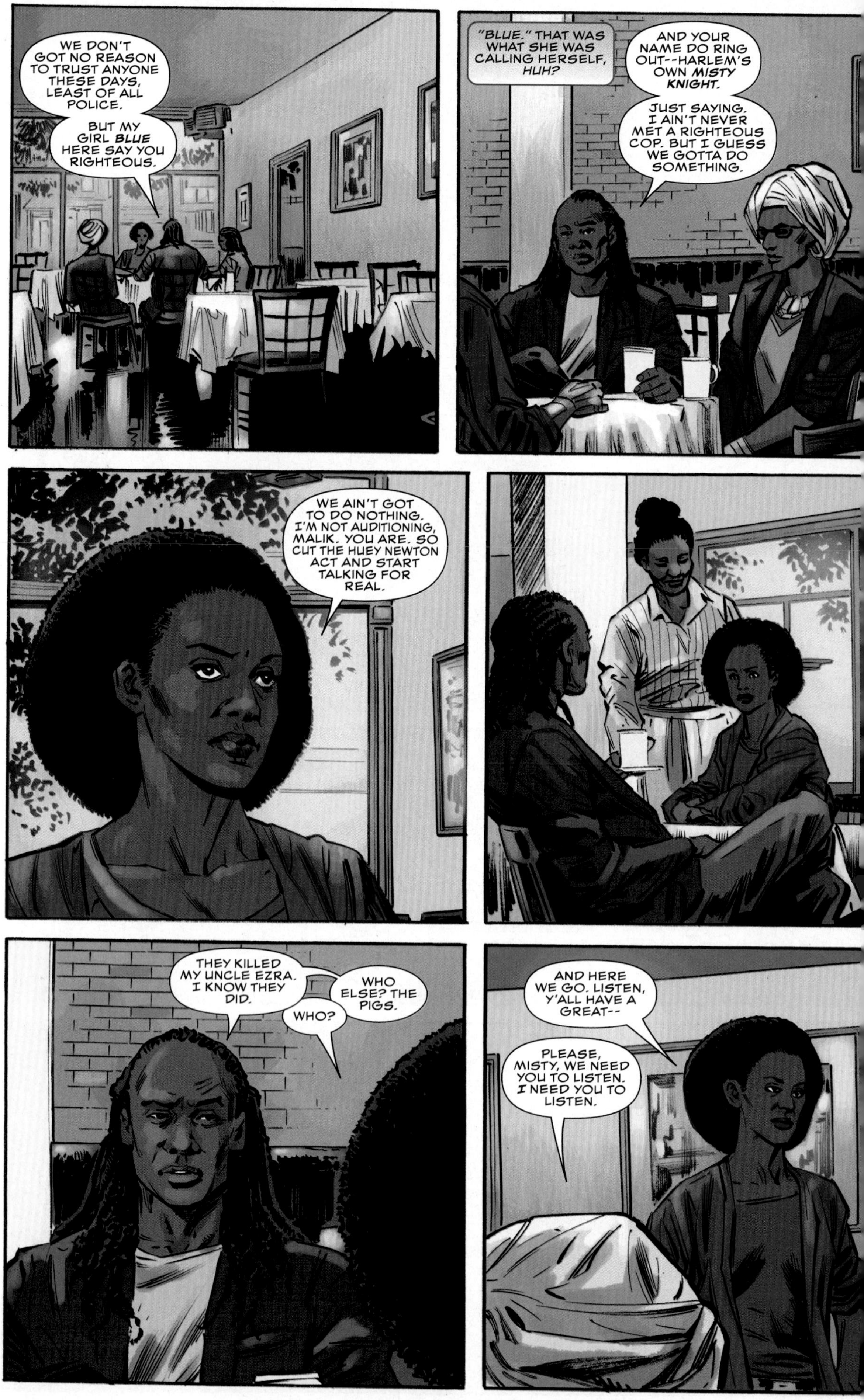
WE DON'T GOT NO REASON TO TRUST ANYONE THESE DAYS, LEAST OF ALL POLICE.
BUT MY GIRL BLUE HERE SAY YOU RIGHTEOUS.
"BLUE." THAT WAS WHAT SHE WAS CALLING HERSELF, HUH?
AND YOUR NAME DO RING OUT--HARLEM'S OWN MISTY KNIGHT.
JUST SAYING. I AIN'T NEVER MET A RIGHTEOUS COP. BUT I GUESS WE GOTTA DO SOMETHING.
WE AIN'T GOT TO DO NOTHING. I'M NOT AUDITIONING, MALIK. YOU ARE. SO CUT THE HUEY NEWTON ACT AND START TALKING FOR REAL.
THEY KILLED MY UNCLE EZRA. I KNOW THEY DID.
WHO?
WHO ELSE? THE PIGS.
AND HERE WE GO. LISTEN, Y'ALL HAVE A GREAT--
PLEASE, MISTY, WE NEED YOU TO LISTEN. I NEED YOU TO LISTEN.

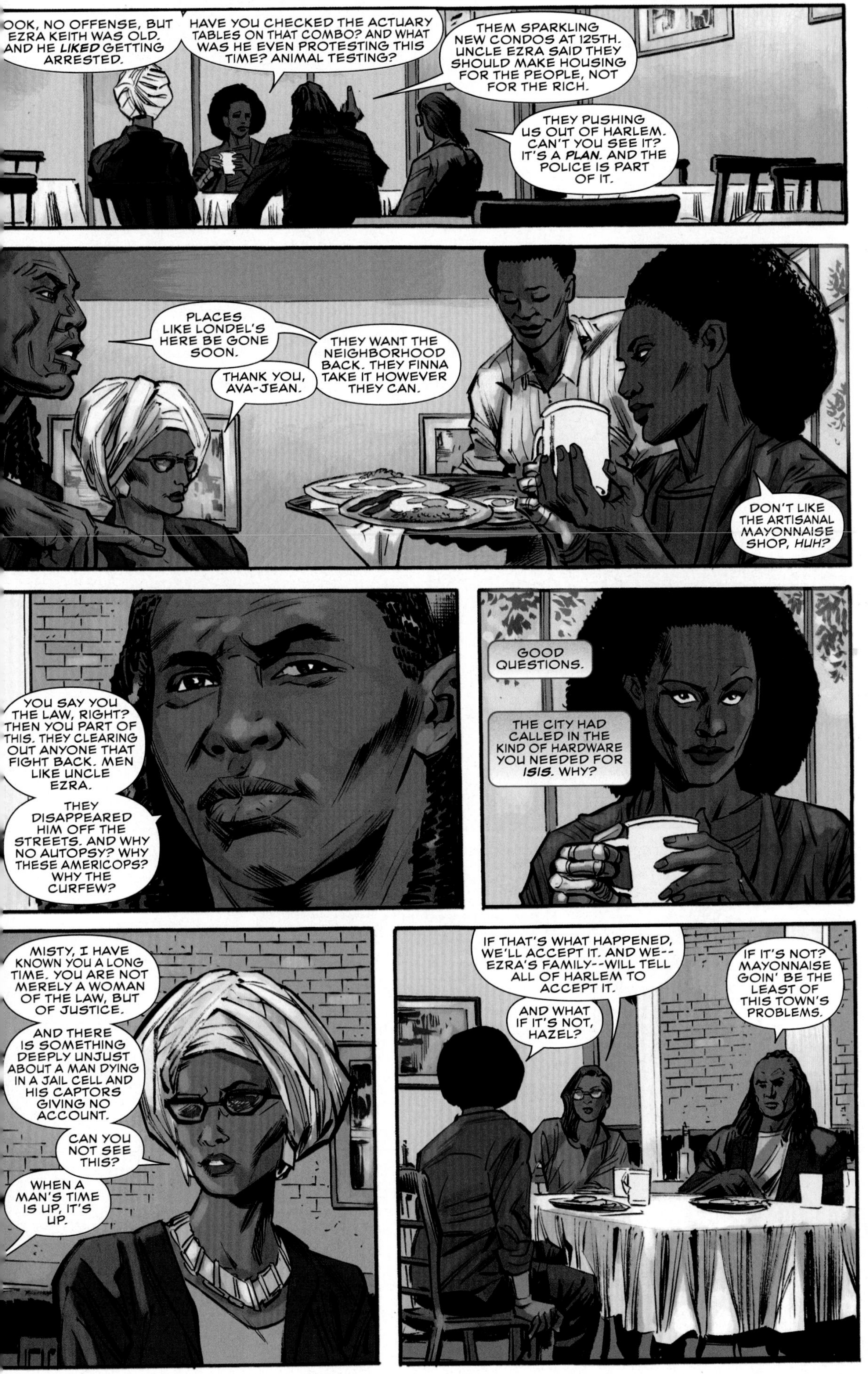
OOK, NO OFFENSE, BUT EZRA KEITH WAS OLD. AND HE *LIKED* GETTING ARRESTED.
HAVE YOU CHECKED THE ACTUARY TABLES ON THAT COMBO? AND WHAT WAS HE EVEN PROTESTING THIS TIME? ANIMAL TESTING?
THEM SPARKLING NEW CONDOS AT 125TH. UNCLE EZRA SAID THEY SHOULD MAKE HOUSING FOR THE PEOPLE, NOT FOR THE RICH.
THEY PUSHING US OUT OF HARLEM. CAN'T YOU SEE IT? IT'S A *PLAN*. AND THE POLICE IS PART OF IT.
PLACES LIKE LONDEL'S HERE BE GONE SOON.
THANK YOU, AVA-JEAN.
THEY WANT THE NEIGHBORHOOD BACK. THEY FINNA TAKE IT HOWEVER THEY CAN.
DON'T LIKE THE ARTISANAL MAYONNAISE SHOP, *HUH?*
YOU SAY YOU THE LAW, RIGHT? THEN YOU PART OF THIS. THEY CLEARING OUT ANYONE THAT FIGHT BACK. MEN LIKE UNCLE EZRA.
THEY DISAPPEARED HIM OFF THE STREETS. AND WHY NO AUTOPSY? WHY THESE AMERICOPS? WHY THE CURFEW?
GOOD QUESTIONS.
THE CITY HAD CALLED IN THE KIND OF HARDWARE YOU NEEDED FOR *ISIS*. WHY?
MISTY, I HAVE KNOWN YOU A LONG TIME. YOU ARE NOT MERELY A WOMAN OF THE LAW, BUT OF JUSTICE.
AND THERE IS SOMETHING DEEPLY UNJUST ABOUT A MAN DYING IN A JAIL CELL AND HIS CAPTORS GIVING NO ACCOUNT.
CAN YOU NOT SEE THIS?
WHEN A MAN'S TIME IS UP, IT'S UP.
IF THAT'S WHAT HAPPENED, WE'LL ACCEPT IT. AND WE-- EZRA'S FAMILY--WILL TELL ALL OF HARLEM TO ACCEPT IT.
AND WHAT IF IT'S NOT, HAZEL?
IF IT'S NOT? MAYONNAISE GOIN' BE THE LEAST OF THIS TOWN'S PROBLEMS.

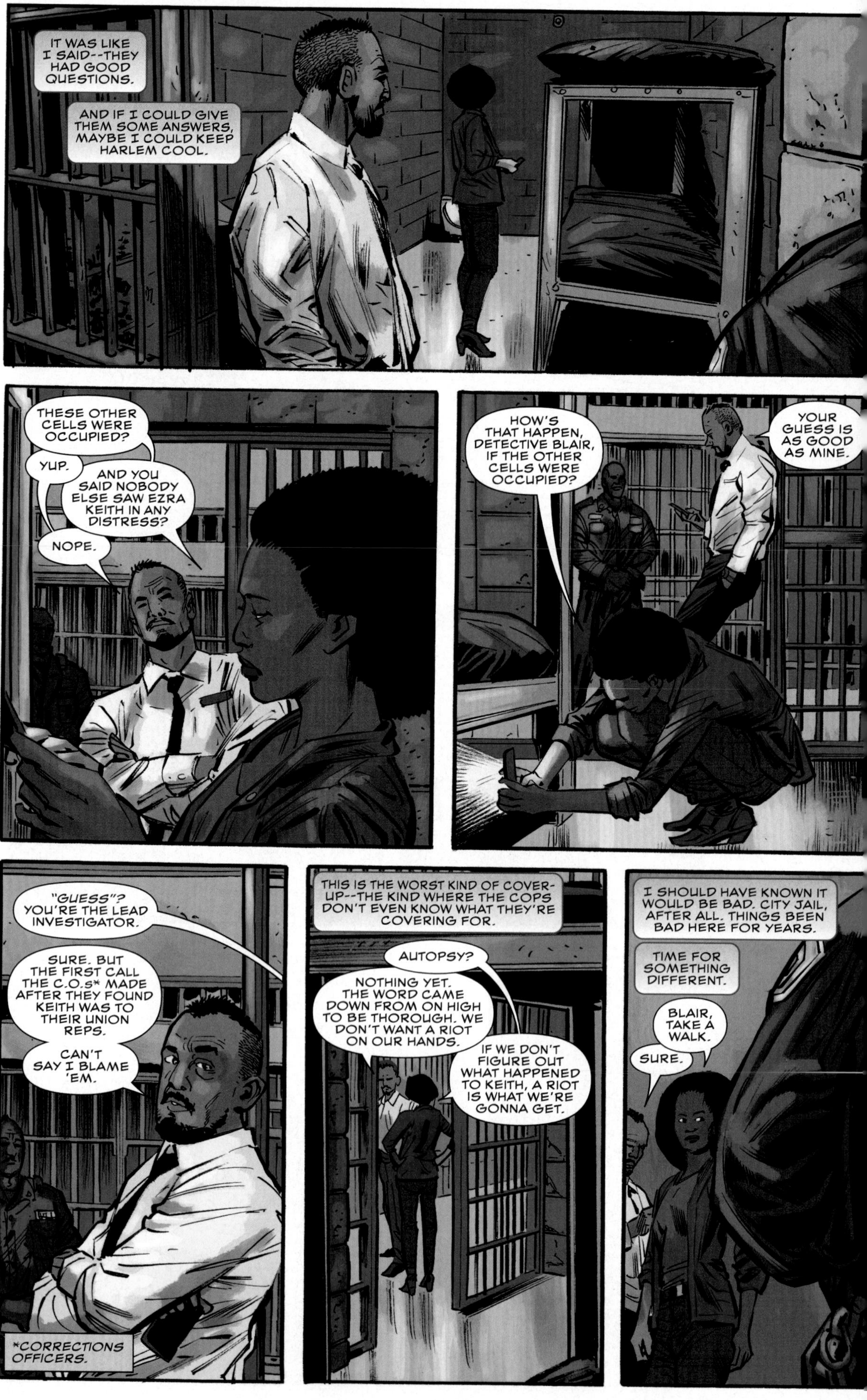

IT WAS LIKE I SAID--THEY HAD GOOD QUESTIONS.
AND IF I COULD GIVE THEM SOME ANSWERS, MAYBE I COULD KEEP HARLEM COOL.
THESE OTHER CELLS WERE OCCUPIED?
YUP.
AND YOU SAID NOBODY ELSE SAW EZRA KEITH IN ANY DISTRESS?
NOPE.
HOW'S THAT HAPPEN, DETECTIVE BLAIR, IF THE OTHER CELLS WERE OCCUPIED?
YOUR GUESS IS AS GOOD AS MINE.
"GUESS"? YOU'RE THE LEAD INVESTIGATOR.
SURE. BUT THE FIRST CALL THE C.O.s* MADE AFTER THEY FOUND KEITH WAS TO THEIR UNION REPS.
CAN'T SAY I BLAME 'EM.
*CORRECTIONS OFFICERS.
THIS IS THE WORST KIND OF COVER-UP--THE KIND WHERE THE COPS DON'T EVEN KNOW WHAT THEY'RE COVERING FOR.
AUTOPSY?
NOTHING YET. THE WORD CAME DOWN FROM ON HIGH TO BE THOROUGH. WE DON'T WANT A RIOT ON OUR HANDS.
IF WE DON'T FIGURE OUT WHAT HAPPENED TO KEITH, A RIOT IS WHAT WE'RE GONNA GET.
I SHOULD HAVE KNOWN IT WOULD BE BAD. CITY JAIL, AFTER ALL. THINGS BEEN BAD HERE FOR YEARS.
TIME FOR SOMETHING DIFFERENT.
BLAIR, TAKE A WALK.
SURE.

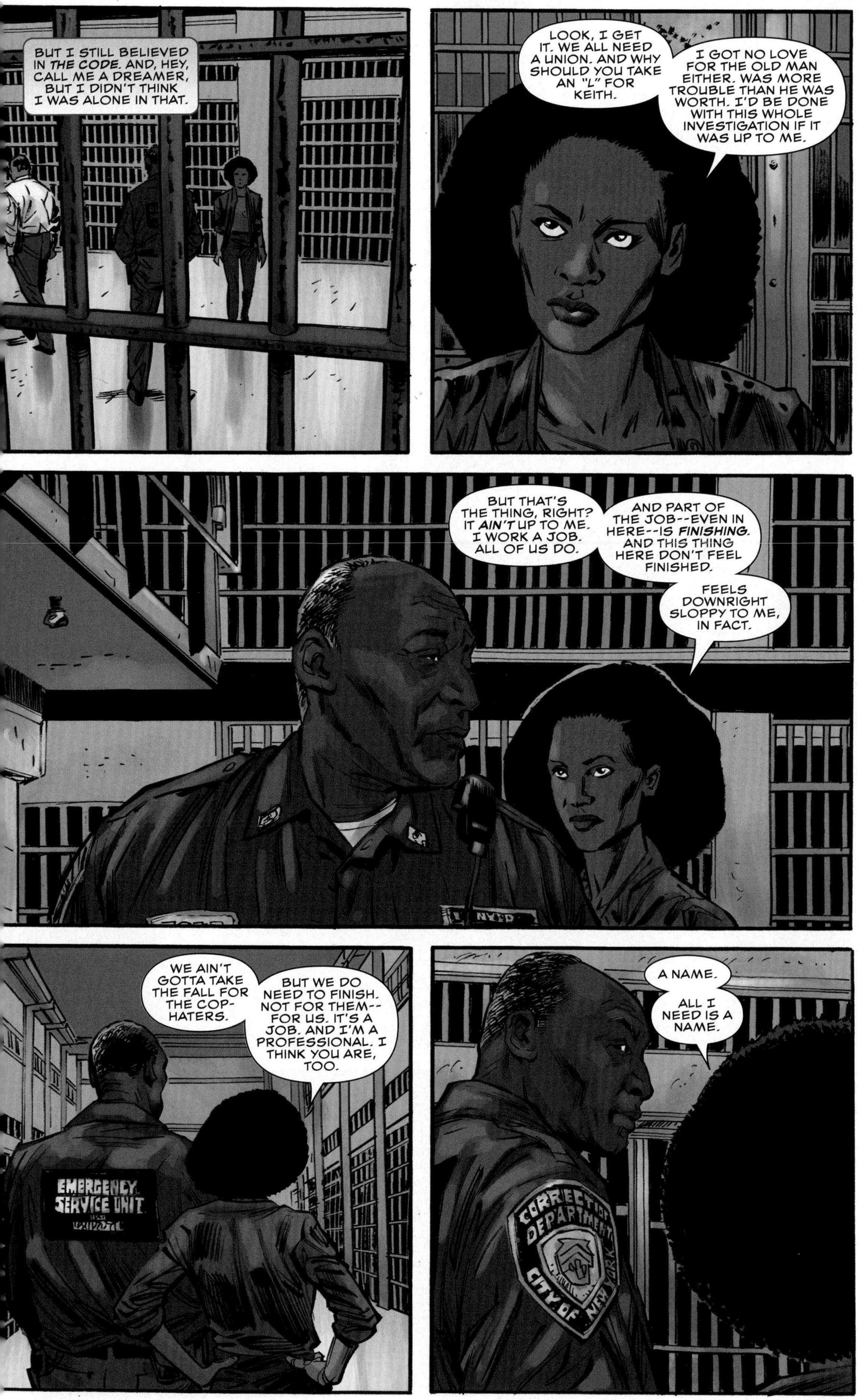
BUT I STILL BELIEVED IN THE CODE. AND, HEY, CALL ME A DREAMER, BUT I DIDN'T THINK I WAS ALONE IN THAT.
LOOK, I GET IT. WE ALL NEED A UNION. AND WHY SHOULD YOU TAKE AN "L" FOR KEITH.
I GOT NO LOVE FOR THE OLD MAN EITHER. WAS MORE TROUBLE THAN HE WAS WORTH. I'D BE DONE WITH THIS WHOLE INVESTIGATION IF IT WAS UP TO ME.
BUT THAT'S THE THING, RIGHT? IT AIN'T UP TO ME. I WORK A JOB. ALL OF US DO.
AND PART OF THE JOB--EVEN IN HERE--IS FINISHING. AND THIS THING HERE DON'T FEEL FINISHED.
FEELS DOWNRIGHT SLOPPY TO ME, IN FACT.
NYCD
WE AIN'T GOTTA TAKE THE FALL FOR THE COP-HATERS.
BUT WE DO NEED TO FINISH. NOT FOR THEM--FOR US. IT'S A JOB. AND I'M A PROFESSIONAL. I THINK YOU ARE, TOO.
EMERGENCY SERVICE UNIT
A NAME.
ALL I NEED IS A NAME.
CORRECTION DEPARTMENT CITY OF NEW YORK

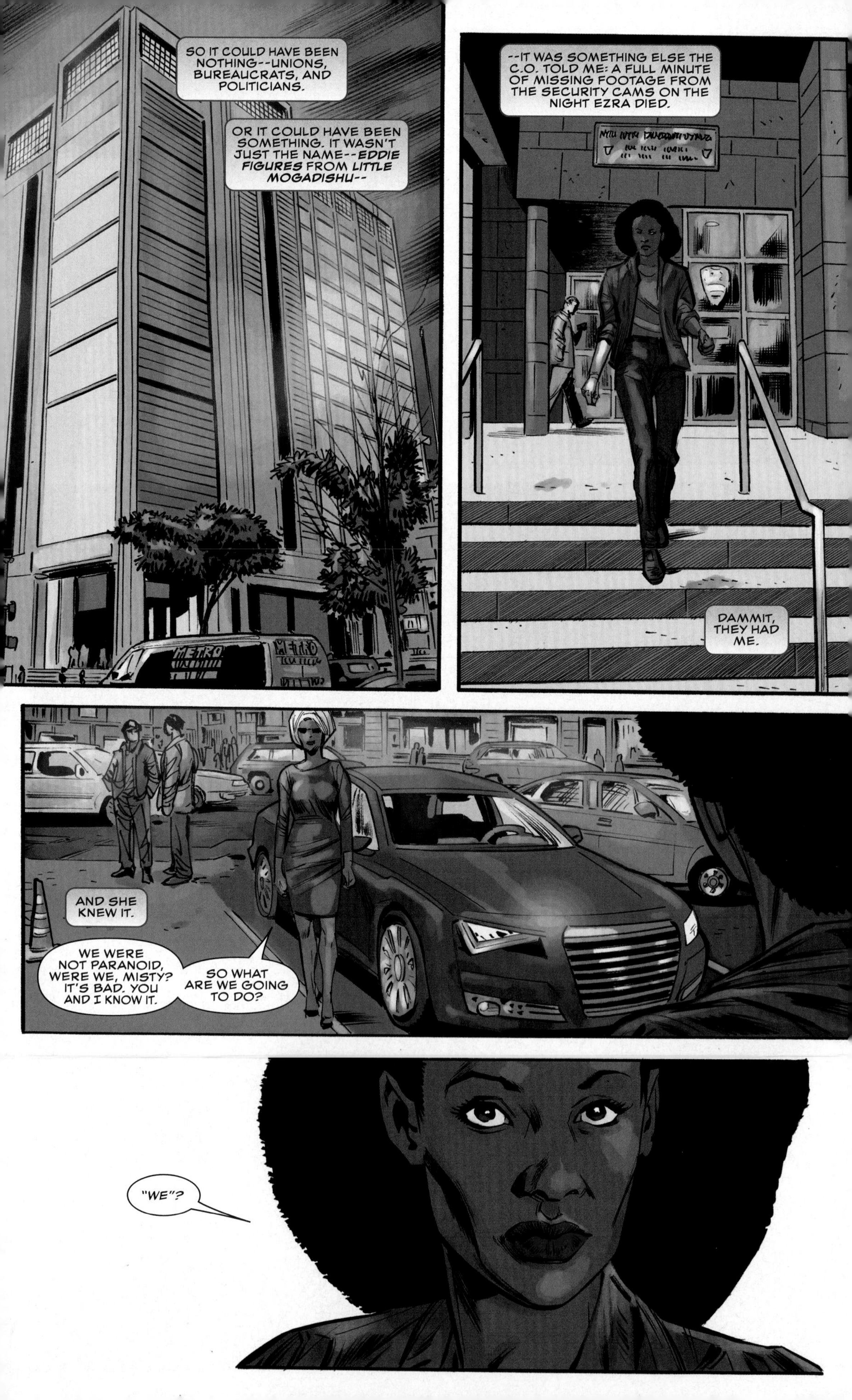
SO IT COULD HAVE BEEN NOTHING--UNIONS, BUREAUCRATS, AND POLITICIANS.
OR IT COULD HAVE BEEN SOMETHING. IT WASN'T JUST THE NAME--EDDIE FIGURES FROM LITTLE MOGADISHU--
METRO
--IT WAS SOMETHING ELSE THE C.O. TOLD ME: A FULL MINUTE OF MISSING FOOTAGE FROM THE SECURITY CAMS ON THE NIGHT EZRA DIED.
DAMMIT, THEY HAD ME.
AND SHE KNEW IT.
WE WERE NOT PARANOID, WERE WE, MISTY? IT'S BAD. YOU AND I KNOW IT.
SO WHAT ARE WE GOING TO DO?
"WE"?

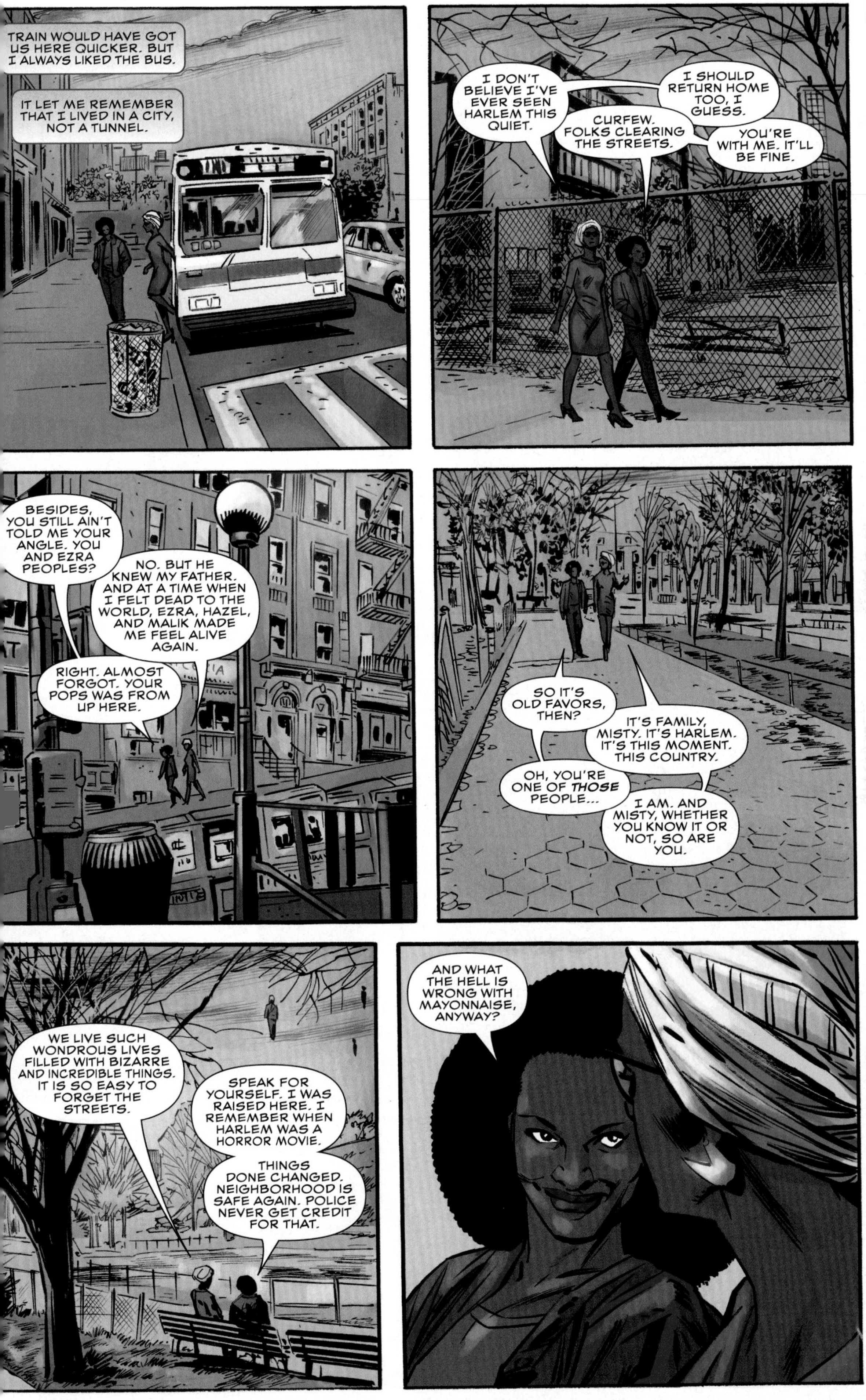

TRAIN WOULD HAVE GOT US HERE QUICKER. BUT I ALWAYS LIKED THE BUS.
IT LET ME REMEMBER THAT I LIVED IN A CITY, NOT A TUNNEL.
I DON'T BELIEVE I'VE EVER SEEN HARLEM THIS QUIET.
CURFEW. FOLKS CLEARING THE STREETS.
I SHOULD RETURN HOME TOO, I GUESS.
YOU'RE WITH ME. IT'LL BE FINE.
BESIDES, YOU STILL AIN'T TOLD ME YOUR ANGLE. YOU AND EZRA PEOPLES?
NO. BUT HE KNEW MY FATHER. AND AT A TIME WHEN I FELT DEAD TO THE WORLD, EZRA, HAZEL, AND MALIK MADE ME FEEL ALIVE AGAIN.
RIGHT. ALMOST FORGOT. YOUR POPS WAS FROM UP HERE.
SO IT'S OLD FAVORS, THEN?
IT'S FAMILY, MISTY. IT'S HARLEM. IT'S THIS MOMENT. THIS COUNTRY.
OH, YOU'RE ONE OF *THOSE* PEOPLE...
I AM. AND MISTY, WHETHER YOU KNOW IT OR NOT, SO ARE YOU.
WE LIVE SUCH WONDROUS LIVES FILLED WITH BIZARRE AND INCREDIBLE THINGS. IT IS SO EASY TO FORGET THE STREETS.
SPEAK FOR YOURSELF. I WAS RAISED HERE. I REMEMBER WHEN HARLEM WAS A HORROR MOVIE.
THINGS DONE CHANGED. NEIGHBORHOOD IS SAFE AGAIN. POLICE NEVER GET CREDIT FOR THAT.
AND WHAT THE HELL IS WRONG WITH MAYONNAISE, ANYWAY?

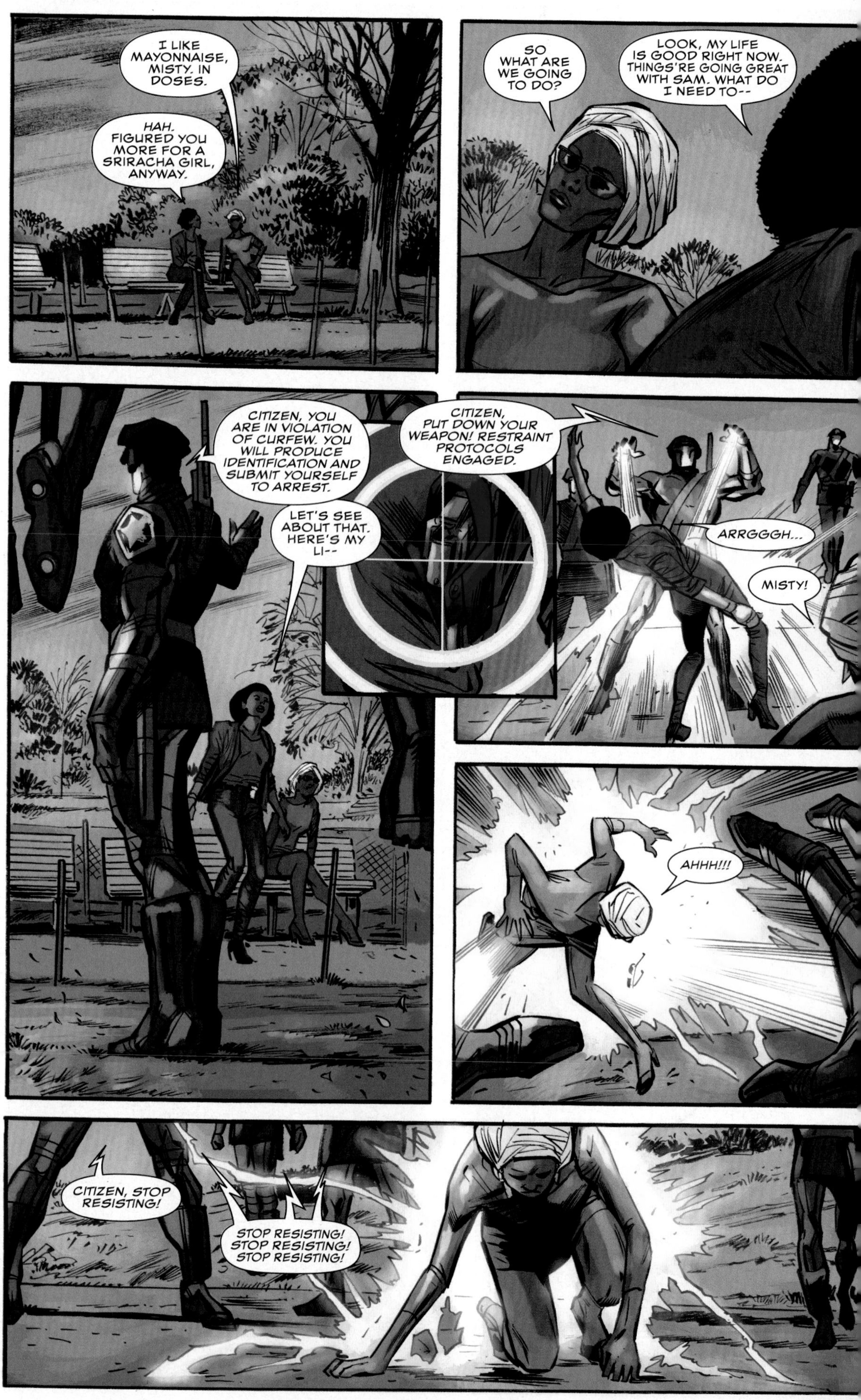
I LIKE MAYONNAISE, MISTY. IN DOSES.
HAH. FIGURED YOU MORE FOR A SRIRACHA GIRL, ANYWAY.
SO WHAT ARE WE GOING TO DO?
LOOK, MY LIFE IS GOOD RIGHT NOW. THINGS'RE GOING GREAT WITH SAM. WHAT DO I NEED TO--
CITIZEN, YOU ARE IN VIOLATION OF CURFEW. YOU WILL PRODUCE IDENTIFICATION AND SUBMIT YOURSELF TO ARREST.
LET'S SEE ABOUT THAT. HERE'S MY LI--
CITIZEN, PUT DOWN YOUR WEAPON! RESTRAINT PROTOCOLS ENGAGED.
ARRGGGH...
MISTY!
AHHH!!!
CITIZEN, STOP RESISTING!
STOP RESISTING! STOP RESISTING! STOP RESISTING!

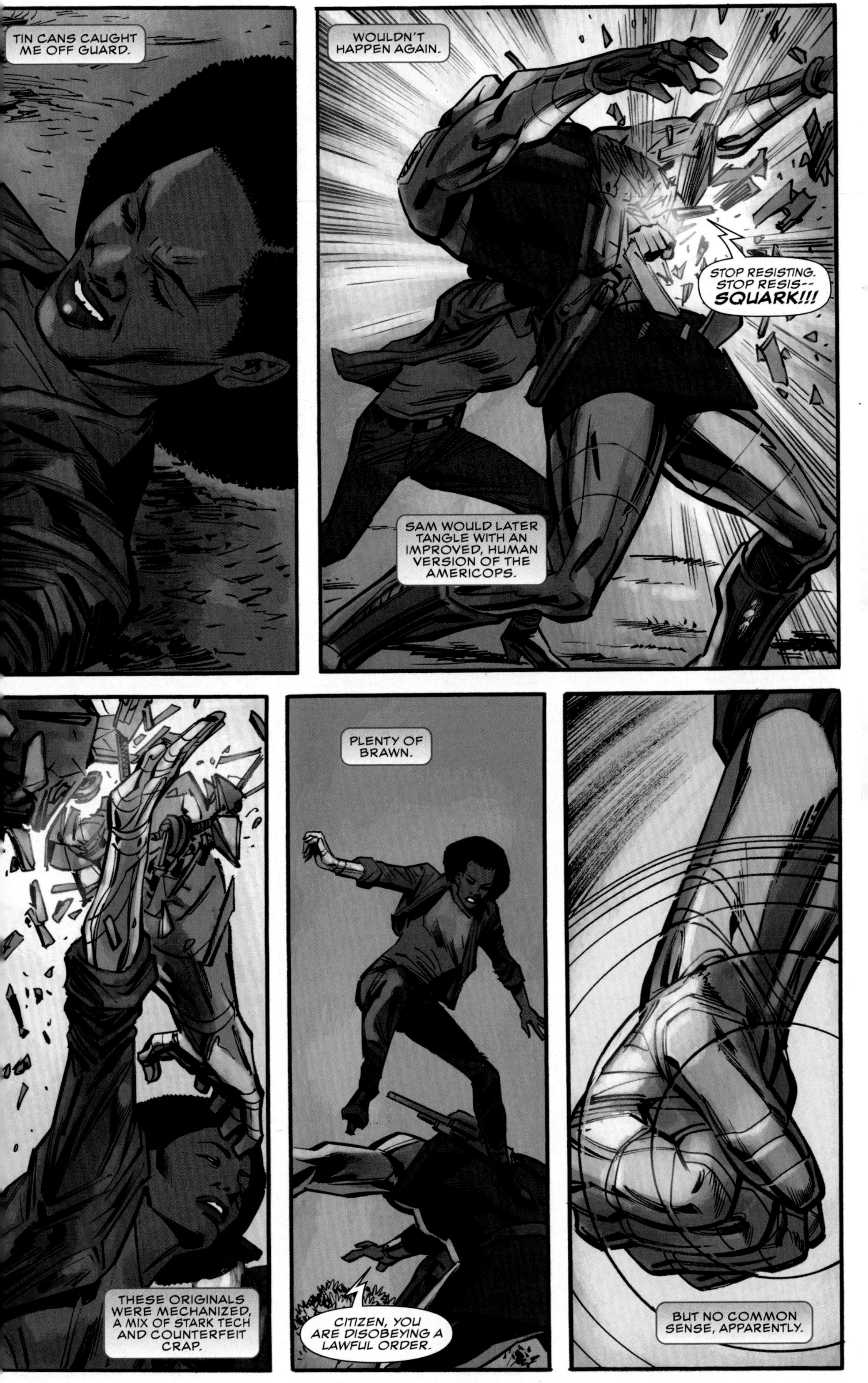
TIN CANS CAUGHT ME OFF GUARD.
WOULDN'T HAPPEN AGAIN.
STOP RESISTING. STOP RESIS-- **SQUARK!!!**
SAM WOULD LATER TANGLE WITH AN IMPROVED, HUMAN VERSION OF THE AMERICOPS.
THESE ORIGINALS WERE MECHANIZED, A MIX OF STARK TECH AND COUNTERFEIT CRAP.
PLENTY OF BRAWN.
CITIZEN, YOU ARE DISOBEYING A LAWFUL ORDER.
BUT NO COMMON SENSE, APPARENTLY.

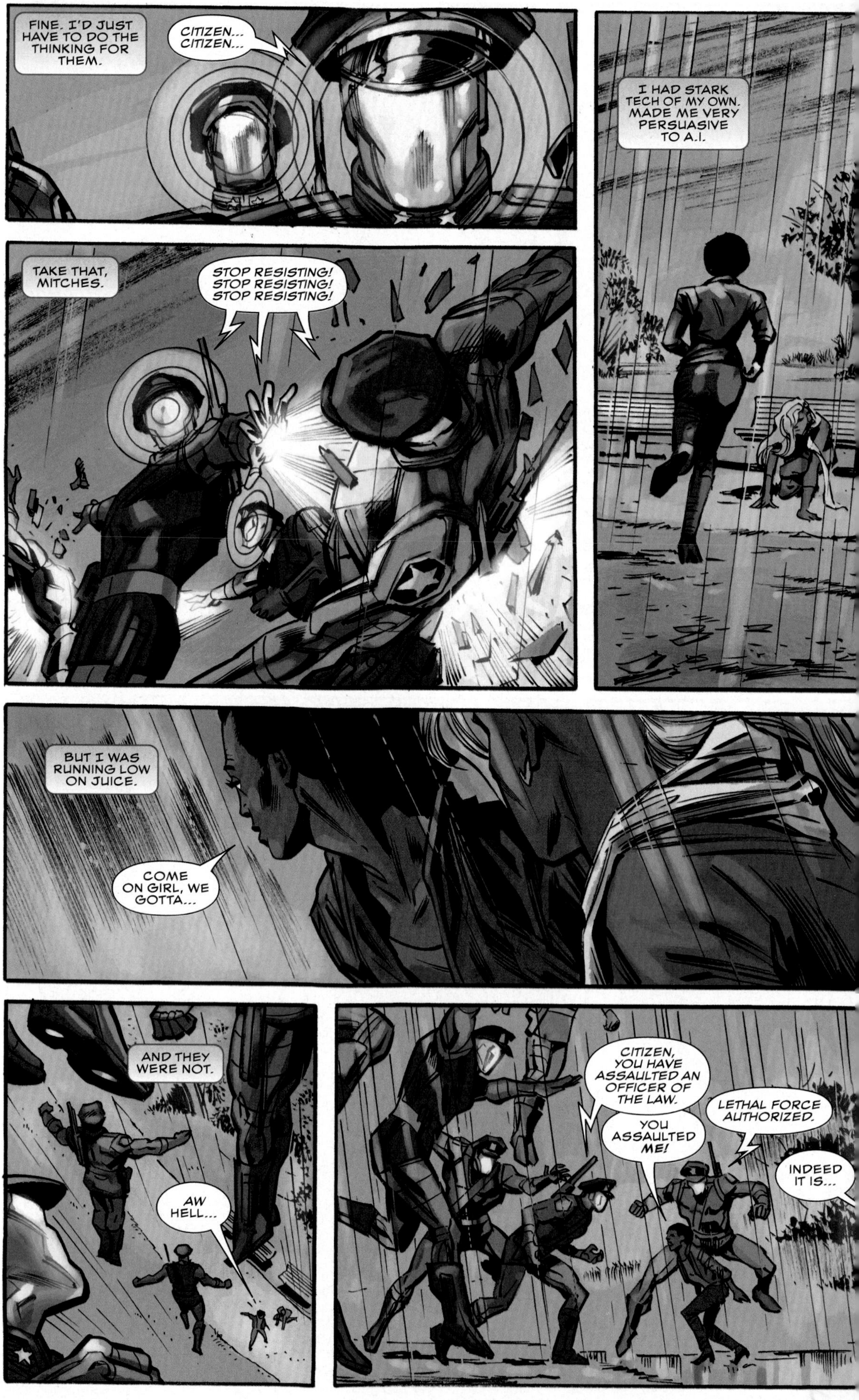
FINE. I'D JUST HAVE TO DO THE THINKING FOR THEM.
CITIZEN... CITIZEN...
I HAD STARK TECH OF MY OWN. MADE ME VERY PERSUASIVE TO A.I.
TAKE THAT, MITCHES.
STOP RESISTING! STOP RESISTING! STOP RESISTING!
BUT I WAS RUNNING LOW ON JUICE.
COME ON GIRL, WE GOTTA...
AND THEY WERE NOT.
AW HELL...
CITIZEN, YOU HAVE ASSAULTED AN OFFICER OF THE LAW.
YOU ASSAULTED ME!
LETHAL FORCE AUTHORIZED.
INDEED IT IS...

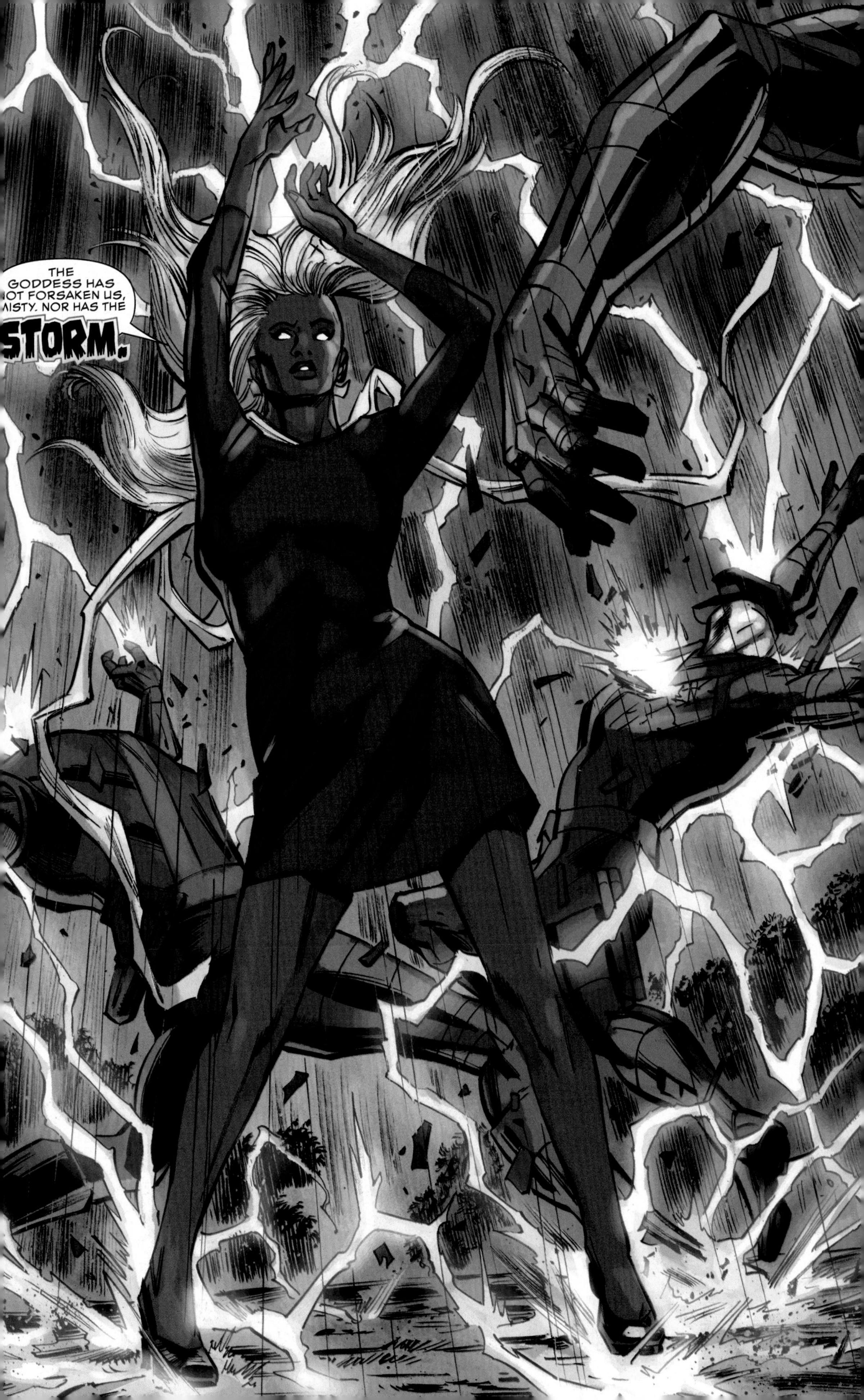
THE GODDESS HAS NOT FORSAKEN US, MISTY. NOR HAS THE STORM.

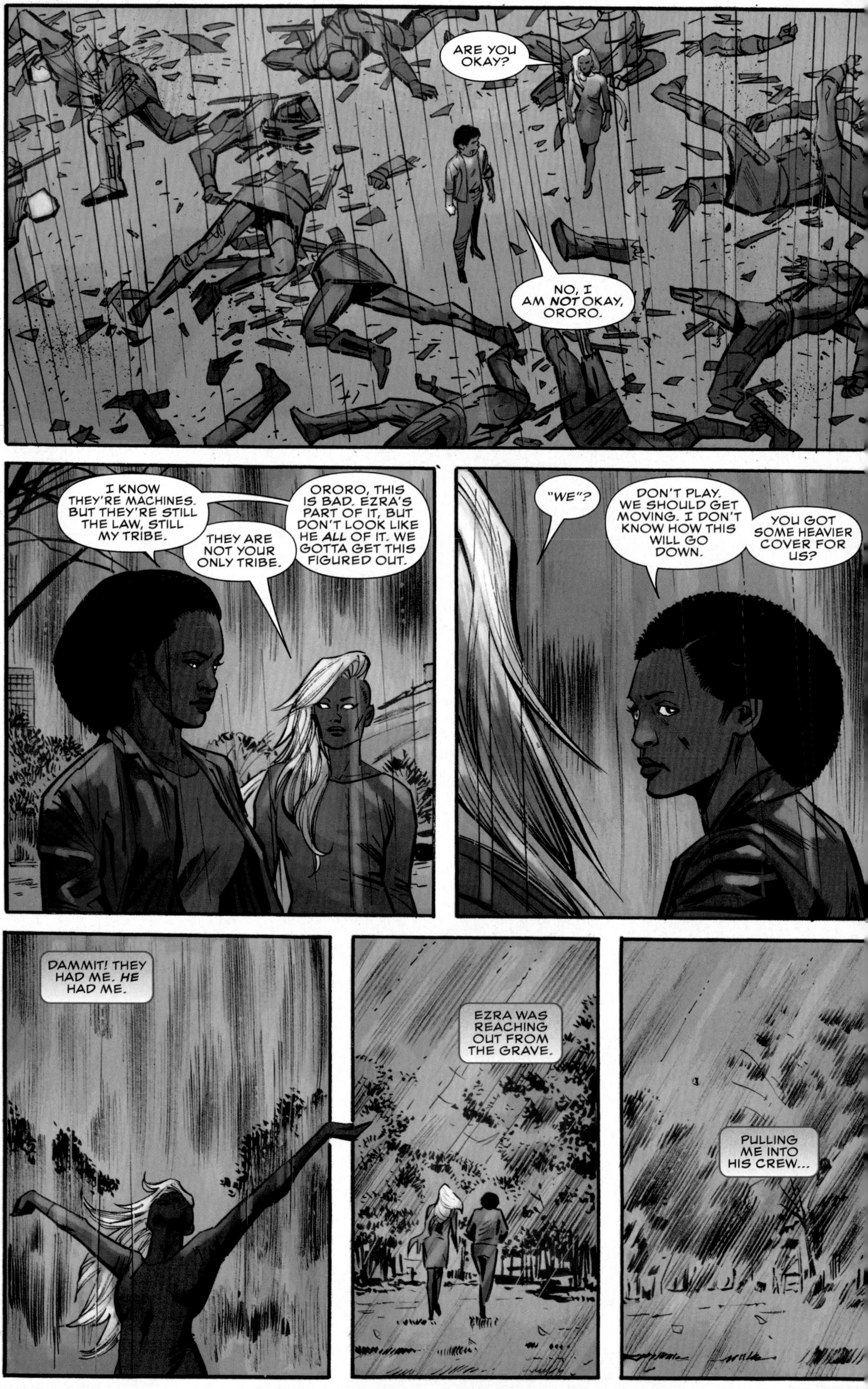
ARE YOU OKAY?
NO, I AM NOT OKAY, ORORO.
I KNOW THEY'RE MACHINES. BUT THEY'RE STILL THE LAW, STILL MY TRIBE.
THEY ARE NOT YOUR ONLY TRIBE.
ORORO, THIS IS BAD. EZRA'S PART OF IT, BUT DON'T LOOK LIKE HE ALL OF IT. WE GOTTA GET THIS FIGURED OUT.
"WE"?
DON'T PLAY. WE SHOULD GET MOVING. I DON'T KNOW HOW THIS WILL GO DOWN.
YOU GOT SOME HEAVIER COVER FOR US?
DAMMIT! THEY HAD ME. HE HAD ME.
EZRA WAS REACHING OUT FROM THE GRAVE.
PULLING ME INTO HIS CREW...

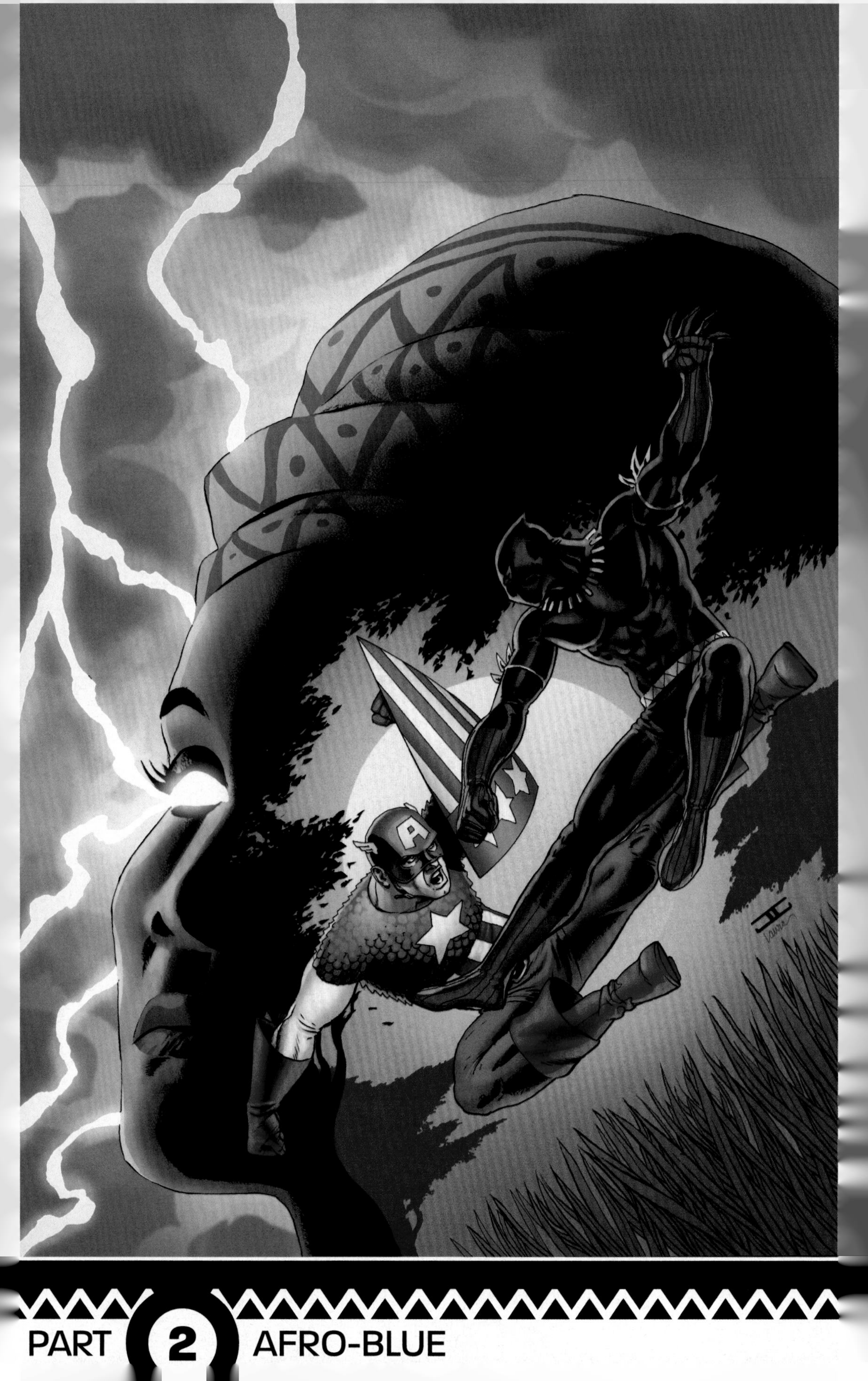

PART 2 AFRO-BLUE

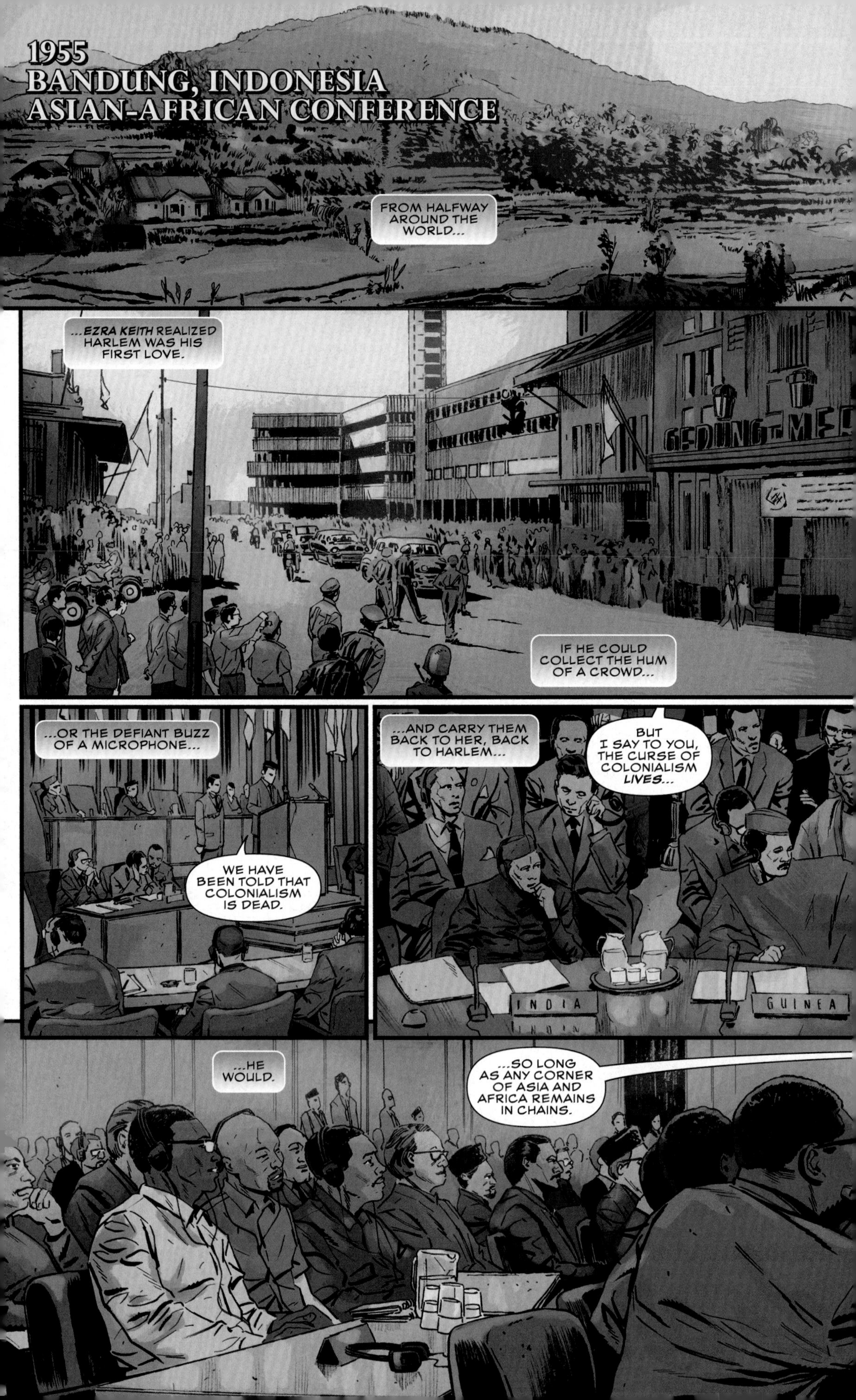
1955
BANDUNG, INDONESIA
ASIAN-AFRICAN CONFERENCE
FROM HALFWAY AROUND THE WORLD...
...EZRA KEITH REALIZED HARLEM WAS HIS FIRST LOVE.
GEDUNG MER
IF HE COULD COLLECT THE HUM OF A CROWD...
...OR THE DEFIANT BUZZ OF A MICROPHONE...
WE HAVE BEEN TOLD THAT COLONIALISM IS DEAD.
...AND CARRY THEM BACK TO HER, BACK TO HARLEM...
BUT I SAY TO YOU, THE CURSE OF COLONIALISM LIVES...
INDIA
GUINEA
...HE WOULD.
...SO LONG AS ANY CORNER OF ASIA AND AFRICA REMAINS IN CHAINS.

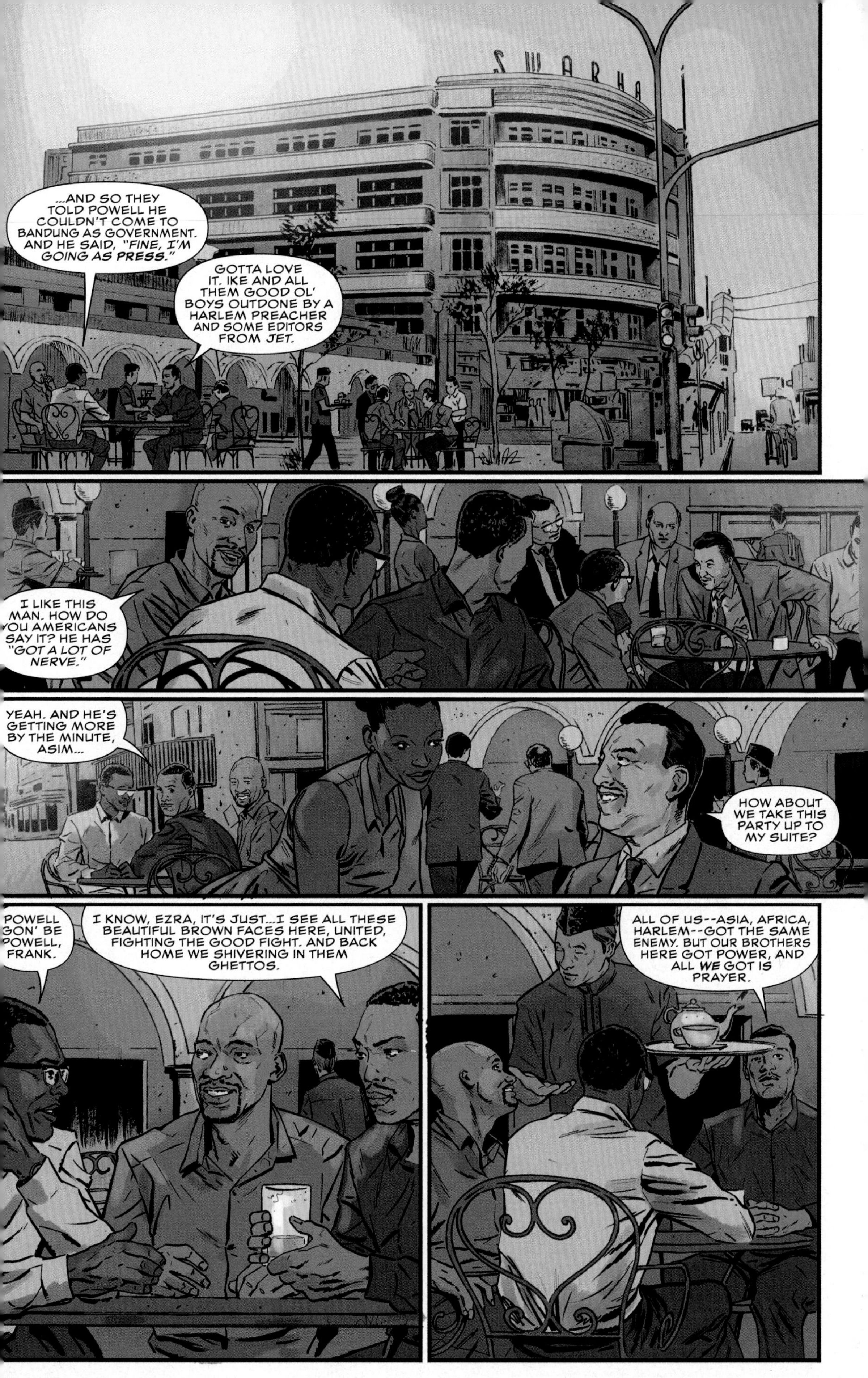
S W A R H A
...AND SO THEY TOLD POWELL HE COULDN'T COME TO BANDUNG AS GOVERNMENT. AND HE SAID, "FINE, I'M GOING AS PRESS."
GOTTA LOVE IT. IKE AND ALL THEM GOOD OL' BOYS OUTDONE BY A HARLEM PREACHER AND SOME EDITORS FROM JET.
I LIKE THIS MAN. HOW DO YOU AMERICANS SAY IT? HE HAS "GOT A LOT OF NERVE."
YEAH. AND HE'S GETTING MORE BY THE MINUTE, ASIM...
HOW ABOUT WE TAKE THIS PARTY UP TO MY SUITE?
POWELL GON' BE POWELL, FRANK.
I KNOW, EZRA, IT'S JUST...I SEE ALL THESE BEAUTIFUL BROWN FACES HERE, UNITED, FIGHTING THE GOOD FIGHT. AND BACK HOME WE SHIVERING IN THEM GHETTOS.
ALL OF US--ASIA, AFRICA, HARLEM--GOT THE SAME ENEMY. BUT OUR BROTHERS HERE GOT POWER, AND ALL WE GOT IS PRAYER.

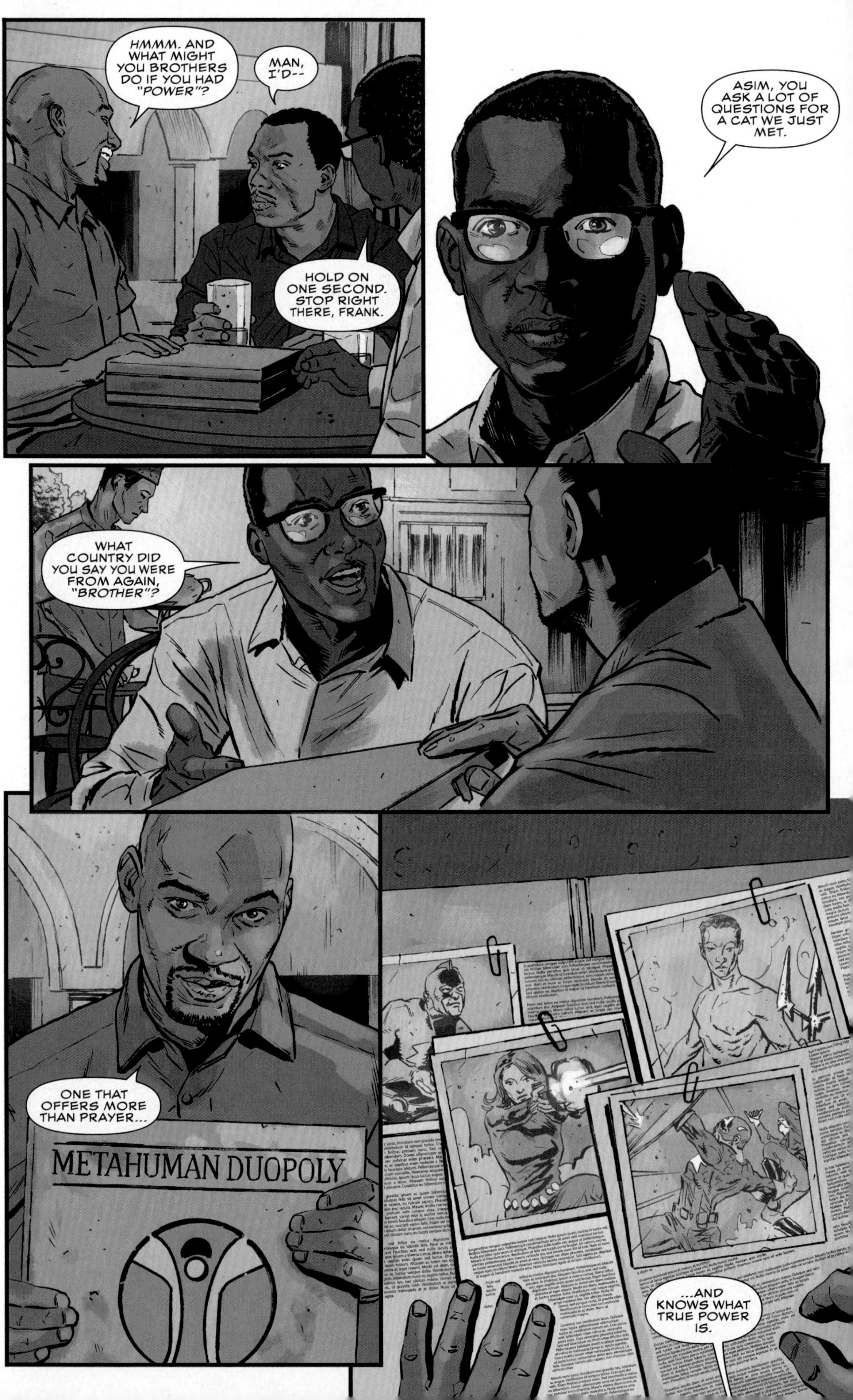
HMMM. AND WHAT MIGHT YOU BROTHERS DO IF YOU HAD "POWER"?
MAN, I'D--
HOLD ON ONE SECOND. STOP RIGHT THERE, FRANK.
ASIM, YOU ASK A LOT OF QUESTIONS FOR A CAT WE JUST MET.
WHAT COUNTRY DID YOU SAY YOU WERE FROM AGAIN, "BROTHER"?
ONE THAT OFFERS MORE THAN PRAYER...
METAHUMAN DUOPOLY
...AND KNOWS WHAT TRUE POWER IS.

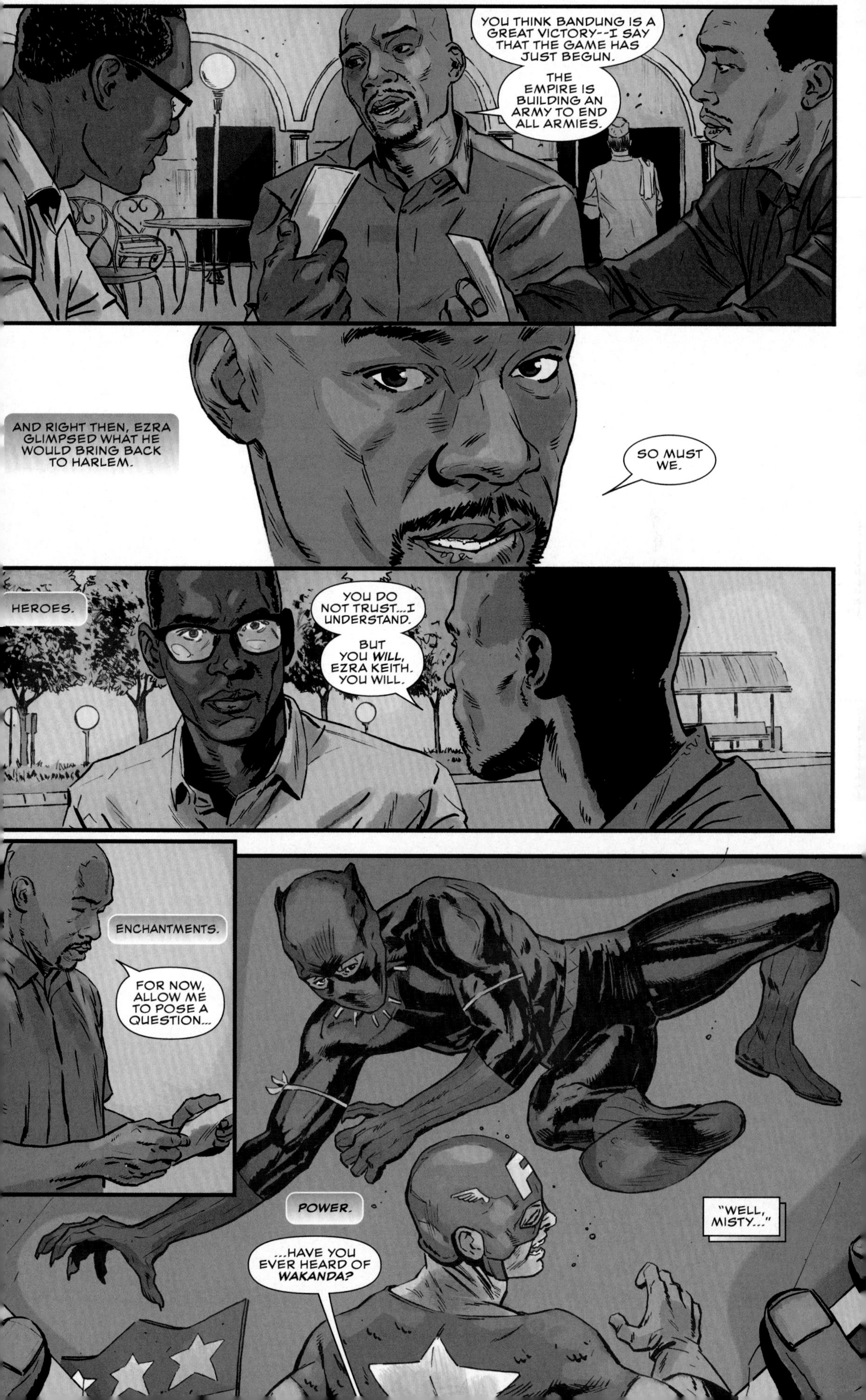
YOU THINK BANDUNG IS A GREAT VICTORY--I SAY THAT THE GAME HAS JUST BEGUN.
THE EMPIRE IS BUILDING AN ARMY TO END ALL ARMIES.
AND RIGHT THEN, EZRA GLIMPSED WHAT HE WOULD BRING BACK TO HARLEM.
SO MUST WE.
HEROES.
YOU DO NOT TRUST...I UNDERSTAND.
BUT YOU *WILL*, EZRA KEITH. YOU WILL.
ENCHANTMENTS.
FOR NOW, ALLOW ME TO POSE A QUESTION...
POWER.
...HAVE YOU EVER HEARD OF ***WAKANDA?***
"WELL, MISTY..."

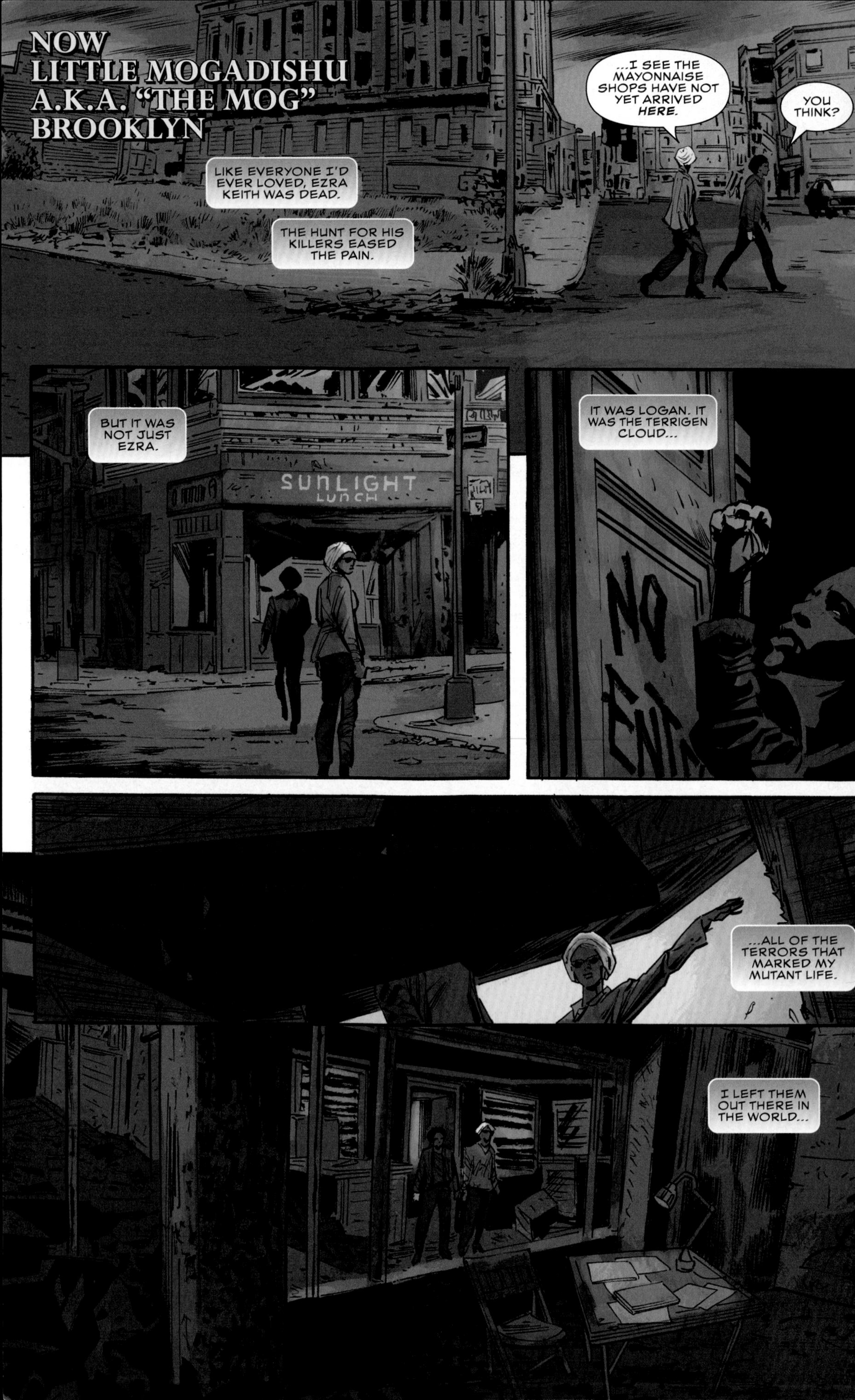
NOW
LITTLE MOGADISHU
A.K.A. "THE MOG"
BROOKLYN
LIKE EVERYONE I'D EVER LOVED, EZRA KEITH WAS DEAD.
THE HUNT FOR HIS KILLERS EASED THE PAIN.
...I SEE THE MAYONNAISE SHOPS HAVE NOT YET ARRIVED HERE.
YOU THINK?
BUT IT WAS NOT JUST EZRA.
SUNLIGHT
LUNCH
IT WAS LOGAN. IT WAS THE TERRIGEN CLOUD...
...ALL OF THE TERRORS THAT MARKED MY MUTANT LIFE.
I LEFT THEM OUT THERE IN THE WORLD...

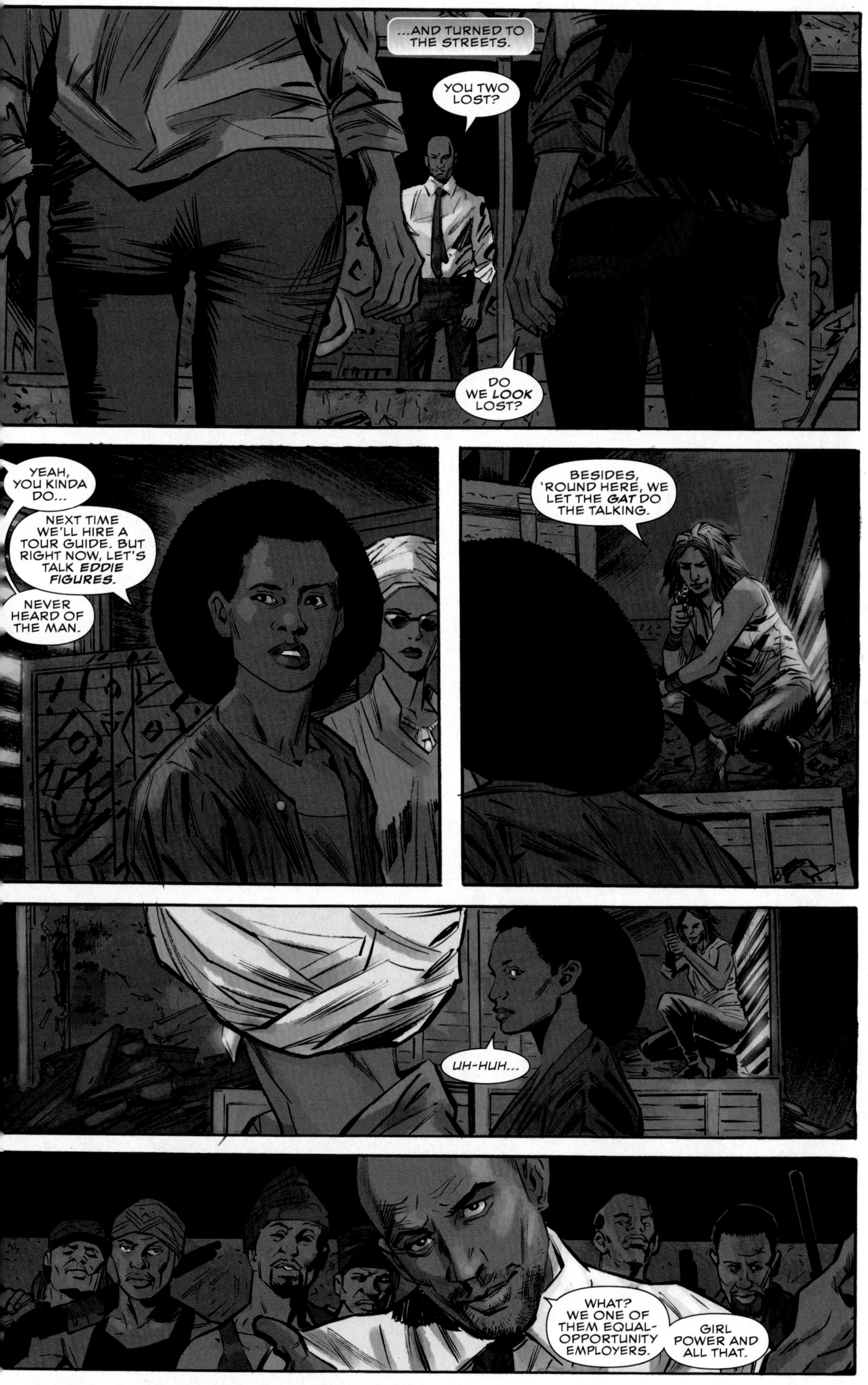
...AND TURNED TO THE STREETS.
YOU TWO LOST?
DO WE LOOK LOST?
YEAH, YOU KINDA DO...
NEXT TIME WE'LL HIRE A TOUR GUIDE. BUT RIGHT NOW, LET'S TALK EDDIE FIGURES.
NEVER HEARD OF THE MAN.
BESIDES, 'ROUND HERE, WE LET THE GAT DO THE TALKING.
UH-HUH...
WHAT? WE ONE OF THEM EQUAL-OPPORTUNITY EMPLOYERS.
GIRL POWER AND ALL THAT.

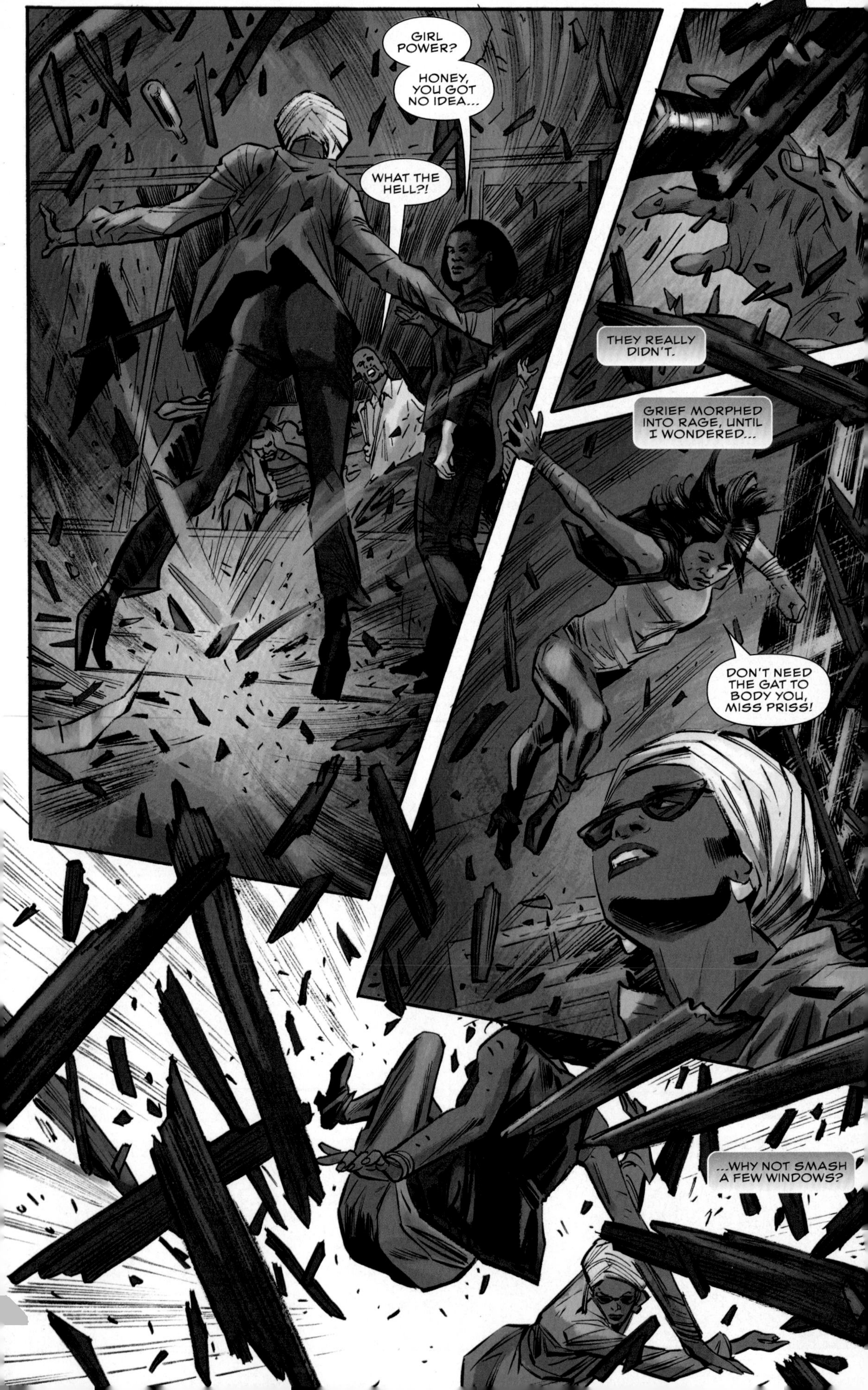
GIRL POWER?
HONEY, YOU GOT NO IDEA...
WHAT THE HELL?!
THEY REALLY DIDN'T.
GRIEF MORPHED INTO RAGE, UNTIL I WONDERED...
DON'T NEED THE GAT TO BODY YOU, MISS PRISS!
...WHY NOT SMASH A FEW WINDOWS?

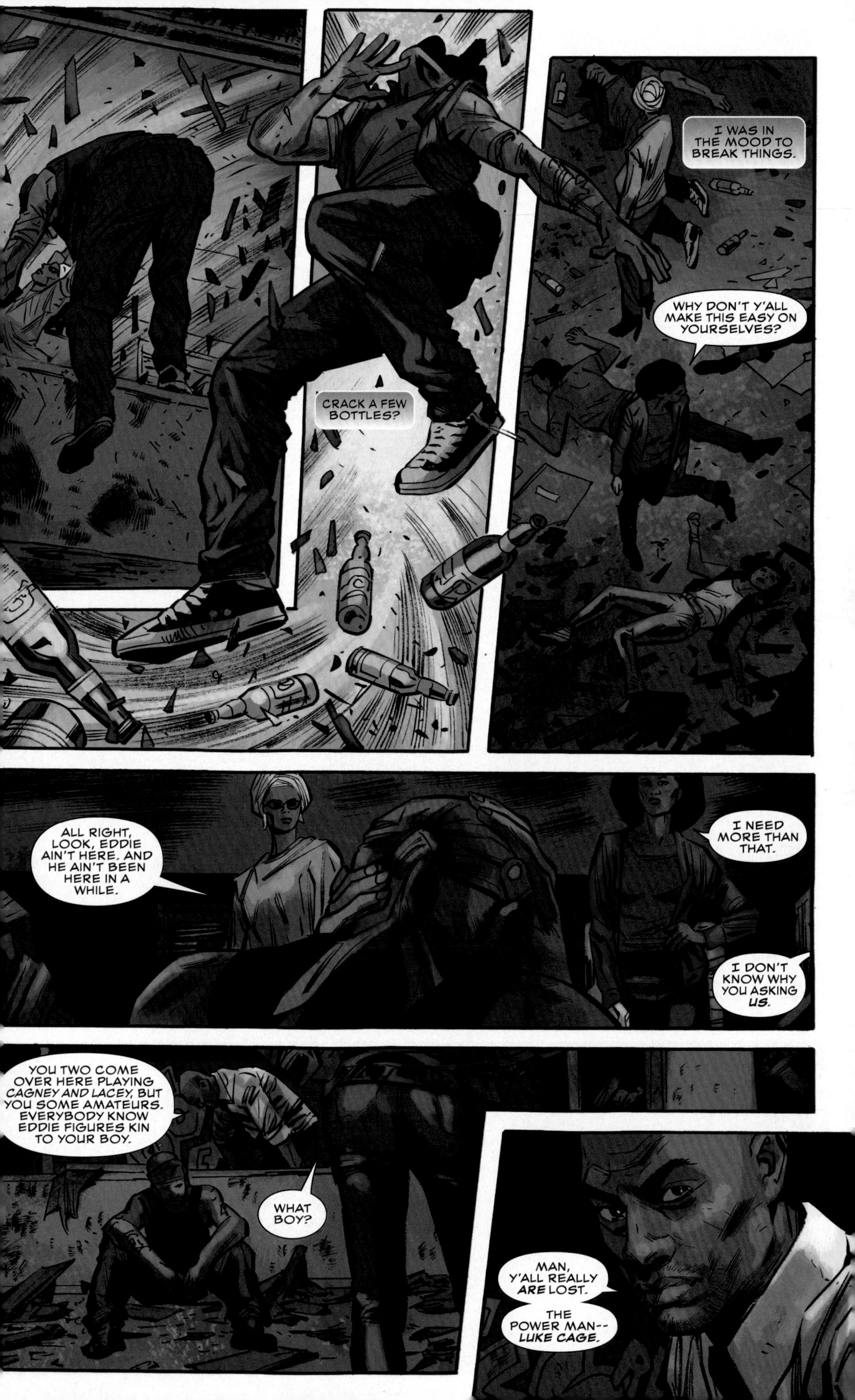
CRACK A FEW BOTTLES?
I WAS IN THE MOOD TO BREAK THINGS.
WHY DON'T Y'ALL MAKE THIS EASY ON YOURSELVES?
ALL RIGHT, LOOK, EDDIE AIN'T HERE. AND HE AIN'T BEEN HERE IN A WHILE.
I NEED MORE THAN THAT.
I DON'T KNOW WHY YOU ASKING *US*.
YOU TWO COME OVER HERE PLAYING *CAGNEY AND LACEY*, BUT YOU SOME AMATEURS. EVERYBODY KNOW EDDIE FIGURES KIN TO YOUR BOY.
WHAT BOY?
MAN, Y'ALL REALLY *ARE* LOST.
THE POWER MAN-- *LUKE CAGE*.

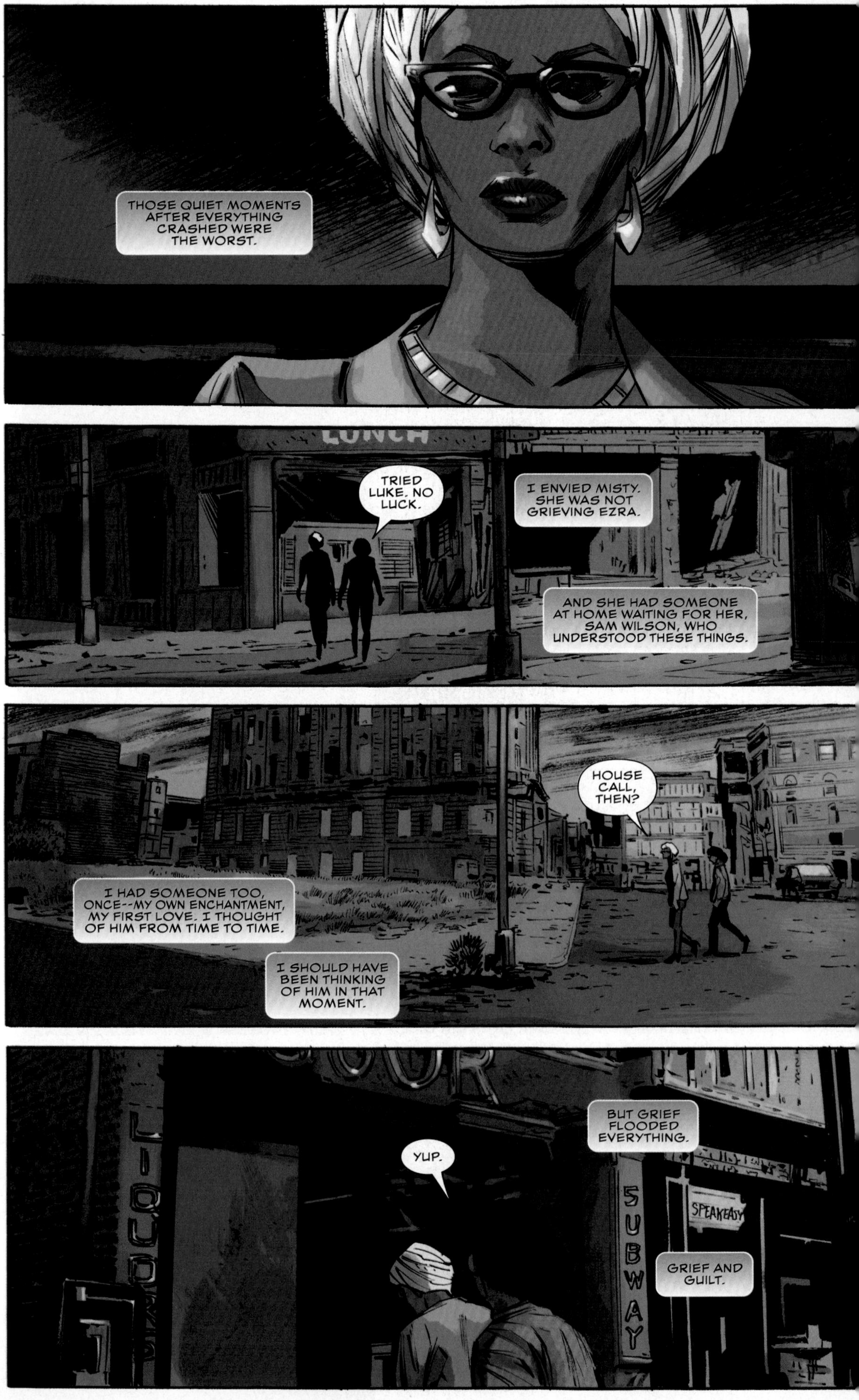
THOSE QUIET MOMENTS AFTER EVERYTHING CRASHED WERE THE WORST.
LUNCH
TRIED LUKE. NO LUCK.
I ENVIED MISTY. SHE WAS NOT GRIEVING EZRA.
AND SHE HAD SOMEONE AT HOME WAITING FOR HER, SAM WILSON, WHO UNDERSTOOD THESE THINGS.
HOUSE CALL, THEN?
I HAD SOMEONE TOO, ONCE--MY OWN ENCHANTMENT, MY FIRST LOVE. I THOUGHT OF HIM FROM TIME TO TIME.
I SHOULD HAVE BEEN THINKING OF HIM IN THAT MOMENT.
BUT GRIEF FLOODED EVERYTHING.
YUP.
SUBWAY
SPEAKEASY
GRIEF AND GUILT.

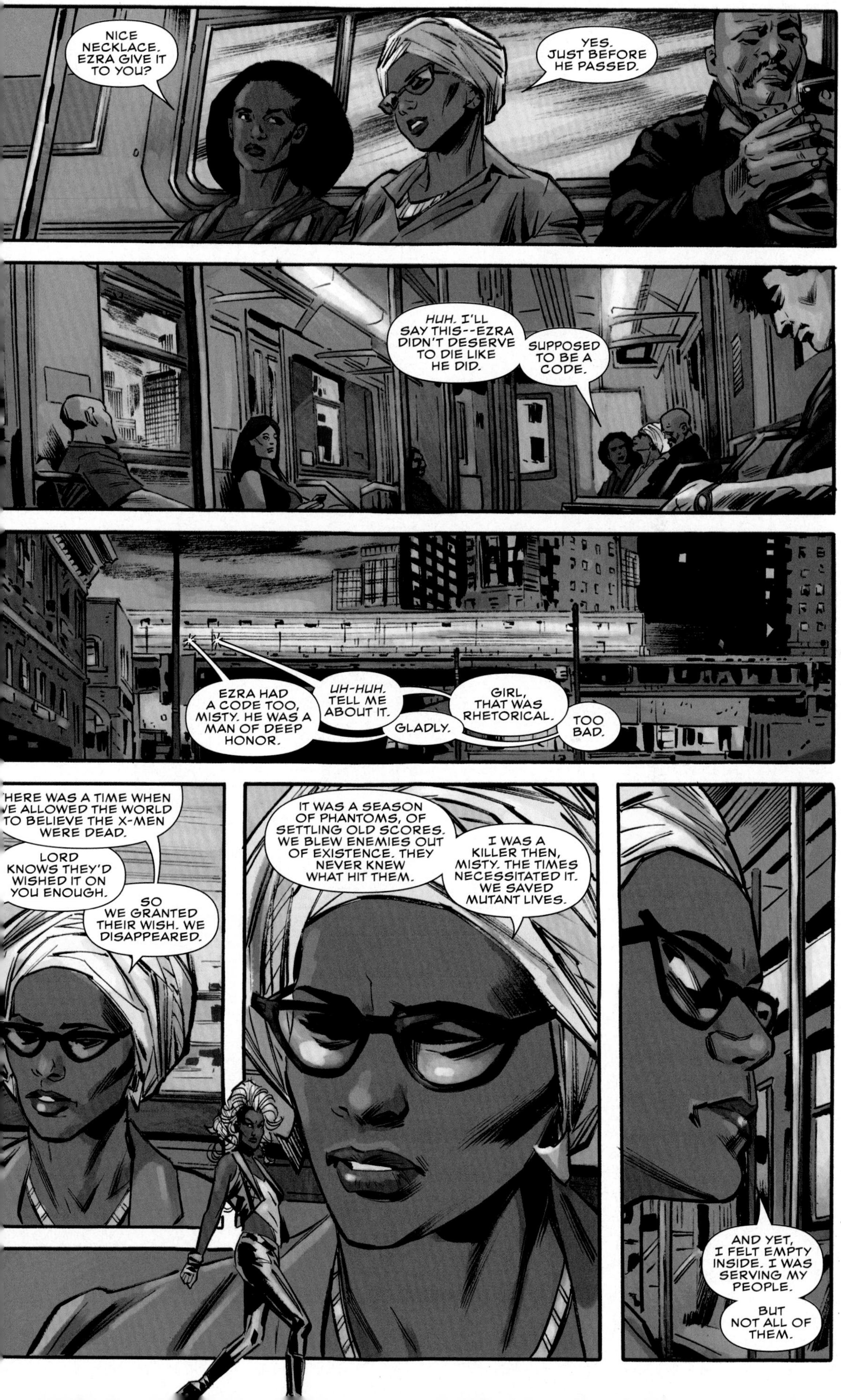
NICE NECKLACE. EZRA GIVE IT TO YOU?
YES. JUST BEFORE HE PASSED.
HUH. I'LL SAY THIS--EZRA DIDN'T DESERVE TO DIE LIKE HE DID.
SUPPOSED TO BE A CODE.
EZRA HAD A CODE TOO, MISTY. HE WAS A MAN OF DEEP HONOR.
UH-HUH. TELL ME ABOUT IT.
GIRL, THAT WAS RHETORICAL.
GLADLY.
TOO BAD.
THERE WAS A TIME WHEN WE ALLOWED THE WORLD TO BELIEVE THE X-MEN WERE DEAD.
LORD KNOWS THEY'D WISHED IT ON YOU ENOUGH.
SO WE GRANTED THEIR WISH. WE DISAPPEARED.
IT WAS A SEASON OF PHANTOMS, OF SETTLING OLD SCORES. WE BLEW ENEMIES OUT OF EXISTENCE. THEY NEVER KNEW WHAT HIT THEM.
I WAS A KILLER THEN, MISTY. THE TIMES NECESSITATED IT. WE SAVED MUTANT LIVES.
AND YET, I FELT EMPTY INSIDE. I WAS SERVING MY PEOPLE.
BUT NOT ALL OF THEM.

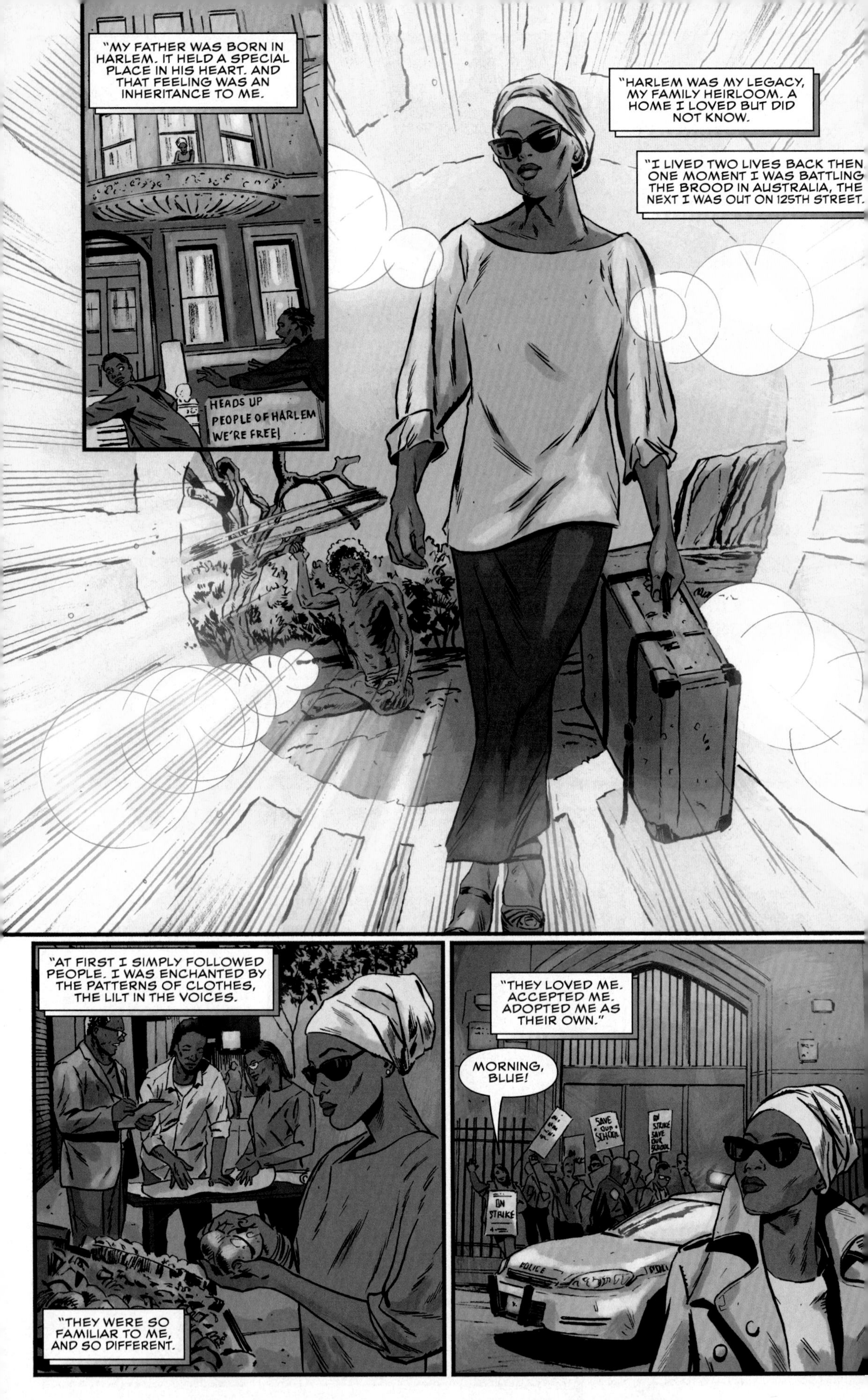
"MY FATHER WAS BORN IN HARLEM. IT HELD A SPECIAL PLACE IN HIS HEART. AND THAT FEELING WAS AN INHERITANCE TO ME.
HEADS UP PEOPLE OF HARLEM WE'RE FREE!
"HARLEM WAS MY LEGACY, MY FAMILY HEIRLOOM. A HOME I LOVED BUT DID NOT KNOW.
"I LIVED TWO LIVES BACK THEN. ONE MOMENT I WAS BATTLING THE BROOD IN AUSTRALIA, THE NEXT I WAS OUT ON 125TH STREET.
"AT FIRST I SIMPLY FOLLOWED PEOPLE. I WAS ENCHANTED BY THE PATTERNS OF CLOTHES, THE LILT IN THE VOICES.
"THEY WERE SO FAMILIAR TO ME, AND SO DIFFERENT.
"THEY LOVED ME. ACCEPTED ME. ADOPTED ME AS THEIR OWN."
MORNING, BLUE!
SAVE OUR SCHOOL
ON STRIKE
POLICE

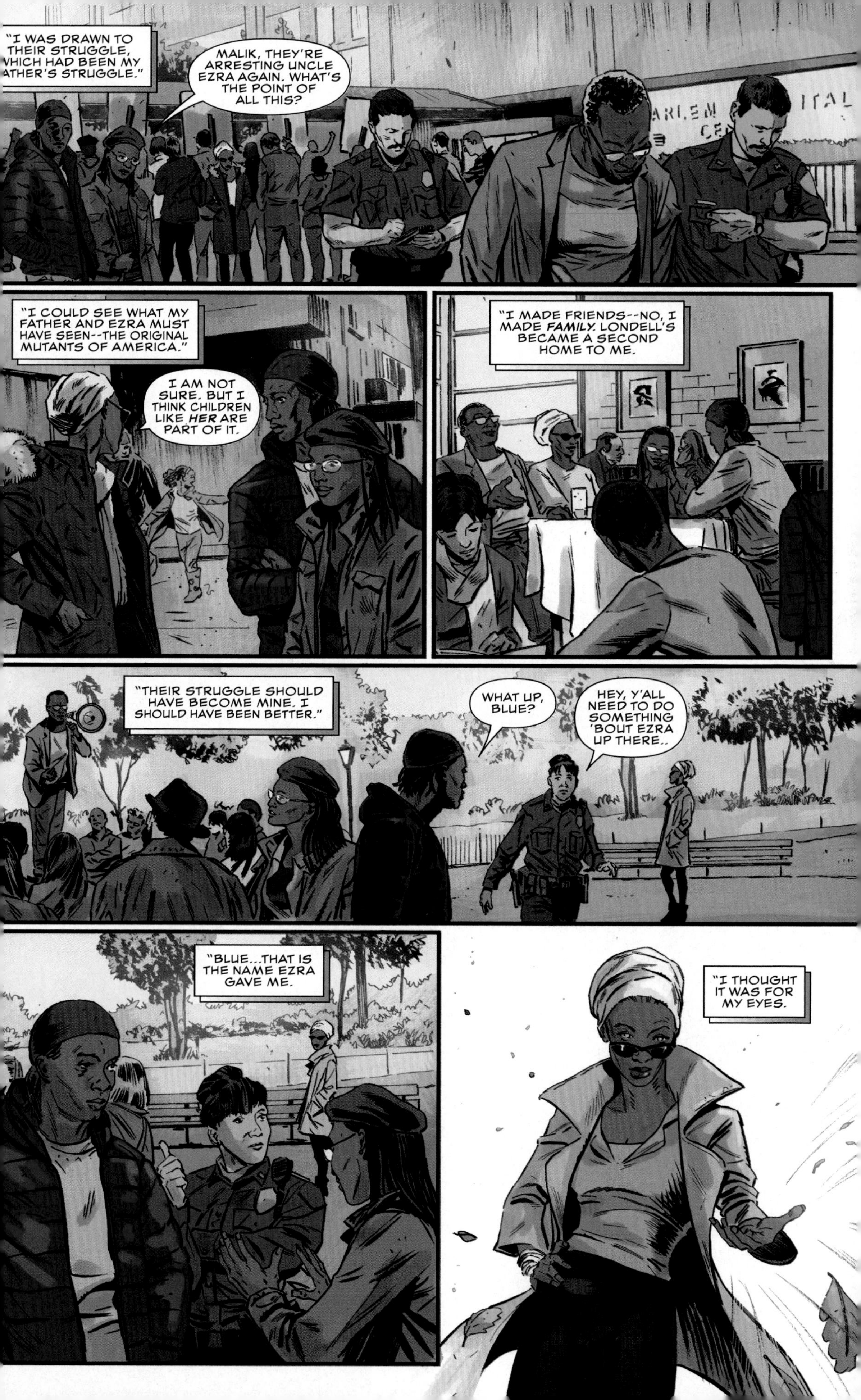
"I WAS DRAWN TO THEIR STRUGGLE, WHICH HAD BEEN MY ATHER'S STRUGGLE."
MALIK, THEY'RE ARRESTING UNCLE EZRA AGAIN. WHAT'S THE POINT OF ALL THIS?
"I COULD SEE WHAT MY FATHER AND EZRA MUST HAVE SEEN--THE ORIGINAL MUTANTS OF AMERICA."
I AM NOT SURE. BUT I THINK CHILDREN LIKE *HER* ARE PART OF IT.
"I MADE FRIENDS--NO, I MADE *FAMILY.* LONDELL'S BECAME A SECOND HOME TO ME.
"THEIR STRUGGLE SHOULD HAVE BECOME MINE. I SHOULD HAVE BEEN BETTER."
WHAT UP, BLUE?
HEY, Y'ALL NEED TO DO SOMETHING 'BOUT EZRA UP THERE..
"BLUE...THAT IS THE NAME EZRA GAVE ME.
"I THOUGHT IT WAS FOR MY EYES.

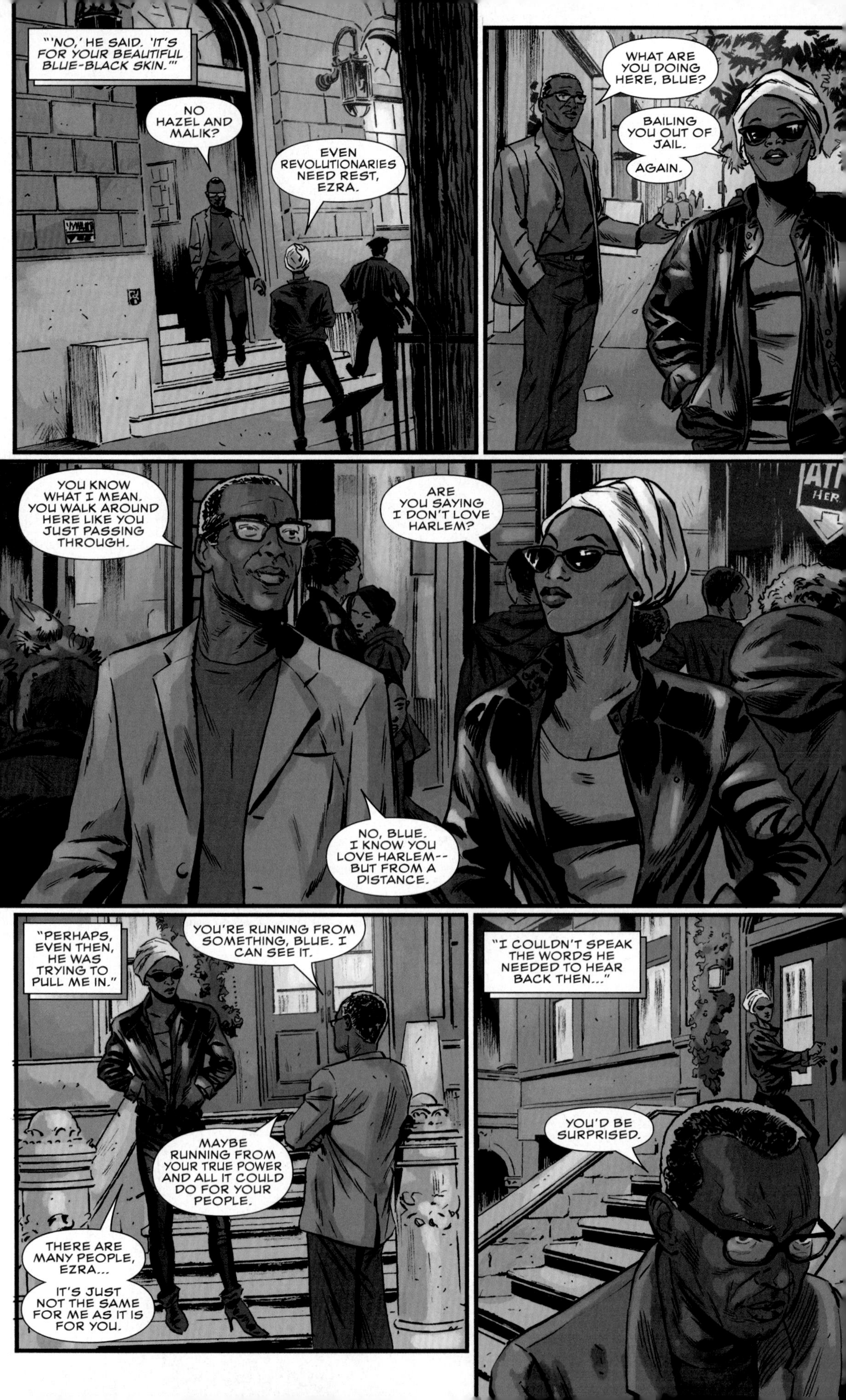
"'NO,' HE SAID. 'IT'S FOR YOUR BEAUTIFUL BLUE-BLACK SKIN.'"
NO HAZEL AND MALIK?
EVEN REVOLUTIONARIES NEED REST, EZRA.
WHAT ARE YOU DOING HERE, BLUE?
BAILING YOU OUT OF JAIL.
AGAIN.
YOU KNOW WHAT I MEAN. YOU WALK AROUND HERE LIKE YOU JUST PASSING THROUGH.
ARE YOU SAYING I DON'T LOVE HARLEM?
NO, BLUE. I KNOW YOU LOVE HARLEM-- BUT FROM A DISTANCE.
"PERHAPS, EVEN THEN, HE WAS TRYING TO PULL ME IN."
YOU'RE RUNNING FROM SOMETHING, BLUE. I CAN SEE IT.
MAYBE RUNNING FROM YOUR TRUE POWER AND ALL IT COULD DO FOR YOUR PEOPLE.
THERE ARE MANY PEOPLE, EZRA...
IT'S JUST NOT THE SAME FOR ME AS IT IS FOR YOU.
"I COULDN'T SPEAK THE WORDS HE NEEDED TO HEAR BACK THEN..."
YOU'D BE SURPRISED.

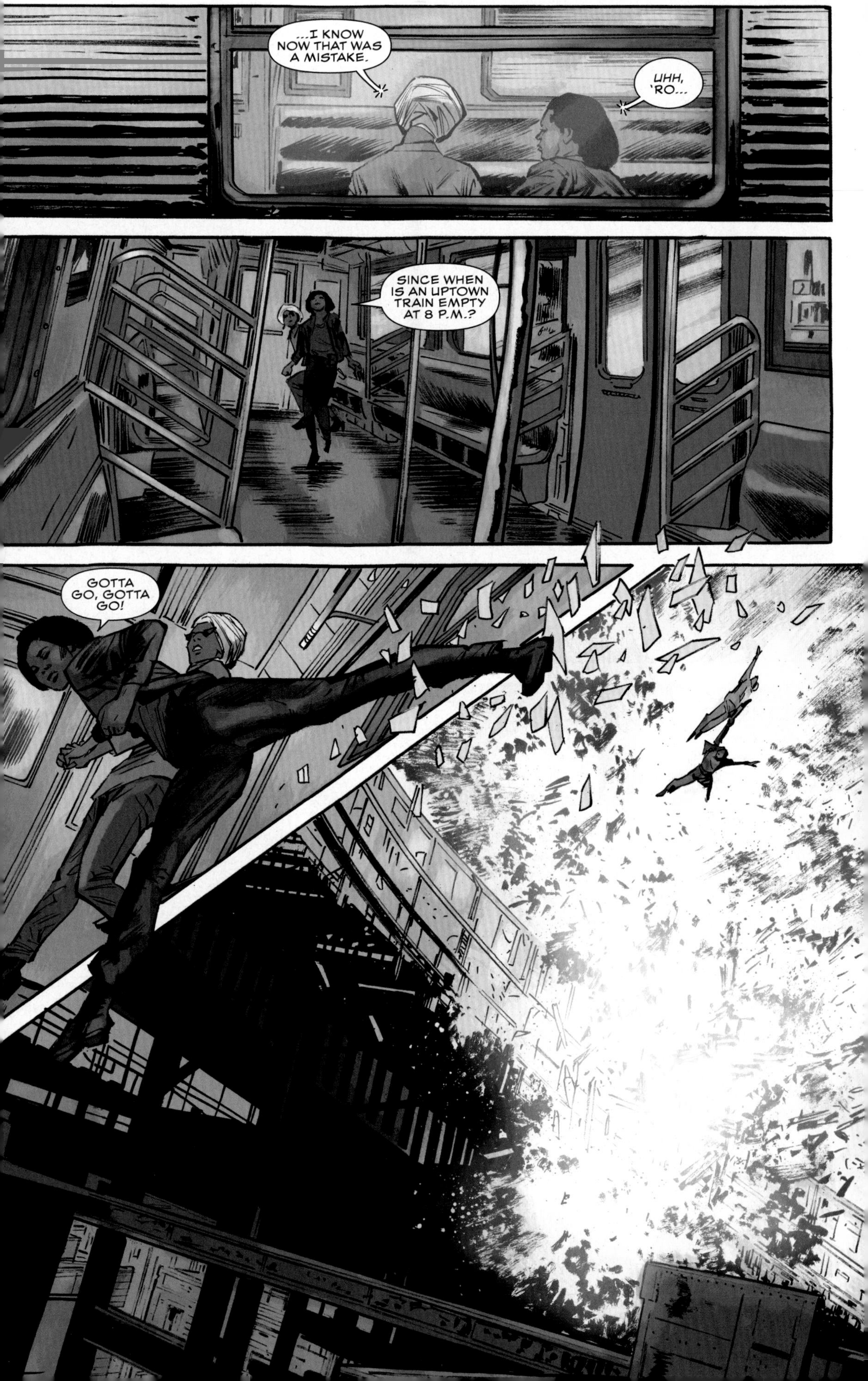
...I KNOW NOW THAT WAS A MISTAKE.
UHH, 'RO...
SINCE WHEN IS AN UPTOWN TRAIN EMPTY AT 8 P.M.?
GOTTA GO, GOTTA GO!

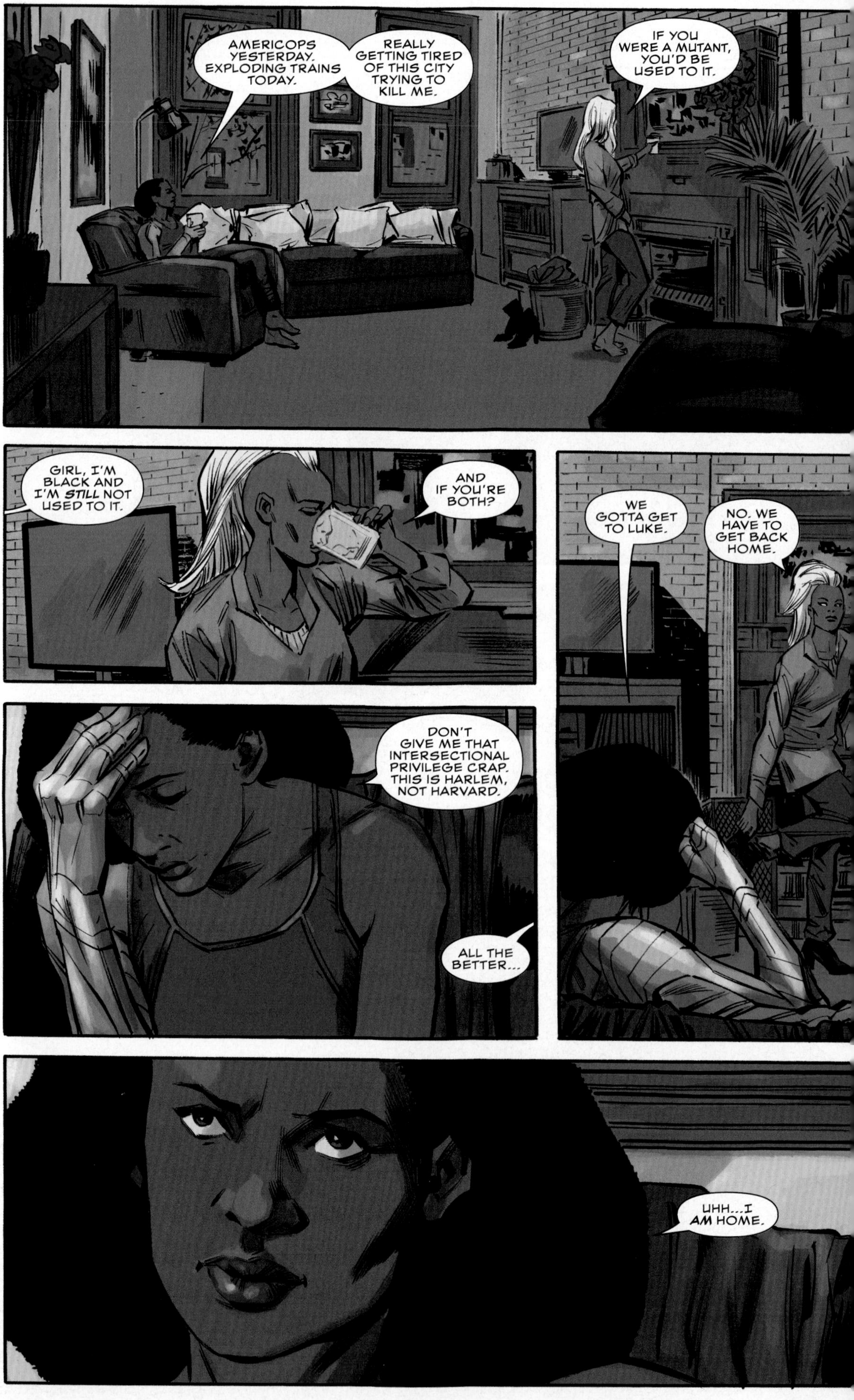
AMERICOPS YESTERDAY. EXPLODING TRAINS TODAY.
REALLY GETTING TIRED OF THIS CITY TRYING TO KILL ME.
IF YOU WERE A MUTANT, YOU'D BE USED TO IT.
GIRL, I'M BLACK AND I'M STILL NOT USED TO IT.
AND IF YOU'RE BOTH?
DON'T GIVE ME THAT INTERSECTIONAL PRIVILEGE CRAP. THIS IS HARLEM, NOT HARVARD.
ALL THE BETTER...
WE GOTTA GET TO LUKE.
NO. WE HAVE TO GET BACK HOME.
UHH...I AM HOME.

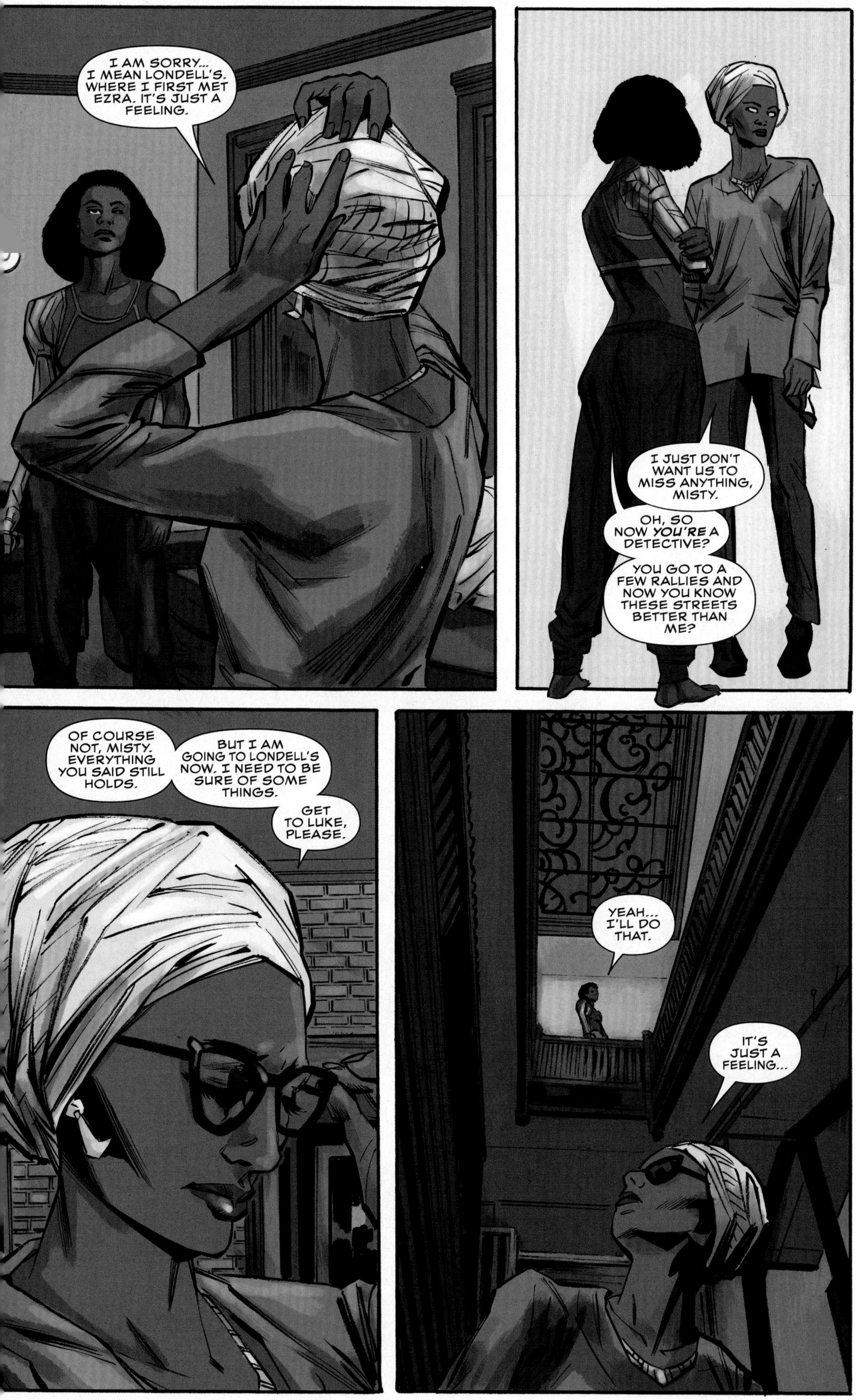
I AM SORRY... I MEAN LONDELL'S. WHERE I FIRST MET EZRA. IT'S JUST A FEELING.
I JUST DON'T WANT US TO MISS ANYTHING, MISTY.
OH, SO NOW *YOU'RE* A DETECTIVE?
YOU GO TO A FEW RALLIES AND NOW YOU KNOW THESE STREETS BETTER THAN ME?
OF COURSE NOT, MISTY. EVERYTHING YOU SAID STILL HOLDS.
BUT I AM GOING TO LONDELL'S NOW. I NEED TO BE SURE OF SOME THINGS.
GET TO LUKE, PLEASE.
YEAH... I'LL DO THAT.
IT'S JUST A FEELING...

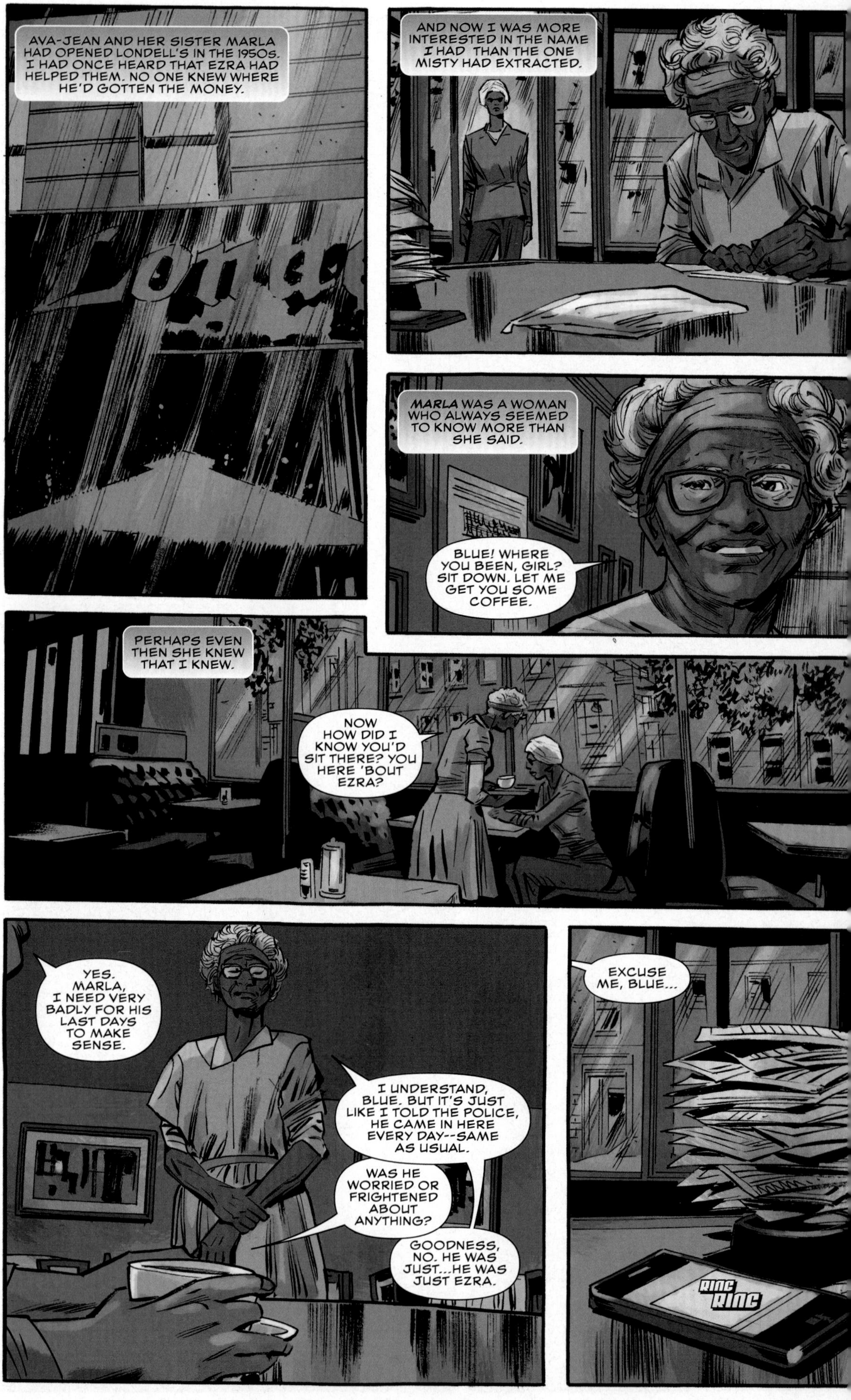
AVA-JEAN AND HER SISTER MARLA HAD OPENED LONDELL'S IN THE 1950s. I HAD ONCE HEARD THAT EZRA HAD HELPED THEM. NO ONE KNEW WHERE HE'D GOTTEN THE MONEY.
AND NOW I WAS MORE INTERESTED IN THE NAME I HAD THAN THE ONE MISTY HAD EXTRACTED.
MARLA WAS A WOMAN WHO ALWAYS SEEMED TO KNOW MORE THAN SHE SAID.
BLUE! WHERE YOU BEEN, GIRL? SIT DOWN. LET ME GET YOU SOME COFFEE.
PERHAPS EVEN THEN SHE KNEW THAT I KNEW.
NOW HOW DID I KNOW YOU'D SIT THERE? YOU HERE 'BOUT EZRA?
YES. MARLA, I NEED VERY BADLY FOR HIS LAST DAYS TO MAKE SENSE.
I UNDERSTAND, BLUE. BUT IT'S JUST LIKE I TOLD THE POLICE, HE CAME IN HERE EVERY DAY--SAME AS USUAL.
WAS HE WORRIED OR FRIGHTENED ABOUT ANYTHING?
GOODNESS, NO. HE WAS JUST...HE WAS JUST EZRA.
EXCUSE ME, BLUE...
RING RING

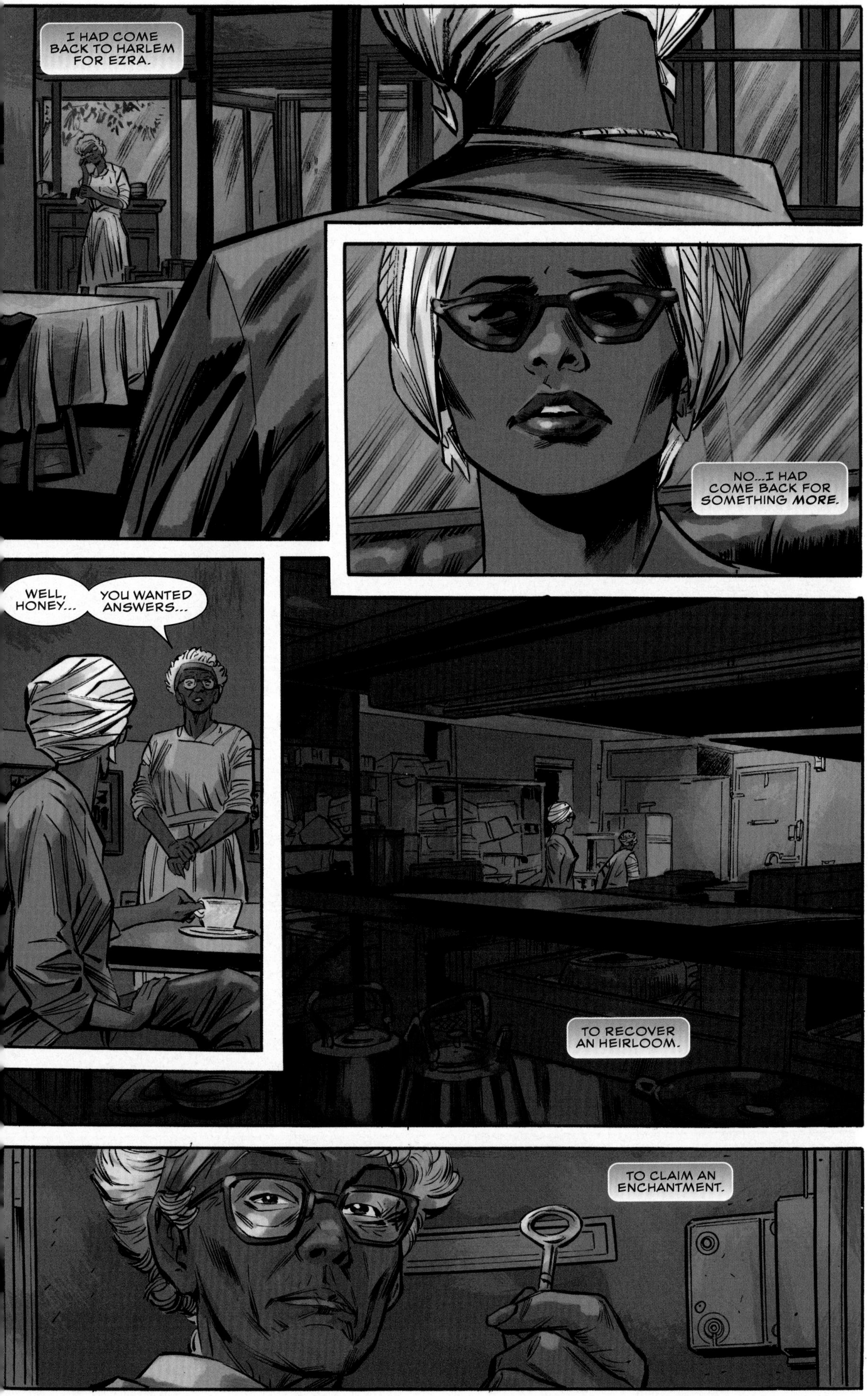
I HAD COME BACK TO HARLEM FOR EZRA.
NO...I HAD COME BACK FOR SOMETHING MORE.
WELL, HONEY...
YOU WANTED ANSWERS...
TO RECOVER AN HEIRLOOM.
TO CLAIM AN ENCHANTMENT.

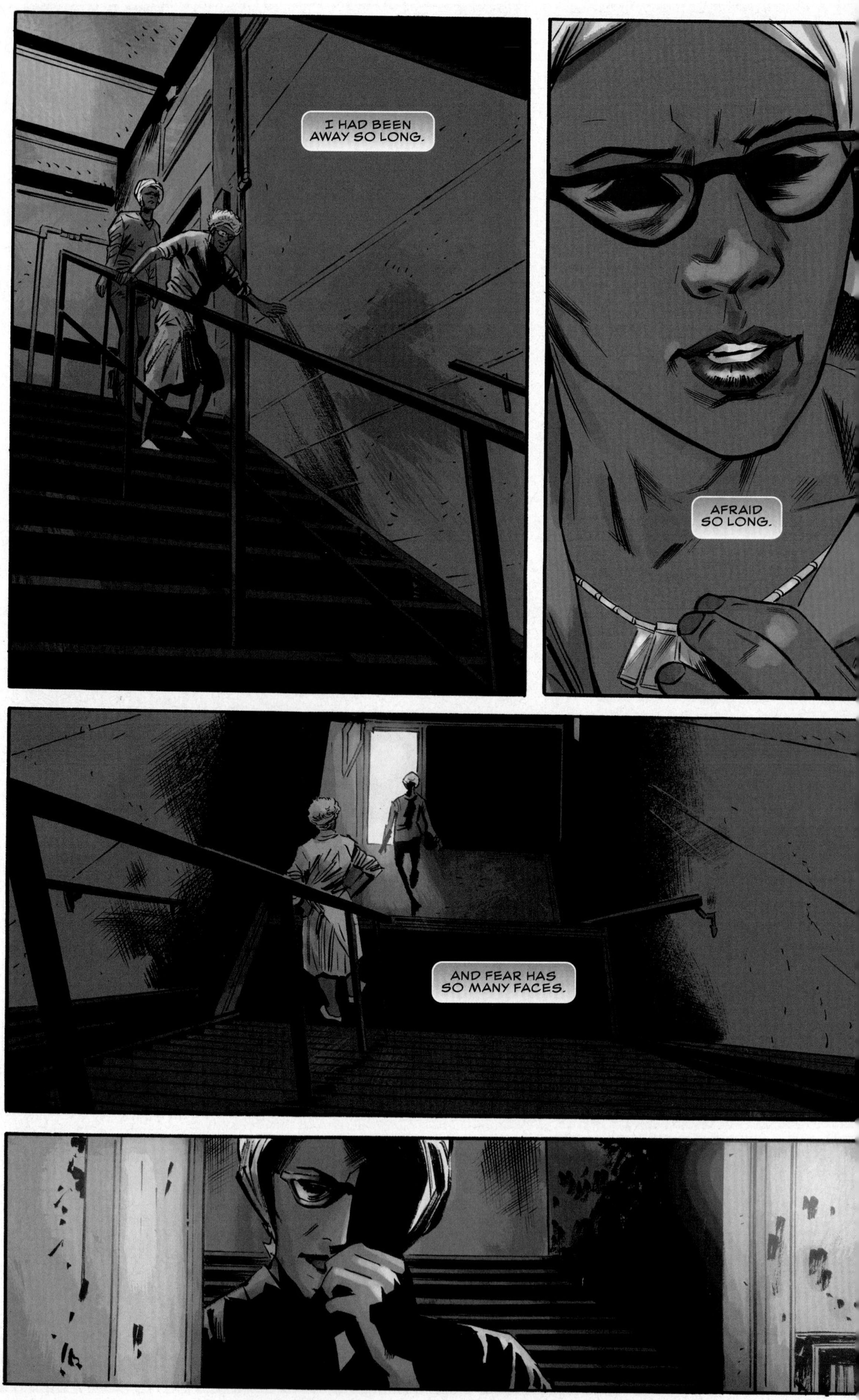
I HAD BEEN AWAY SO LONG.
AFRAID SO LONG.
AND FEAR HAS SO MANY FACES.

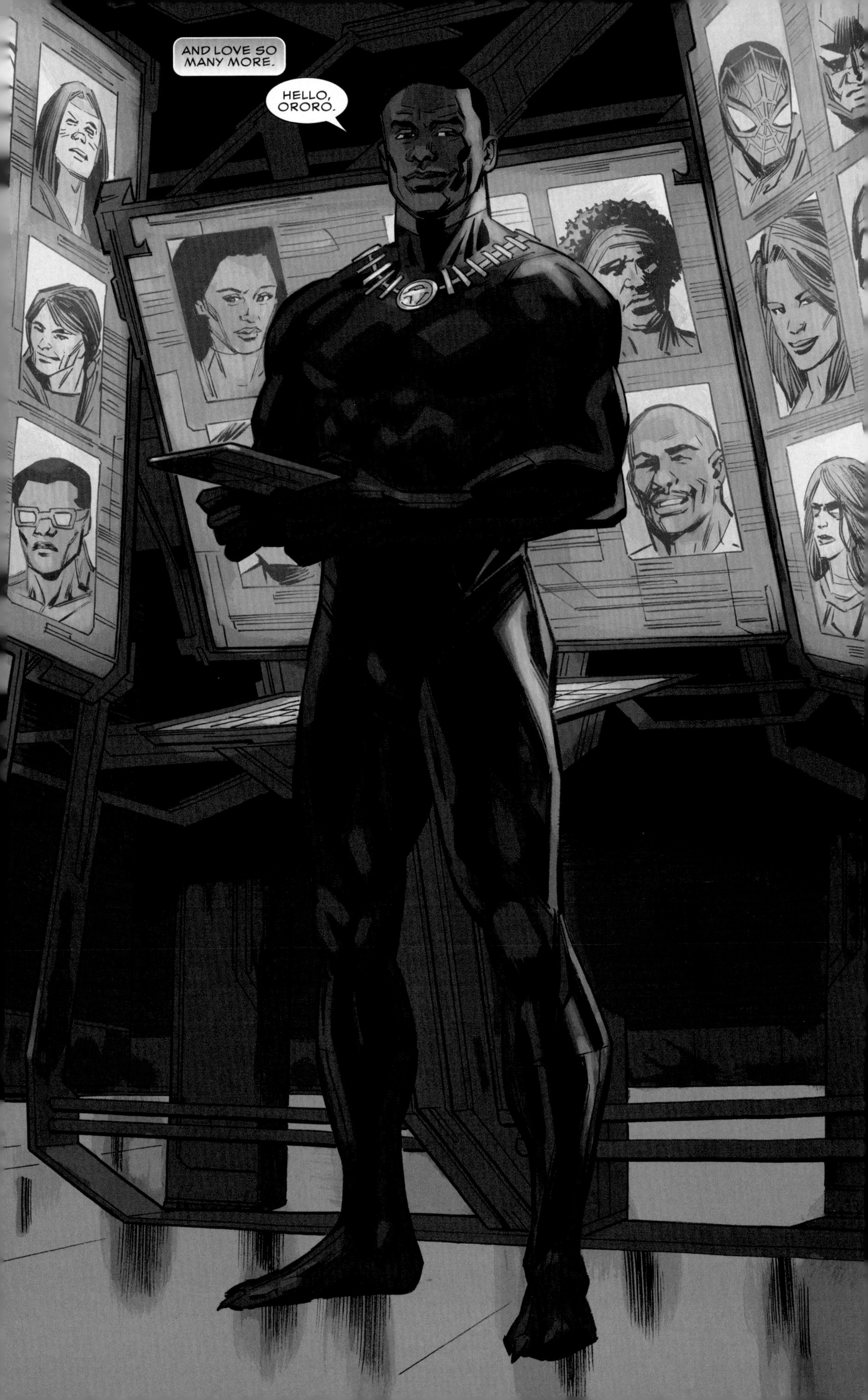
AND LOVE SO MANY MORE.
HELLO, ORORO.

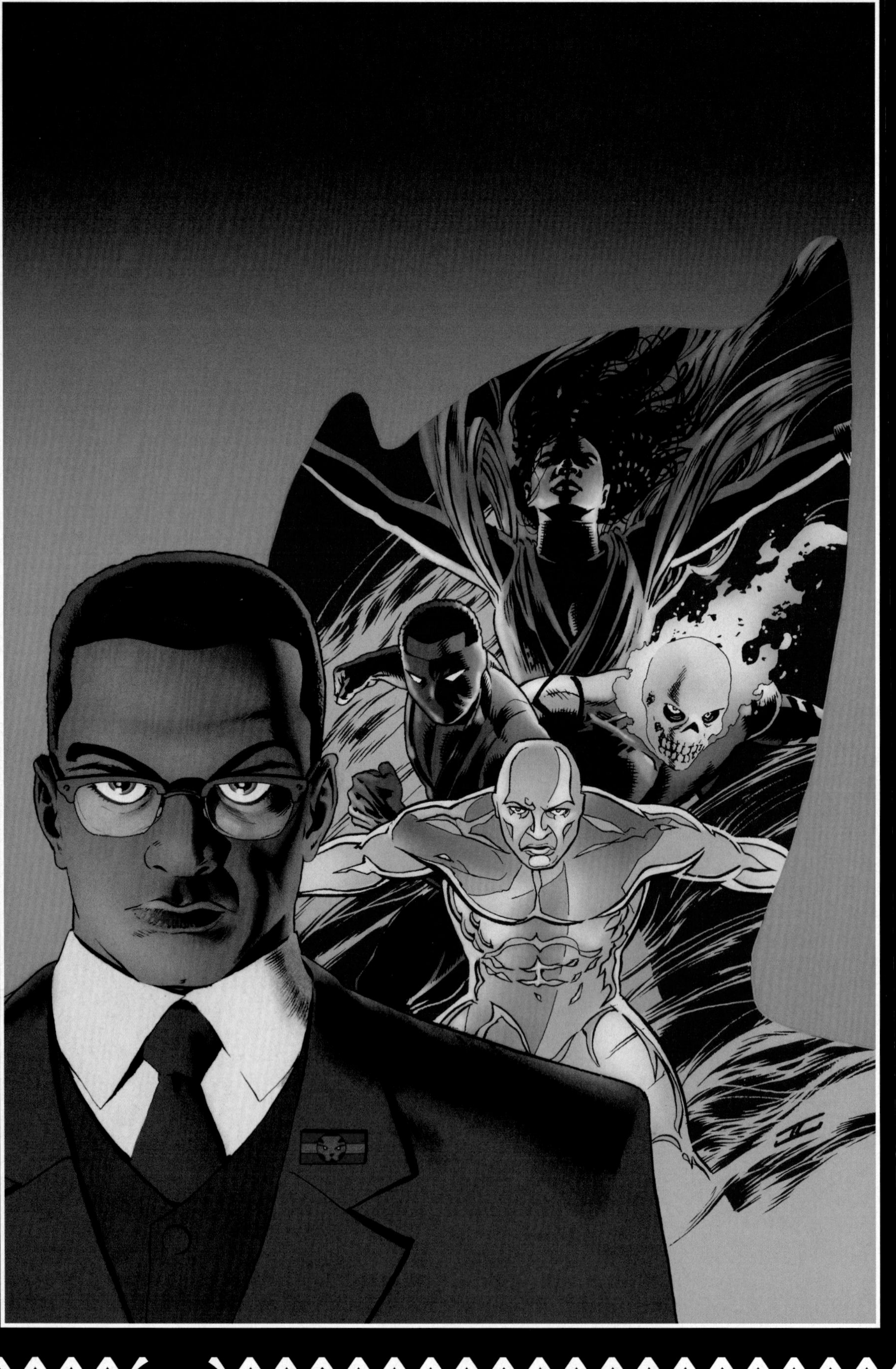

PART 3 BLACK AGAINST THE EMPIRE

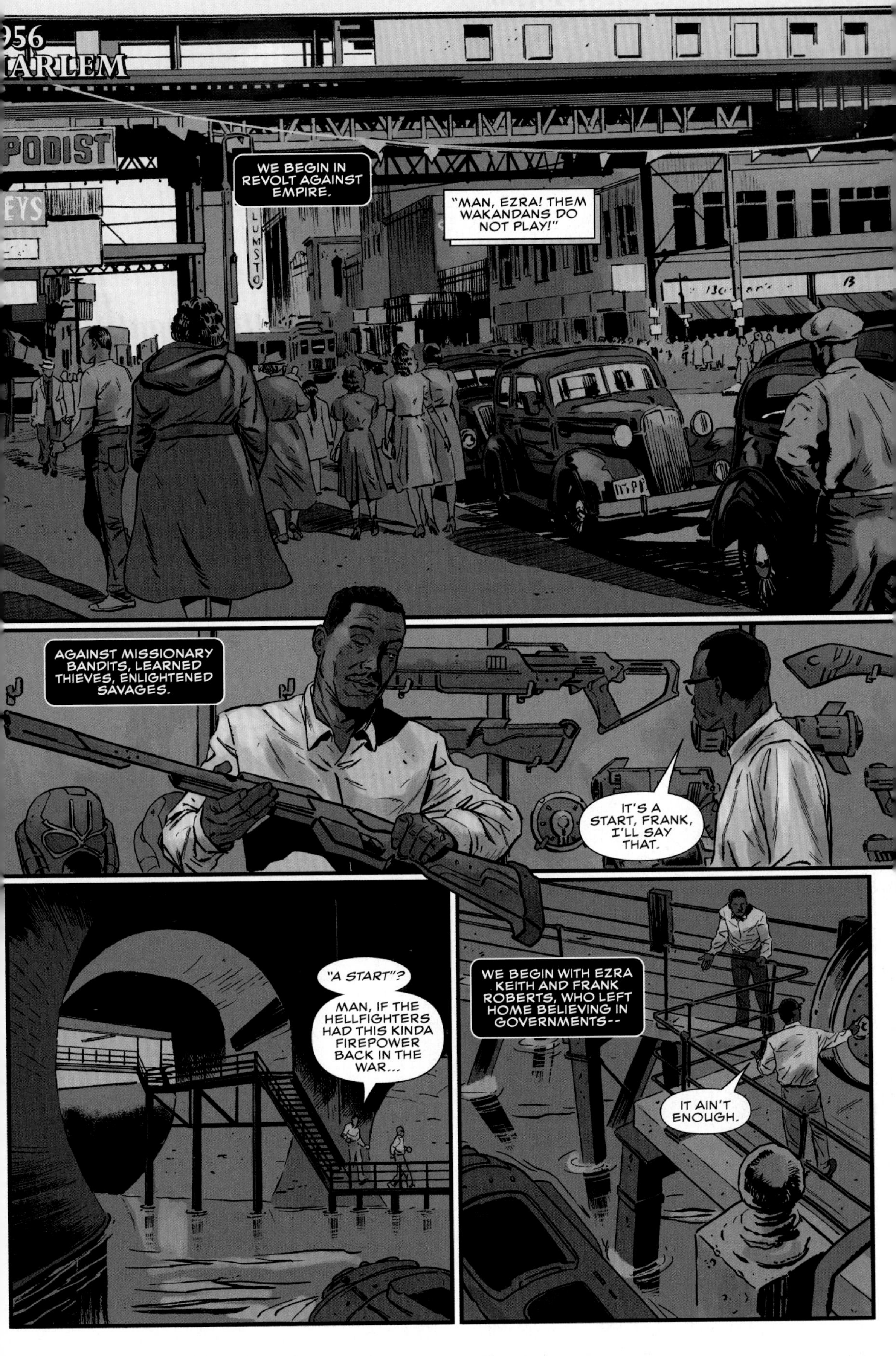
956
ARLEM
WE BEGIN IN REVOLT AGAINST EMPIRE.
"MAN, EZRA! THEM WAKANDANS DO NOT PLAY!"
AGAINST MISSIONARY BANDITS, LEARNED THIEVES, ENLIGHTENED SAVAGES.
IT'S A START, FRANK, I'LL SAY THAT.
"A START"?
MAN, IF THE HELLFIGHTERS HAD THIS KINDA FIREPOWER BACK IN THE WAR...
WE BEGIN WITH EZRA KEITH AND FRANK ROBERTS, WHO LEFT HOME BELIEVING IN GOVERNMENTS--
IT AIN'T ENOUGH.

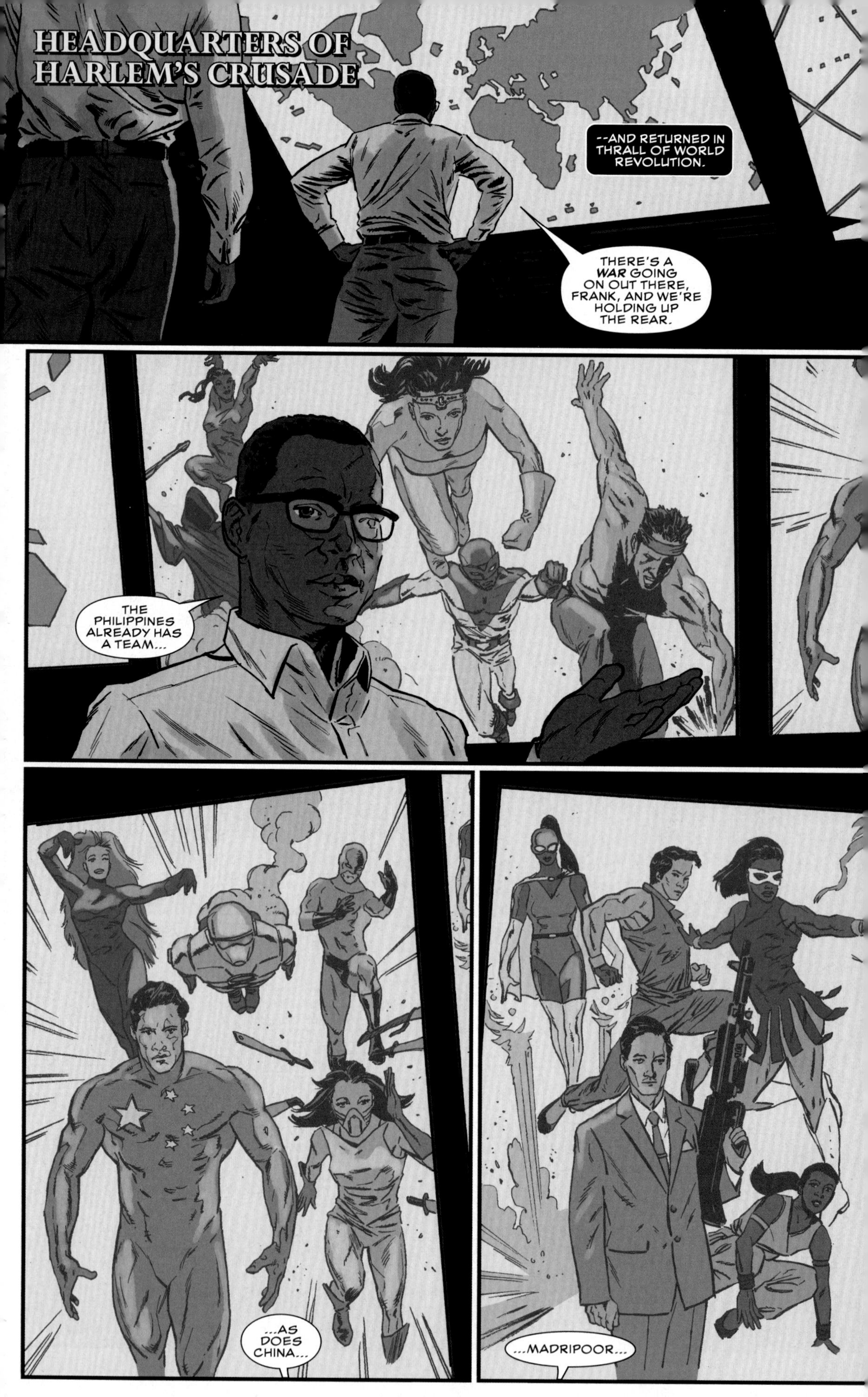
HEADQUARTERS OF HARLEM'S CRUSADE
--AND RETURNED IN THRALL OF WORLD REVOLUTION.
THERE'S A WAR GOING ON OUT THERE, FRANK, AND WE'RE HOLDING UP THE REAR.
THE PHILIPPINES ALREADY HAS A TEAM...
...AS DOES CHINA...
...MADRIPOOR...

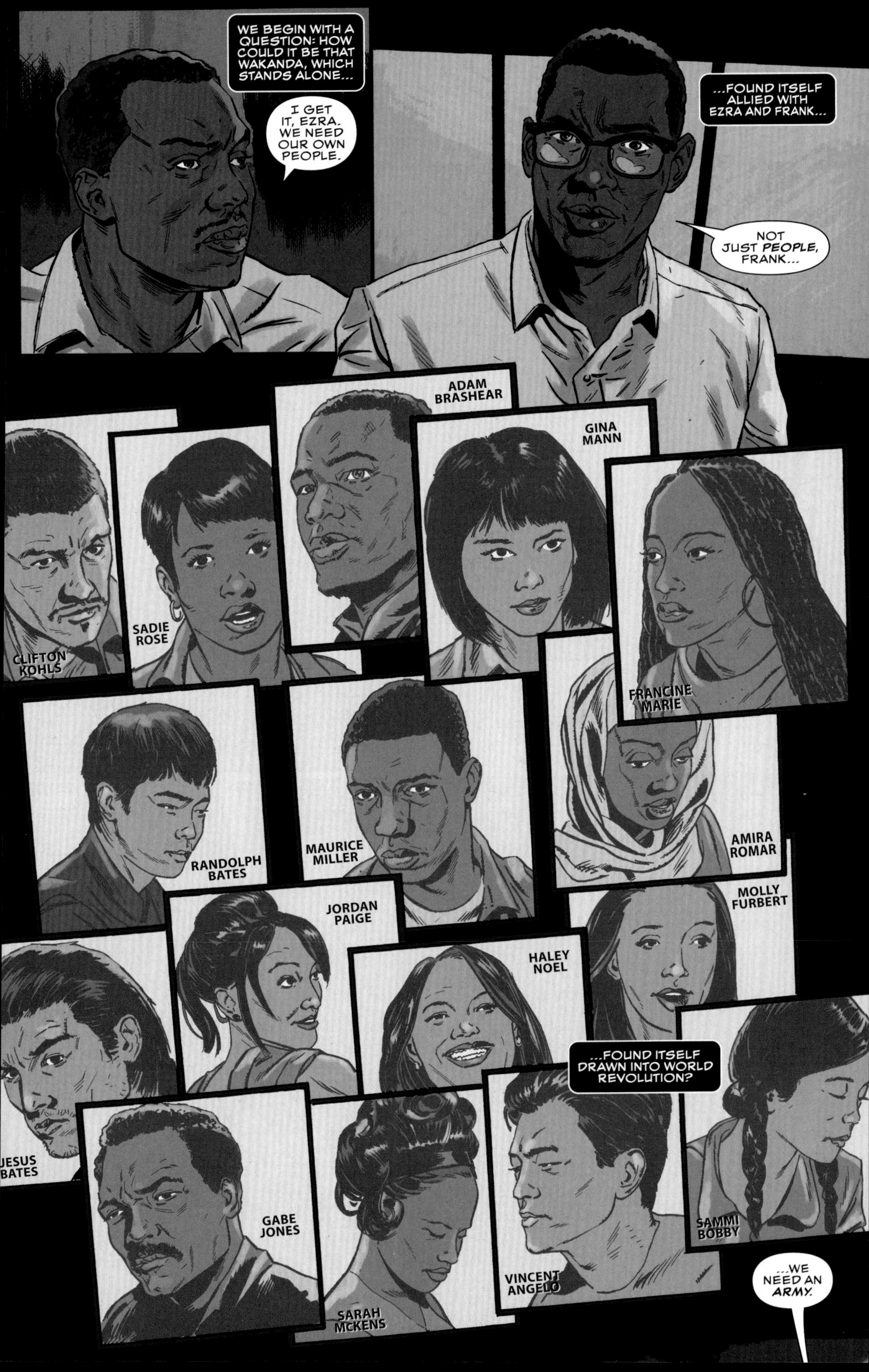
WE BEGIN WITH A QUESTION: HOW COULD IT BE THAT WAKANDA, WHICH STANDS ALONE...
I GET IT, EZRA. WE NEED OUR OWN PEOPLE.
...FOUND ITSELF ALLIED WITH EZRA AND FRANK...
NOT JUST PEOPLE, FRANK...
ADAM BRASHEAR
GINA MANN
CLIFTON KOHLS
SADIE ROSE
FRANCINE MARIE
RANDOLPH BATES
MAURICE MILLER
AMIRA ROMAR
JORDAN PAIGE
MOLLY FURBERT
HALEY NOEL
...FOUND ITSELF DRAWN INTO WORLD REVOLUTION?
JESUS BATES
GABE JONES
SAMMI BOBBY
VINCENT ANGELO
SARAH MCKENS
...WE NEED AN ARMY.

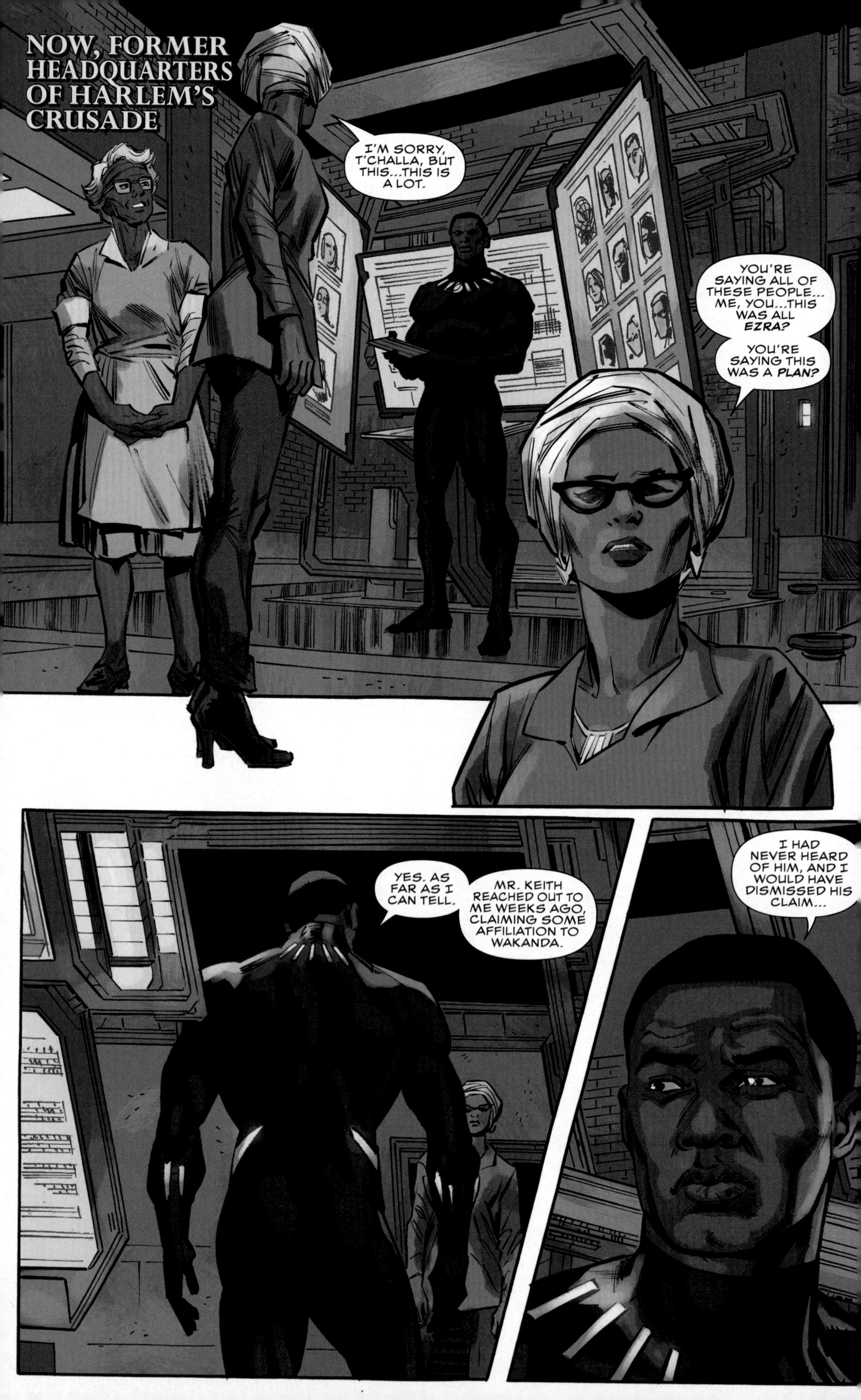
NOW, FORMER HEADQUARTERS OF HARLEM'S CRUSADE
I'M SORRY, T'CHALLA, BUT THIS...THIS IS A LOT.
YOU'RE SAYING ALL OF THESE PEOPLE... ME, YOU...THIS WAS ALL EZRA?
YOU'RE SAYING THIS WAS A PLAN?
YES. AS FAR AS I CAN TELL.
MR. KEITH REACHED OUT TO ME WEEKS AGO, CLAIMING SOME AFFILIATION TO WAKANDA.
I HAD NEVER HEARD OF HIM, AND I WOULD HAVE DISMISSED HIS CLAIM...

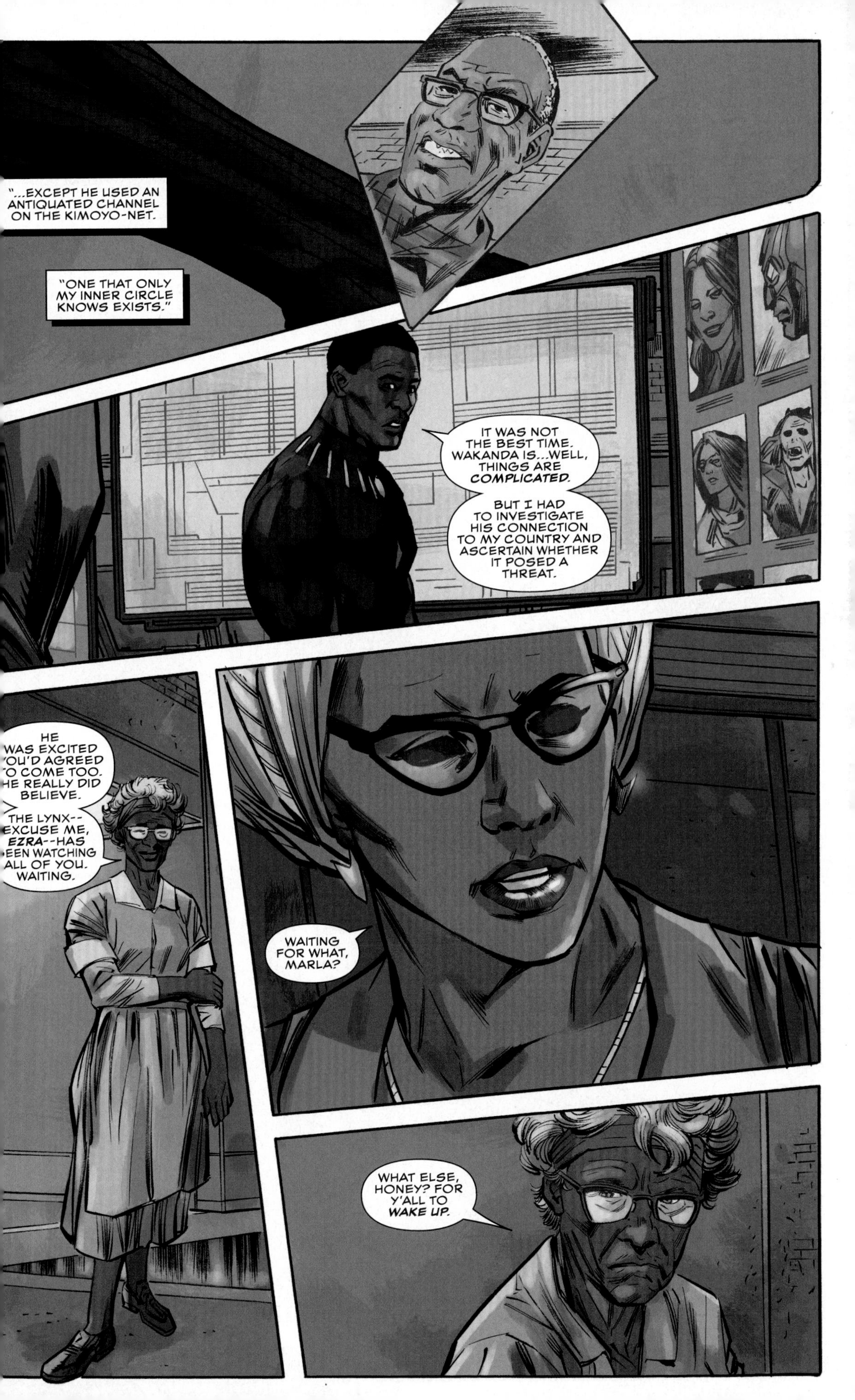
"...EXCEPT HE USED AN ANTIQUATED CHANNEL ON THE KIMOYO-NET.
"ONE THAT ONLY MY INNER CIRCLE KNOWS EXISTS."
IT WAS NOT THE BEST TIME. WAKANDA IS...WELL, THINGS ARE COMPLICATED.
BUT I HAD TO INVESTIGATE HIS CONNECTION TO MY COUNTRY AND ASCERTAIN WHETHER IT POSED A THREAT.
HE WAS EXCITED YOU'D AGREED TO COME TOO. HE REALLY DID BELIEVE.
THE LYNX--EXCUSE ME, EZRA--HAS BEEN WATCHING ALL OF YOU. WAITING.
WAITING FOR WHAT, MARLA?
WHAT ELSE, HONEY? FOR Y'ALL TO WAKE UP.

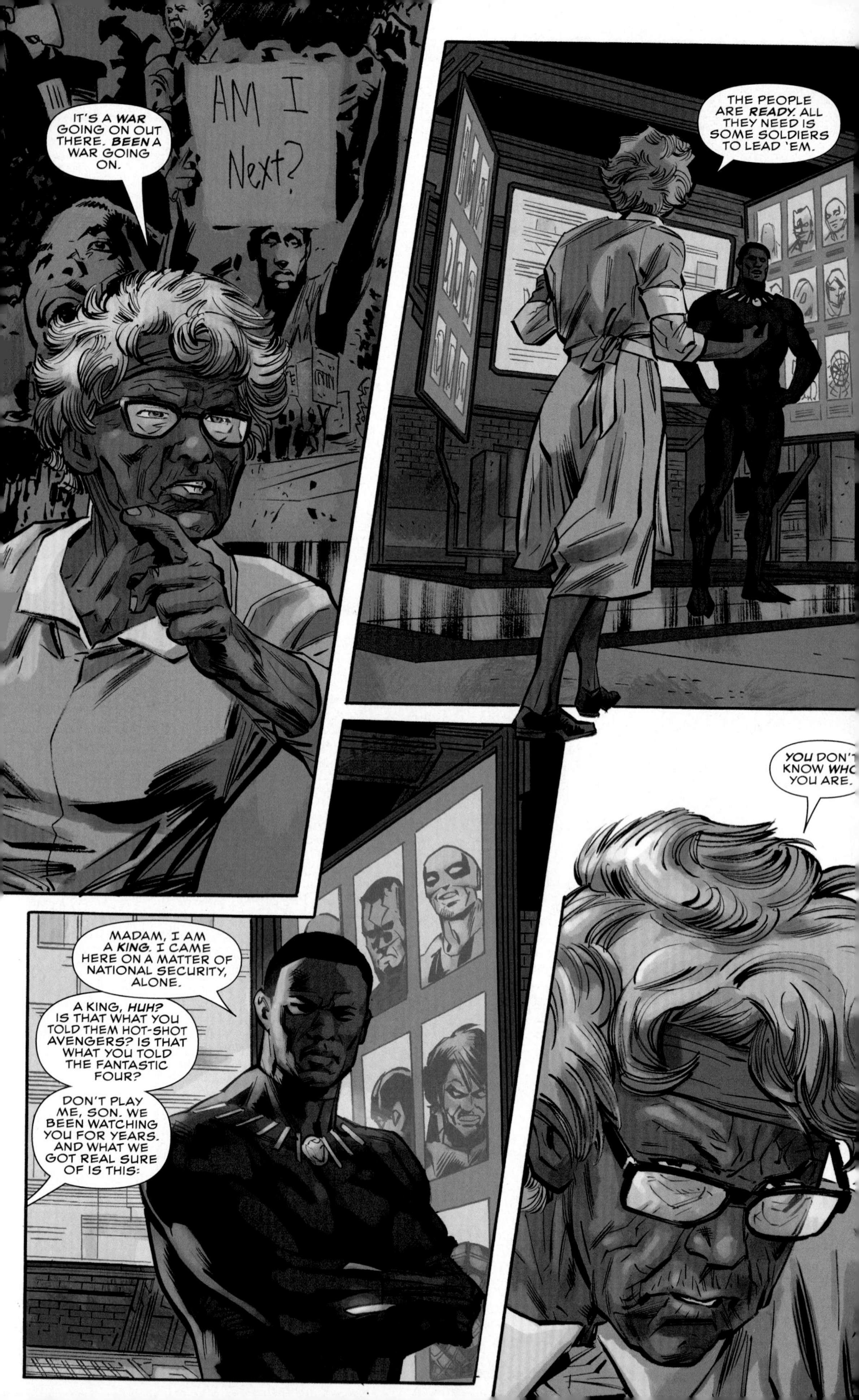
AM I Next?
IT'S A WAR GOING ON OUT THERE. BEEN A WAR GOING ON.
THE PEOPLE ARE READY. ALL THEY NEED IS SOME SOLDIERS TO LEAD 'EM.
MADAM, I AM A KING. I CAME HERE ON A MATTER OF NATIONAL SECURITY, ALONE.
A KING, HUH? IS THAT WHAT YOU TOLD THEM HOT-SHOT AVENGERS? IS THAT WHAT YOU TOLD THE FANTASTIC FOUR?
DON'T PLAY ME, SON. WE BEEN WATCHING YOU FOR YEARS. AND WHAT WE GOT REAL SURE OF IS THIS:
YOU DON'T KNOW WHO YOU ARE.

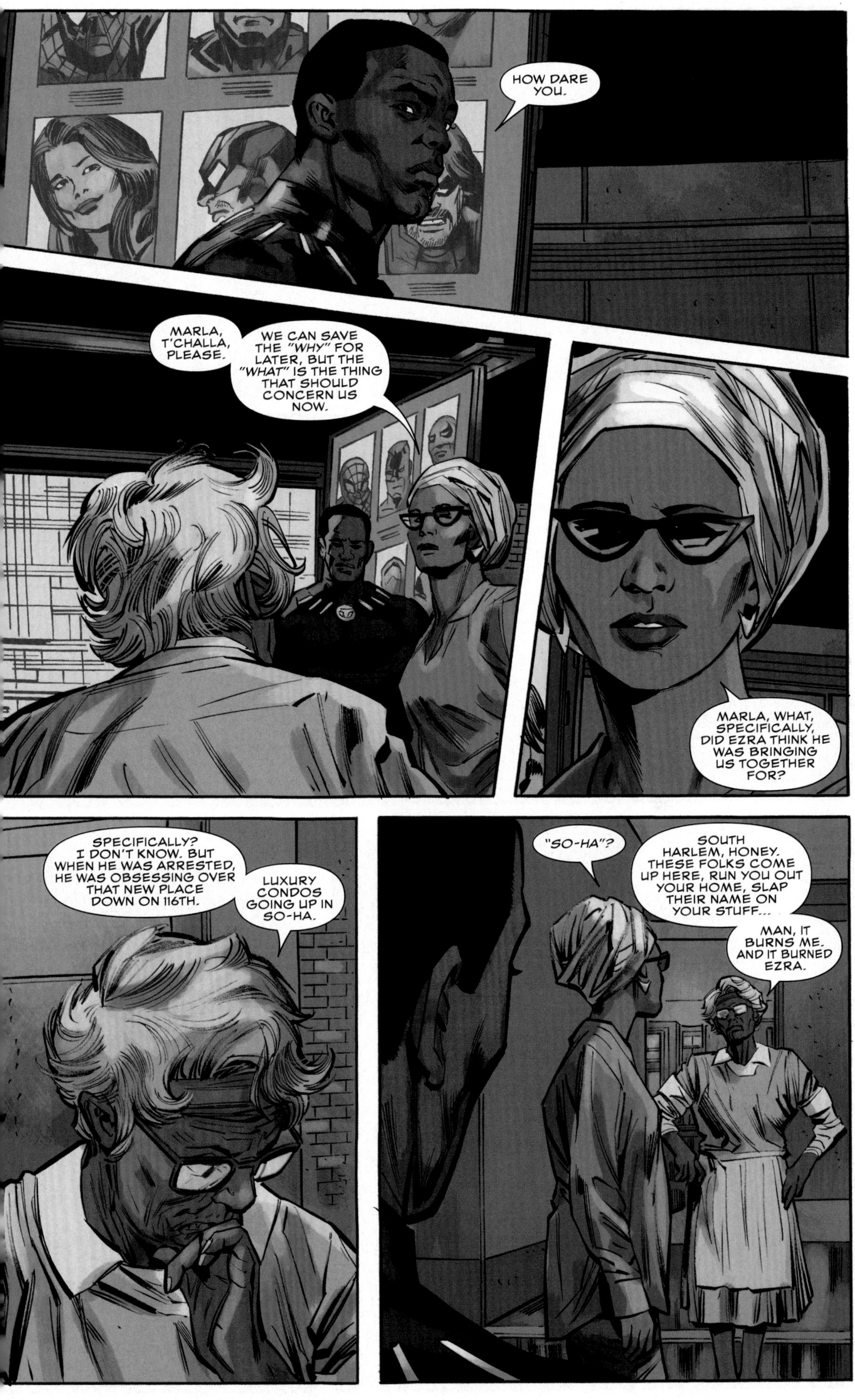
HOW DARE YOU.
MARLA, T'CHALLA, PLEASE.
WE CAN SAVE THE "WHY" FOR LATER, BUT THE "WHAT" IS THE THING THAT SHOULD CONCERN US NOW.
MARLA, WHAT, SPECIFICALLY, DID EZRA THINK HE WAS BRINGING US TOGETHER FOR?
SPECIFICALLY? I DON'T KNOW. BUT WHEN HE WAS ARRESTED, HE WAS OBSESSING OVER THAT NEW PLACE DOWN ON 116TH.
LUXURY CONDOS GOING UP IN SO-HA.
"SO-HA"?
SOUTH HARLEM, HONEY. THESE FOLKS COME UP HERE, RUN YOU OUT YOUR HOME, SLAP THEIR NAME ON YOUR STUFF...
MAN, IT BURNS ME. AND IT BURNED EZRA.

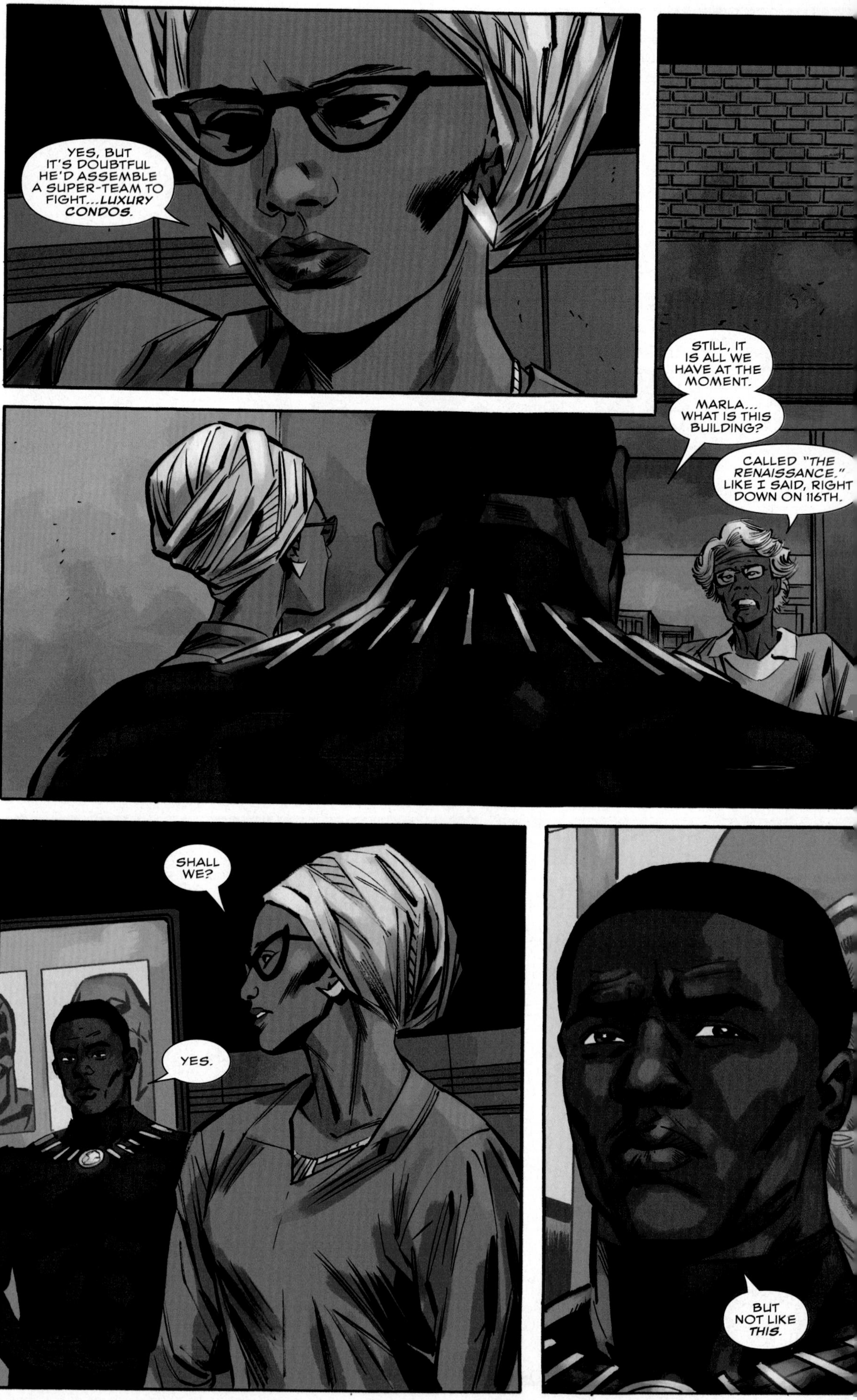
YES, BUT IT'S DOUBTFUL HE'D ASSEMBLE A SUPER-TEAM TO FIGHT...*LUXURY CONDOS*.
STILL, IT IS ALL WE HAVE AT THE MOMENT.
MARLA... WHAT IS THIS BUILDING?
CALLED *"THE RENAISSANCE."* LIKE I SAID, RIGHT DOWN ON 116TH.
SHALL WE?
YES.
BUT NOT LIKE *THIS*.

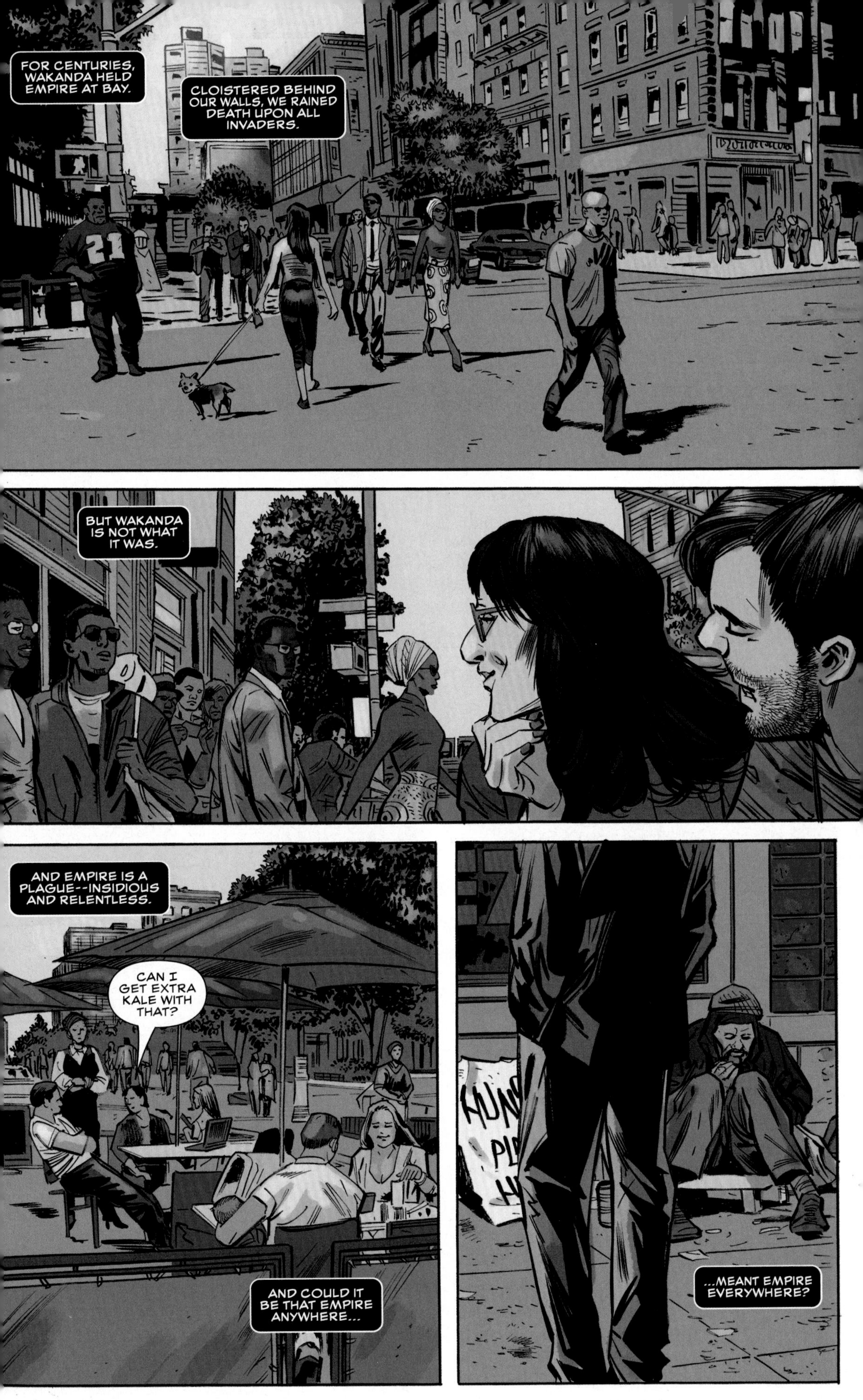
FOR CENTURIES, WAKANDA HELD EMPIRE AT BAY.
CLOISTERED BEHIND OUR WALLS, WE RAINED DEATH UPON ALL INVADERS.
BUT WAKANDA IS NOT WHAT IT WAS.
AND EMPIRE IS A PLAGUE--INSIDIOUS AND RELENTLESS.
CAN I GET EXTRA KALE WITH THAT?
AND COULD IT BE THAT EMPIRE ANYWHERE...
...MEANT EMPIRE EVERYWHERE?

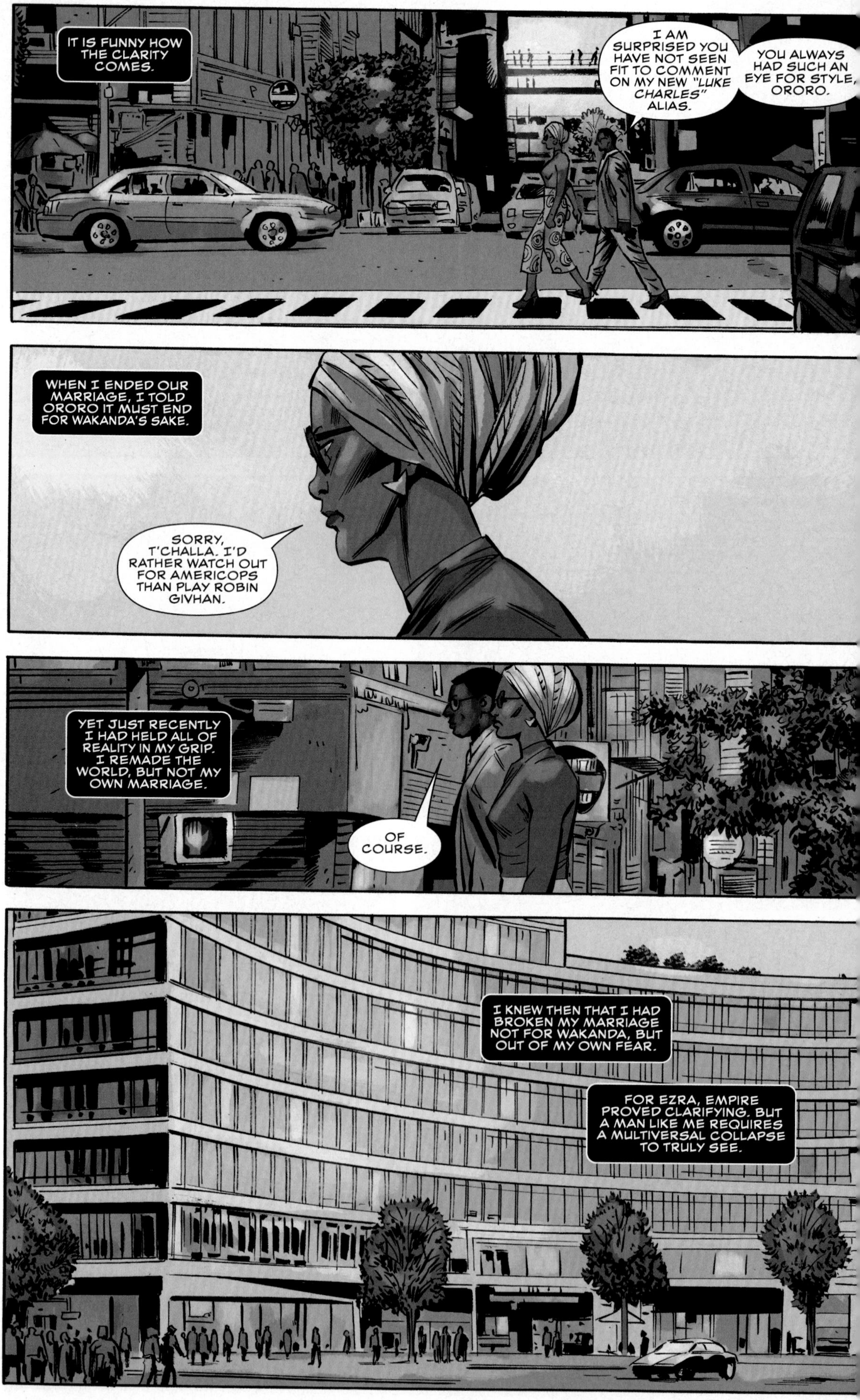
IT IS FUNNY HOW THE CLARITY COMES.
I AM SURPRISED YOU HAVE NOT SEEN FIT TO COMMENT ON MY NEW "LUKE CHARLES" ALIAS.
YOU ALWAYS HAD SUCH AN EYE FOR STYLE, ORORO.
WHEN I ENDED OUR MARRIAGE, I TOLD ORORO IT MUST END FOR WAKANDA'S SAKE.
SORRY, T'CHALLA. I'D RATHER WATCH OUT FOR AMERICOPS THAN PLAY ROBIN GIVHAN.
YET JUST RECENTLY I HAD HELD ALL OF REALITY IN MY GRIP. I REMADE THE WORLD, BUT NOT MY OWN MARRIAGE.
OF COURSE.
I KNEW THEN THAT I HAD BROKEN MY MARRIAGE NOT FOR WAKANDA, BUT OUT OF MY OWN FEAR.
FOR EZRA, EMPIRE PROVED CLARIFYING. BUT A MAN LIKE ME REQUIRES A MULTIVERSAL COLLAPSE TO TRULY SEE.

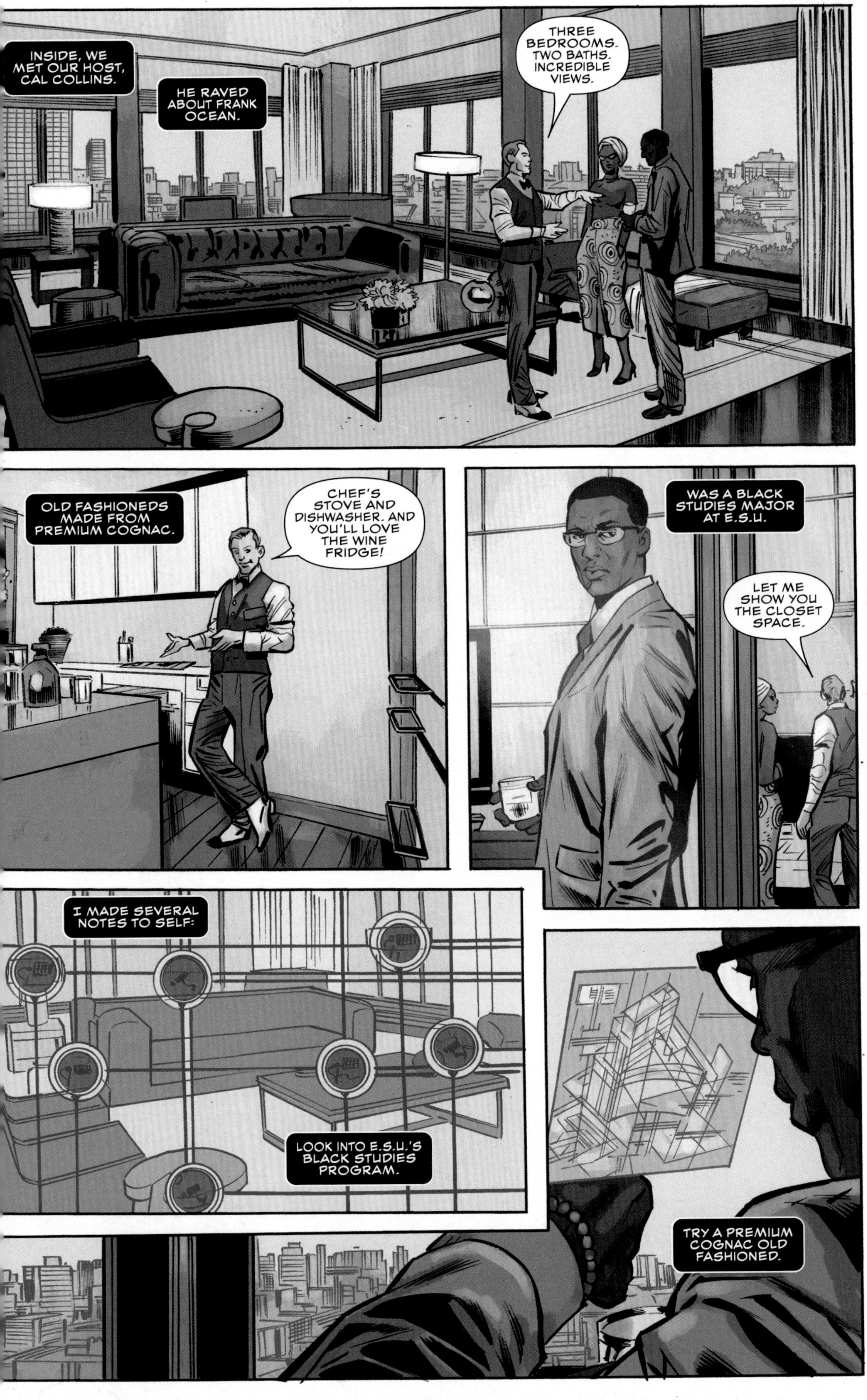
INSIDE, WE MET OUR HOST, CAL COLLINS.
HE RAVED ABOUT FRANK OCEAN.
THREE BEDROOMS. TWO BATHS. INCREDIBLE VIEWS.
OLD FASHIONEDS MADE FROM PREMIUM COGNAC.
CHEF'S STOVE AND DISHWASHER. AND YOU'LL LOVE THE WINE FRIDGE!
WAS A BLACK STUDIES MAJOR AT E.S.U.
LET ME SHOW YOU THE CLOSET SPACE.
I MADE SEVERAL NOTES TO SELF:
LOOK INTO E.S.U.'S BLACK STUDIES PROGRAM.
TRY A PREMIUM COGNAC OLD FASHIONED.

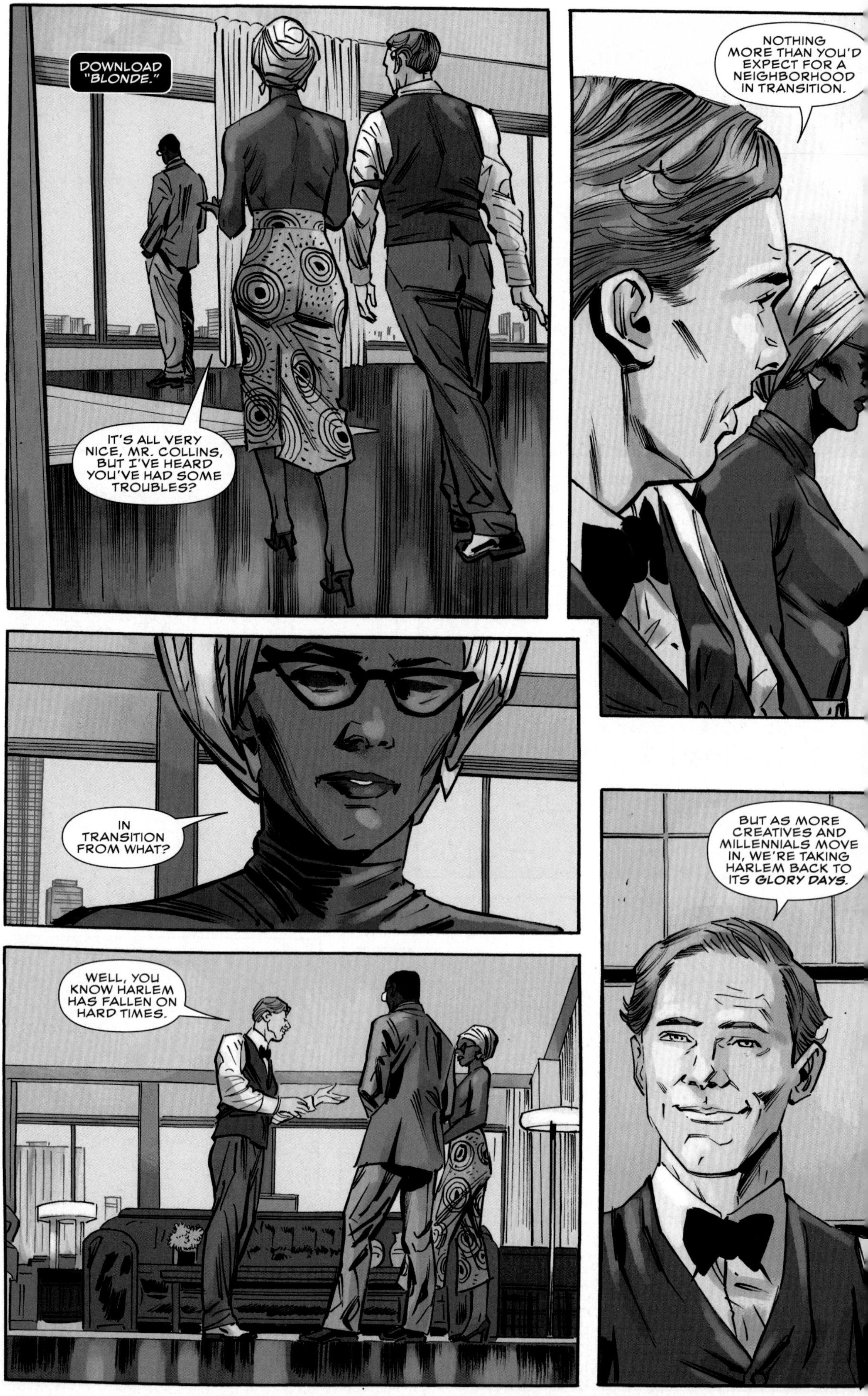
DOWNLOAD "BLONDE."
IT'S ALL VERY NICE, MR. COLLINS, BUT I'VE HEARD YOU'VE HAD SOME TROUBLES?
NOTHING MORE THAN YOU'D EXPECT FOR A NEIGHBORHOOD IN TRANSITION.
IN TRANSITION FROM WHAT?
WELL, YOU KNOW HARLEM HAS FALLEN ON HARD TIMES.
BUT AS MORE CREATIVES AND MILLENNIALS MOVE IN, WE'RE TAKING HARLEM BACK TO ITS GLORY DAYS.

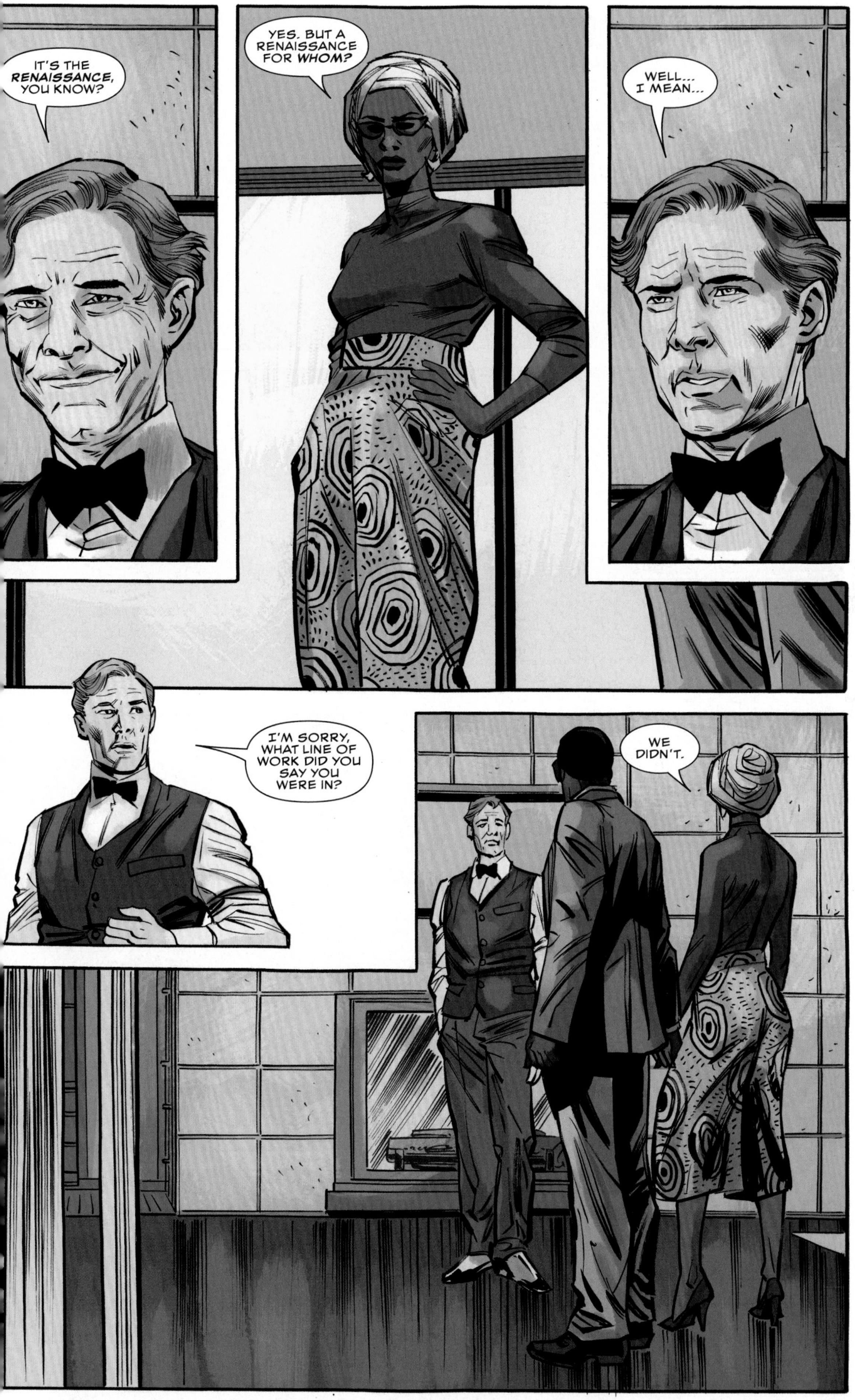
IT'S THE *RENAISSANCE*, YOU KNOW?
YES. BUT A RENAISSANCE FOR *WHOM?*
WELL... I MEAN...
I'M SORRY, WHAT LINE OF WORK DID YOU SAY YOU WERE IN?
WE DIDN'T.

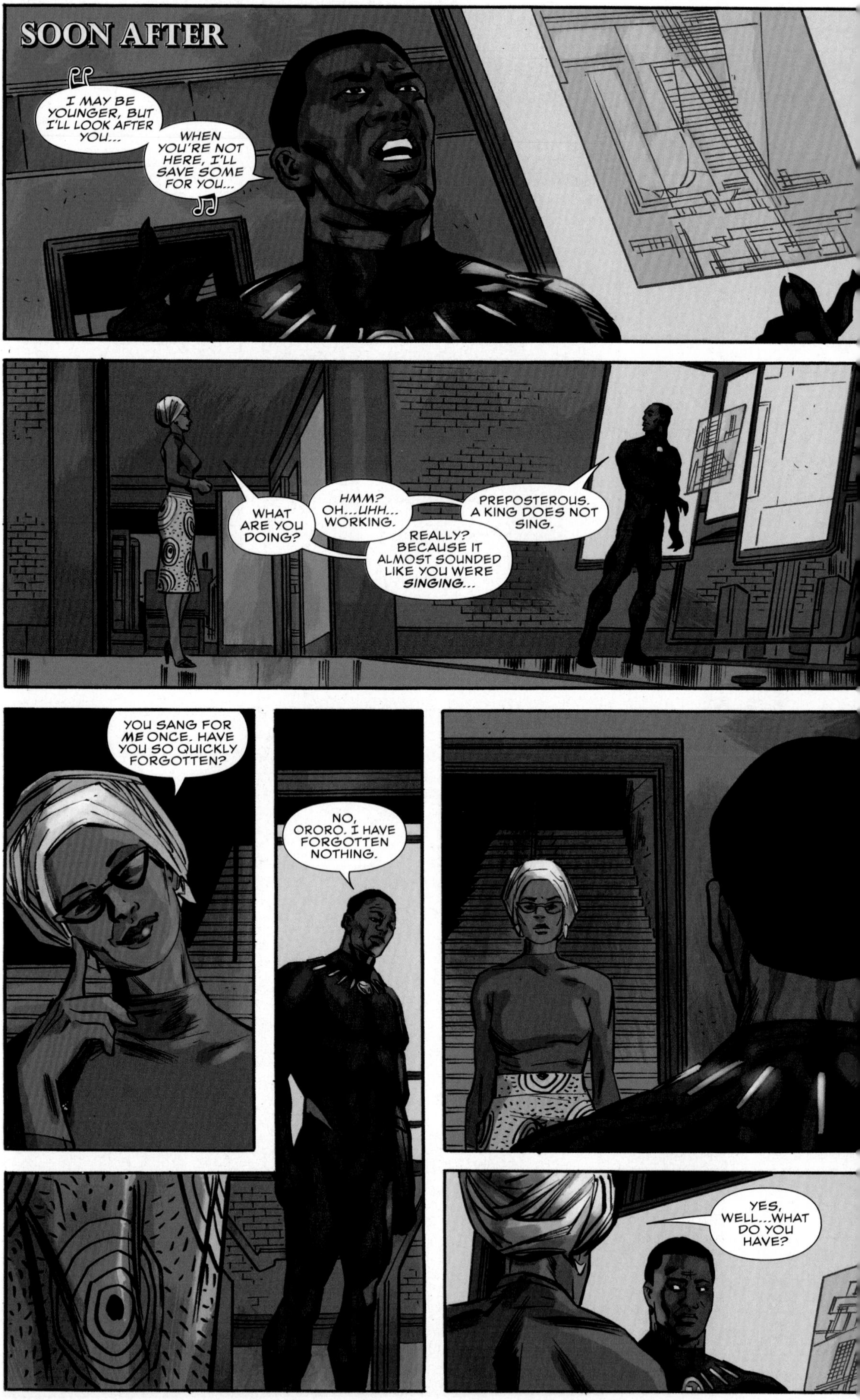
SOON AFTER
I MAY BE YOUNGER, BUT I'LL LOOK AFTER YOU...
WHEN YOU'RE NOT HERE, I'LL SAVE SOME FOR YOU...
WHAT ARE YOU DOING?
HMM? OH...UHH... WORKING.
REALLY? BECAUSE IT ALMOST SOUNDED LIKE YOU WERE SINGING...
PREPOSTEROUS. A KING DOES NOT SING.
YOU SANG FOR ME ONCE. HAVE YOU SO QUICKLY FORGOTTEN?
NO, ORORO. I HAVE FORGOTTEN NOTHING.
YES, WELL...WHAT DO YOU HAVE?

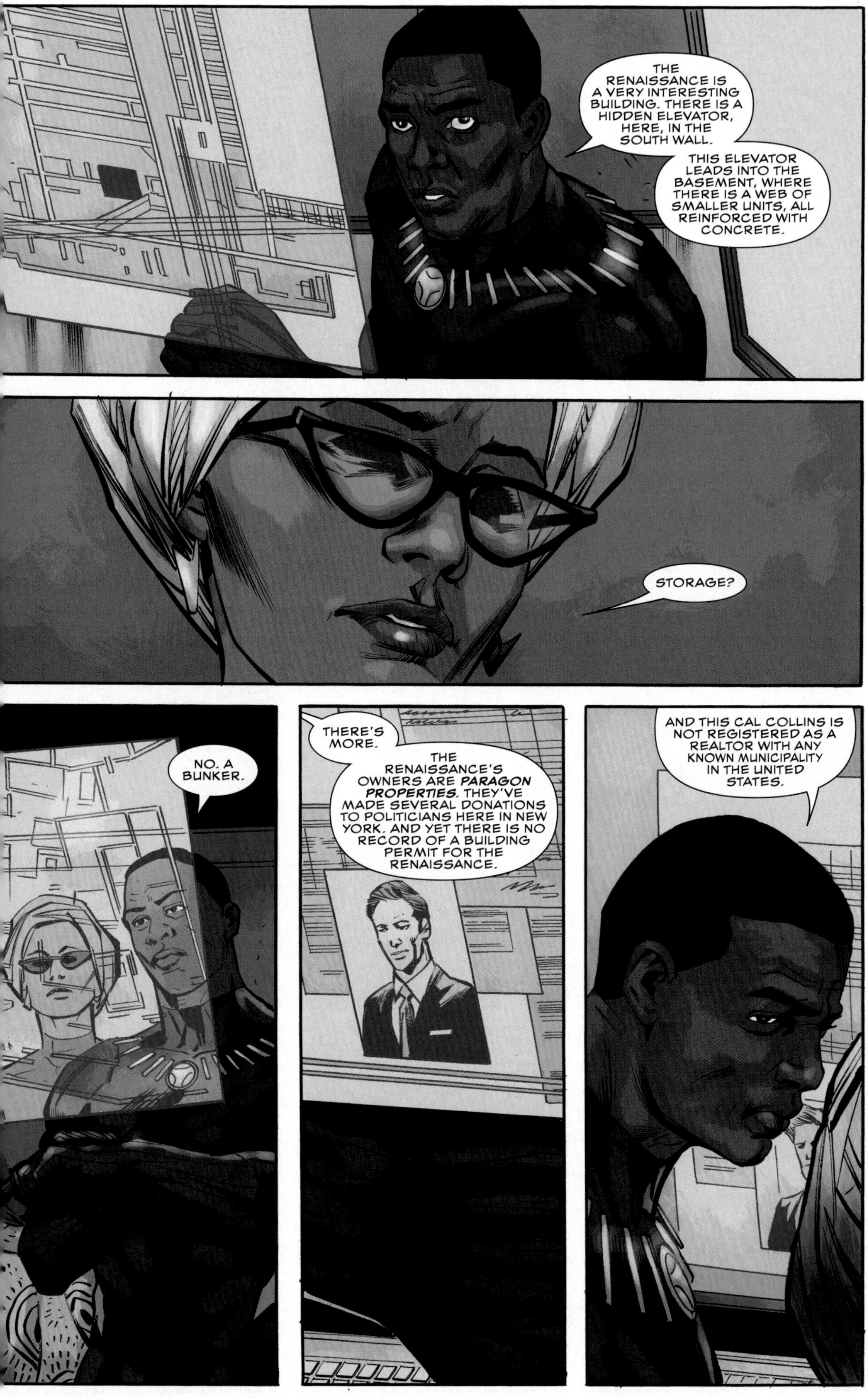
THE RENAISSANCE IS A VERY INTERESTING BUILDING. THERE IS A HIDDEN ELEVATOR, HERE, IN THE SOUTH WALL.
THIS ELEVATOR LEADS INTO THE BASEMENT, WHERE THERE IS A WEB OF SMALLER UNITS, ALL REINFORCED WITH CONCRETE.
STORAGE?
NO. A BUNKER.
THERE'S MORE.
THE RENAISSANCE'S OWNERS ARE *PARAGON PROPERTIES.* THEY'VE MADE SEVERAL DONATIONS TO POLITICIANS HERE IN NEW YORK. AND YET THERE IS NO RECORD OF A BUILDING PERMIT FOR THE RENAISSANCE.
AND THIS CAL COLLINS IS NOT REGISTERED AS A REALTOR WITH ANY KNOWN MUNICIPALITY IN THE UNITED STATES.

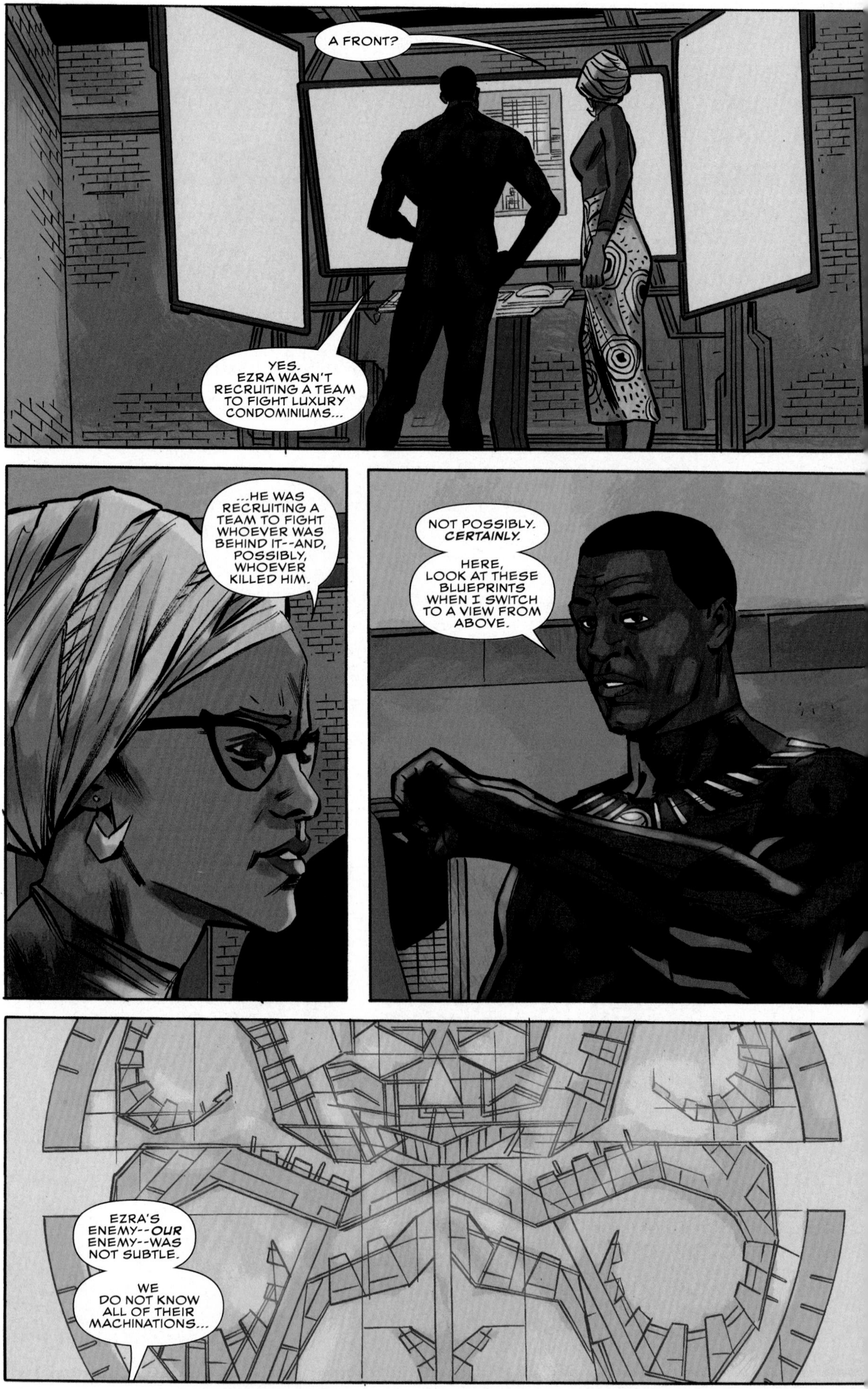
A FRONT?
YES. EZRA WASN'T RECRUITING A TEAM TO FIGHT LUXURY CONDOMINIUMS...
...HE WAS RECRUITING A TEAM TO FIGHT WHOEVER WAS BEHIND IT--AND, POSSIBLY, WHOEVER KILLED HIM.
NOT POSSIBLY. *CERTAINLY.*
HERE, LOOK AT THESE BLUEPRINTS WHEN I SWITCH TO A VIEW FROM ABOVE.
EZRA'S ENEMY--*OUR* ENEMY--WAS NOT SUBTLE.
WE DO NOT KNOW ALL OF THEIR MACHINATIONS...

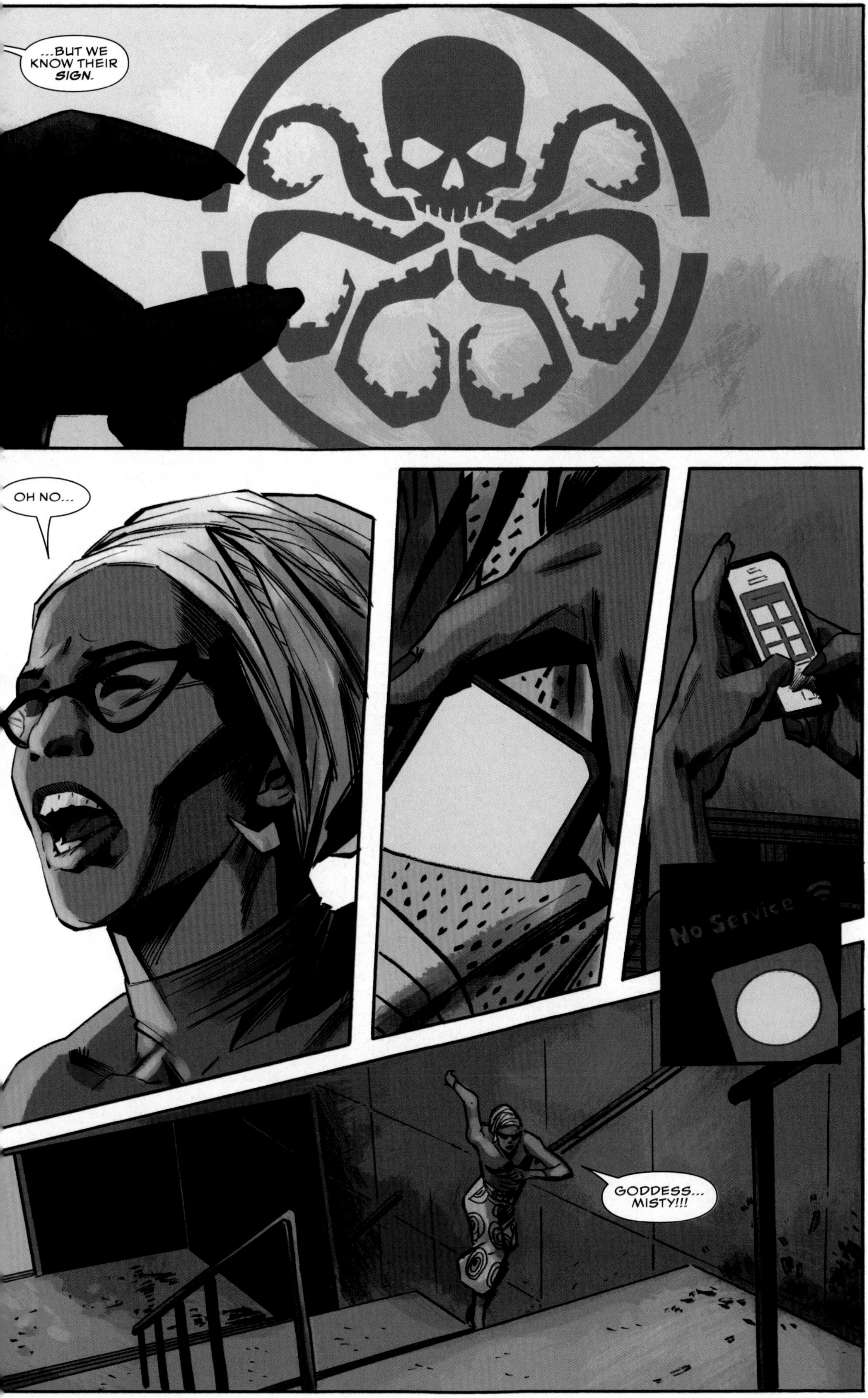
...BUT WE KNOW THEIR *SIGN*.
OH NO...
No Service
GODDESS... MISTY!!!

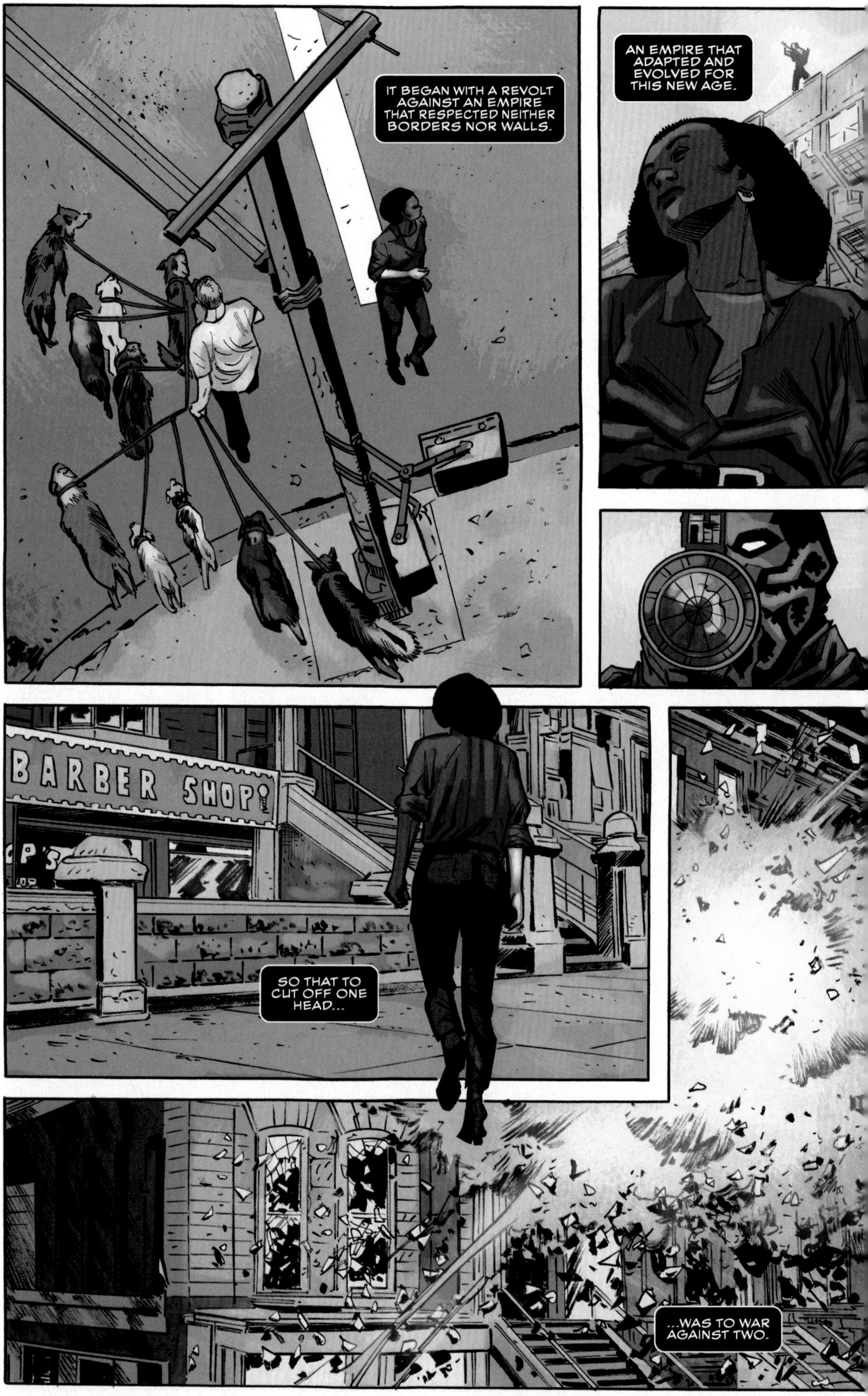
IT BEGAN WITH A REVOLT AGAINST AN EMPIRE THAT RESPECTED NEITHER BORDERS NOR WALLS.
AN EMPIRE THAT ADAPTED AND EVOLVED FOR THIS NEW AGE.
BARBER SHOP
SO THAT TO CUT OFF ONE HEAD...
...WAS TO WAR AGAINST TWO.

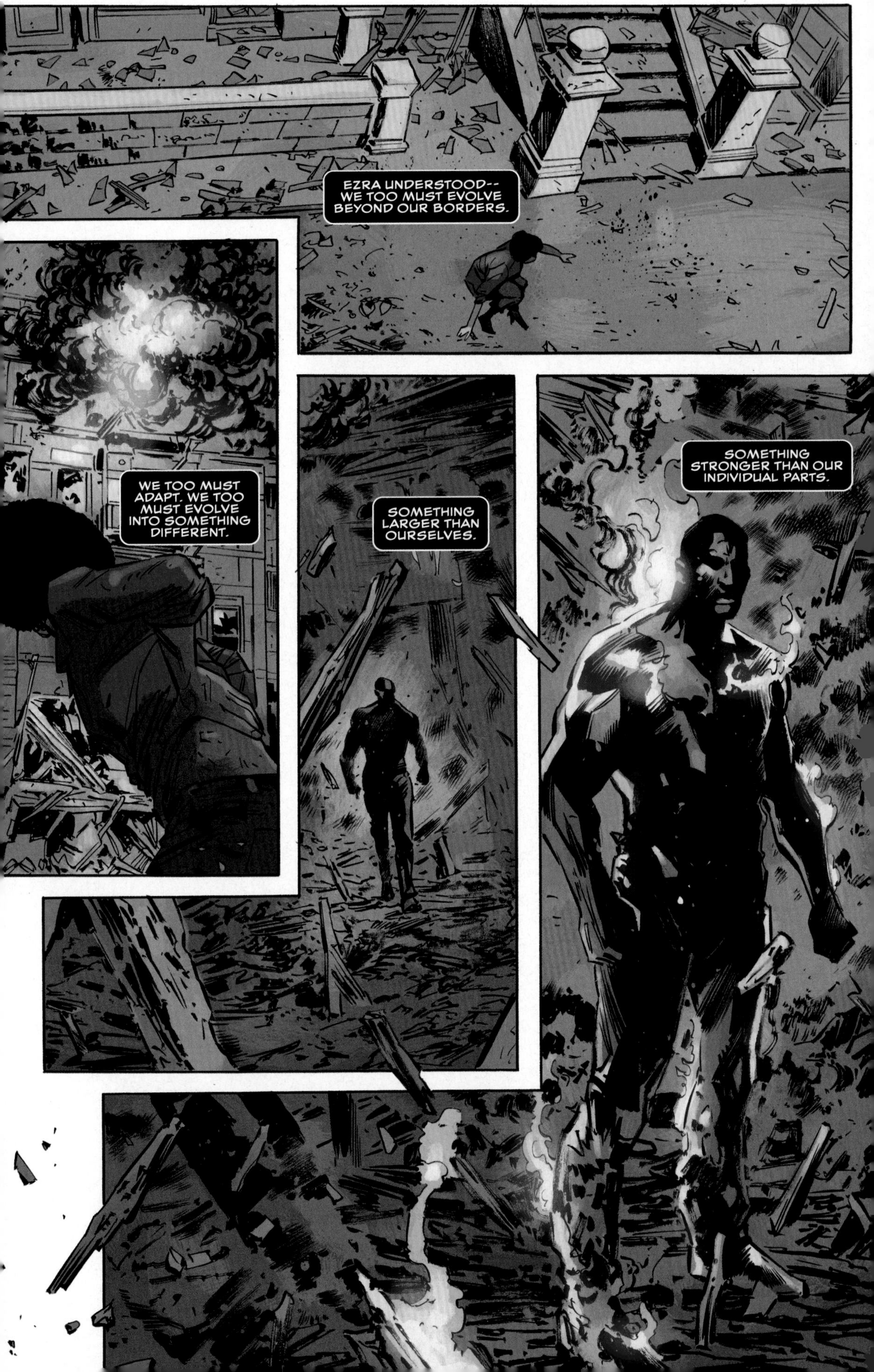
EZRA UNDERSTOOD--
WE TOO MUST EVOLVE
BEYOND OUR BORDERS.
WE TOO MUST ADAPT. WE TOO MUST EVOLVE INTO SOMETHING DIFFERENT.
SOMETHING LARGER THAN OURSELVES.
SOMETHING STRONGER THAN OUR INDIVIDUAL PARTS.

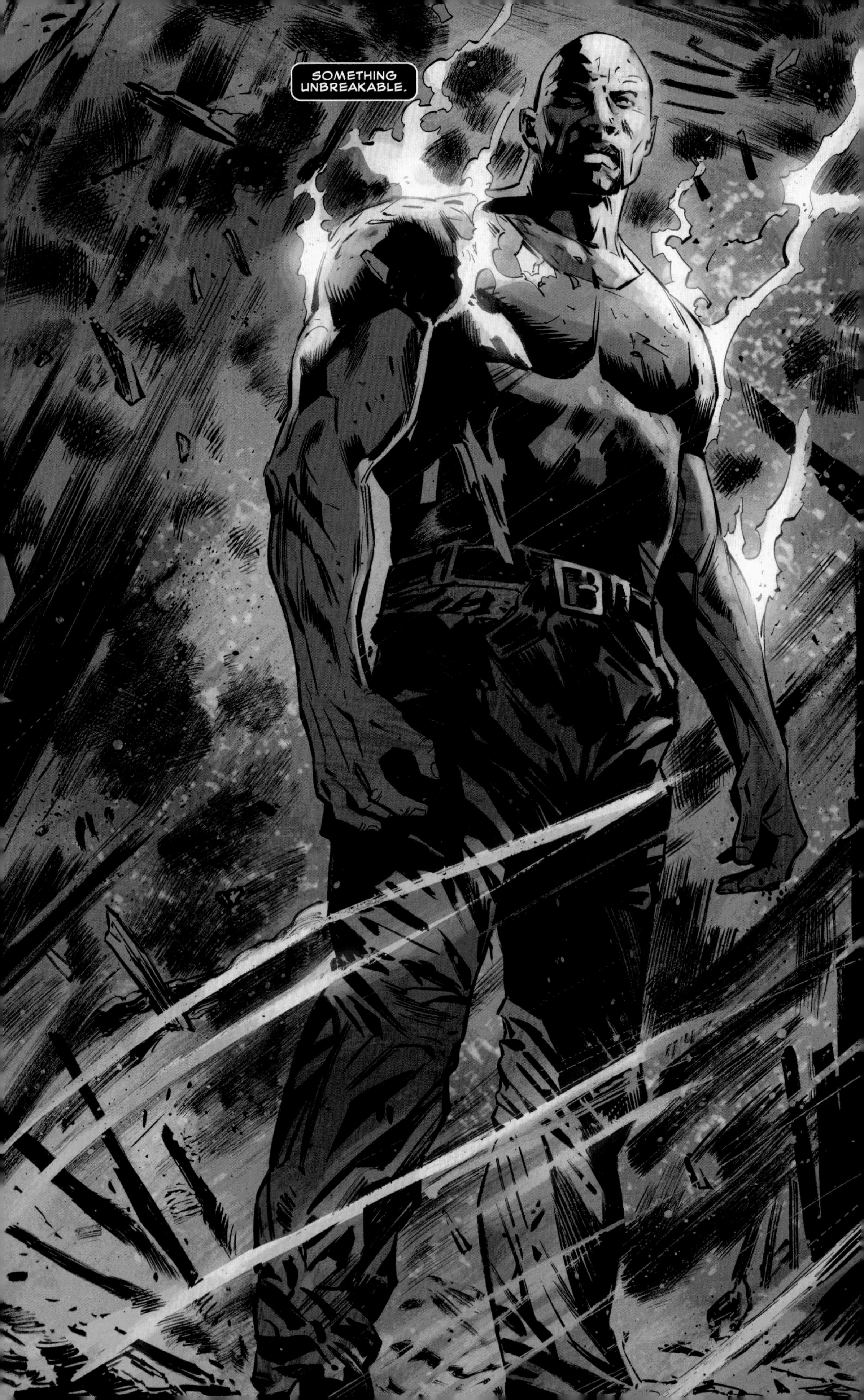
SOMETHING UNBREAKABLE.

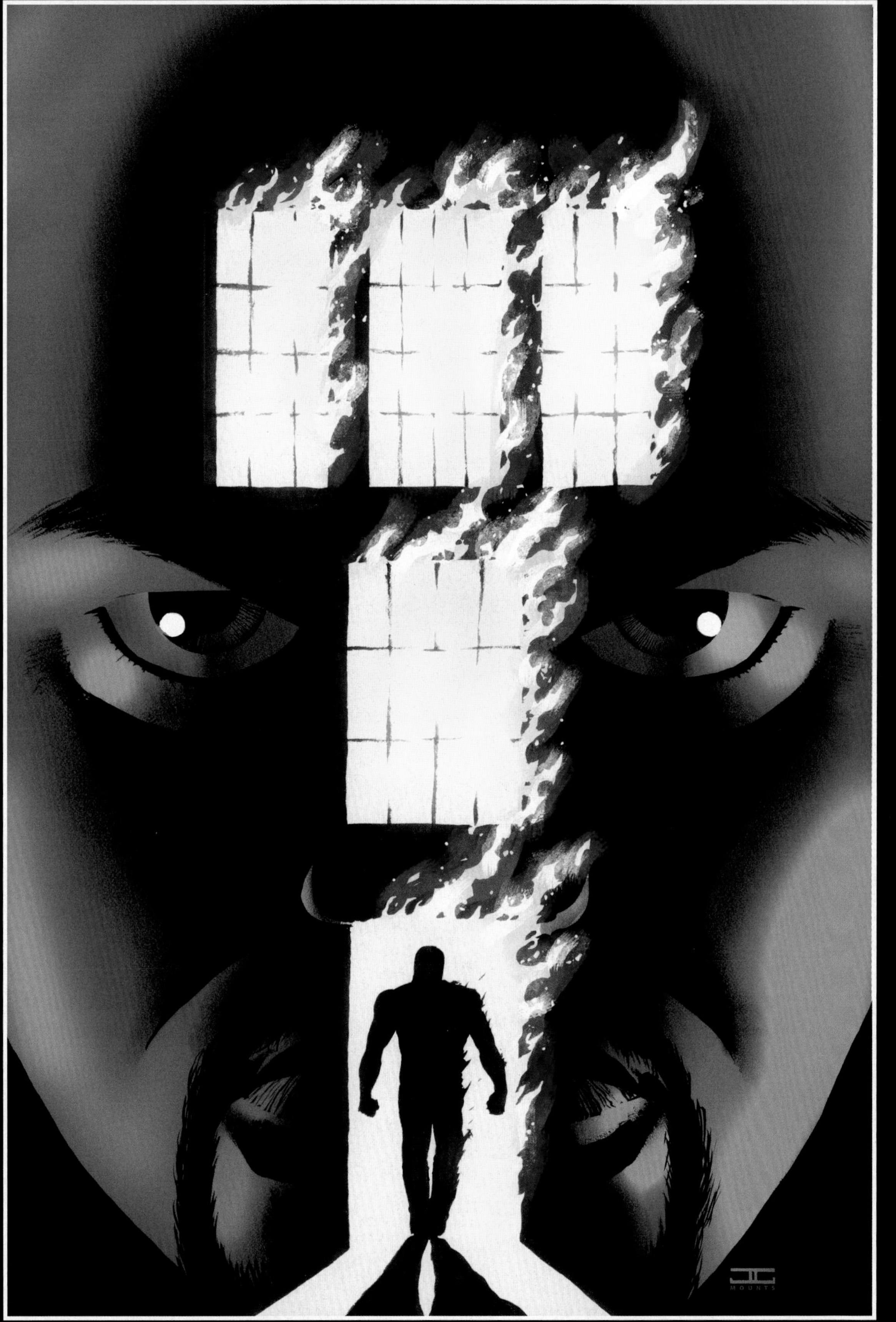
MOUNTS

PART 4 NOTHING BUT A MAN

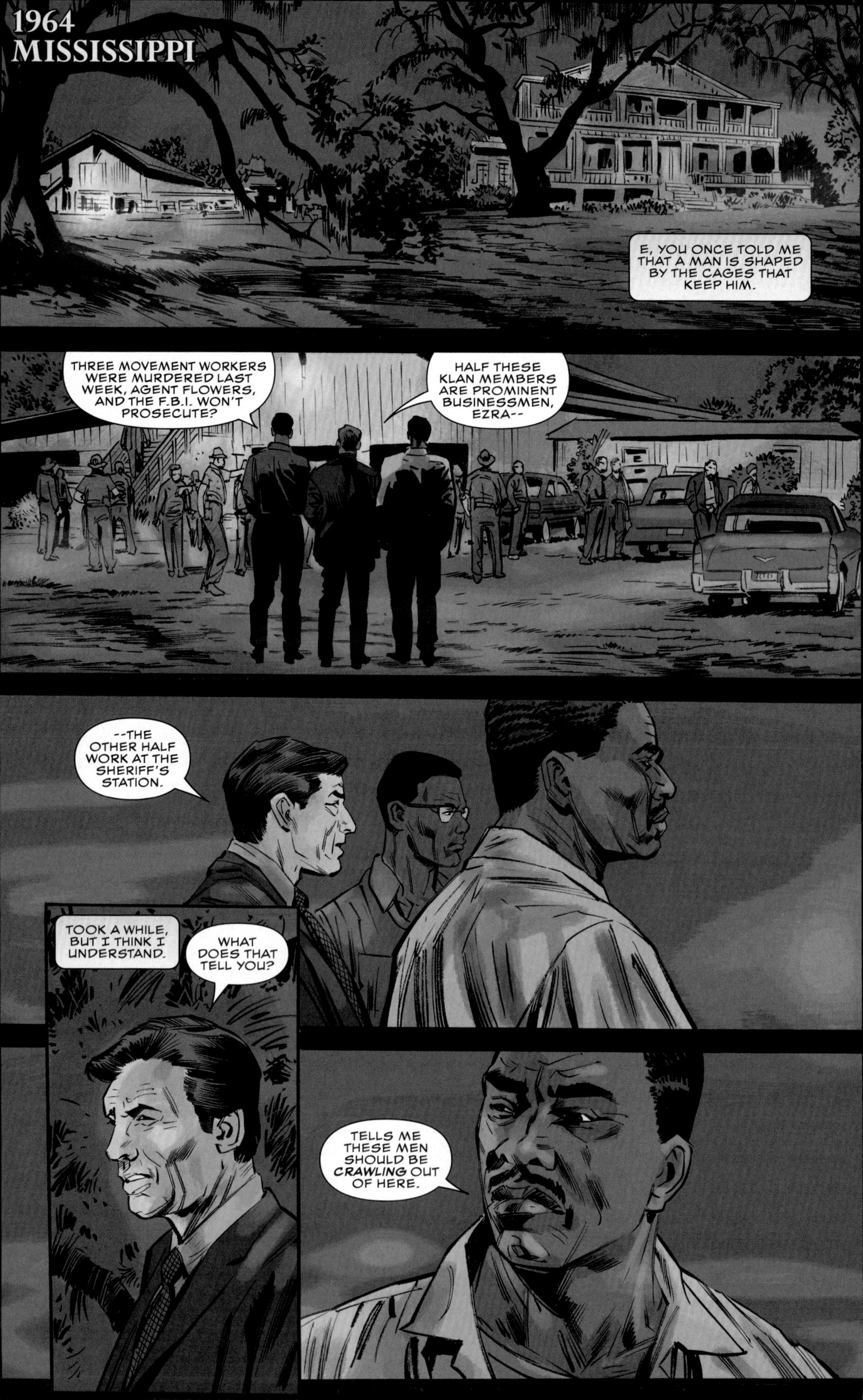
1964 MISSISSIPPI
E, YOU ONCE TOLD ME THAT A MAN IS SHAPED BY THE CAGES THAT KEEP HIM.
THREE MOVEMENT WORKERS WERE MURDERED LAST WEEK, AGENT FLOWERS, AND THE F.B.I. WON'T PROSECUTE?
HALF THESE KLAN MEMBERS ARE PROMINENT BUSINESSMEN, EZRA--
--THE OTHER HALF WORK AT THE SHERIFF'S STATION.
TOOK A WHILE, BUT I THINK I UNDERSTAND.
WHAT DOES THAT TELL YOU?
TELLS ME THESE MEN SHOULD BE *CRAWLING* OUT OF HERE.

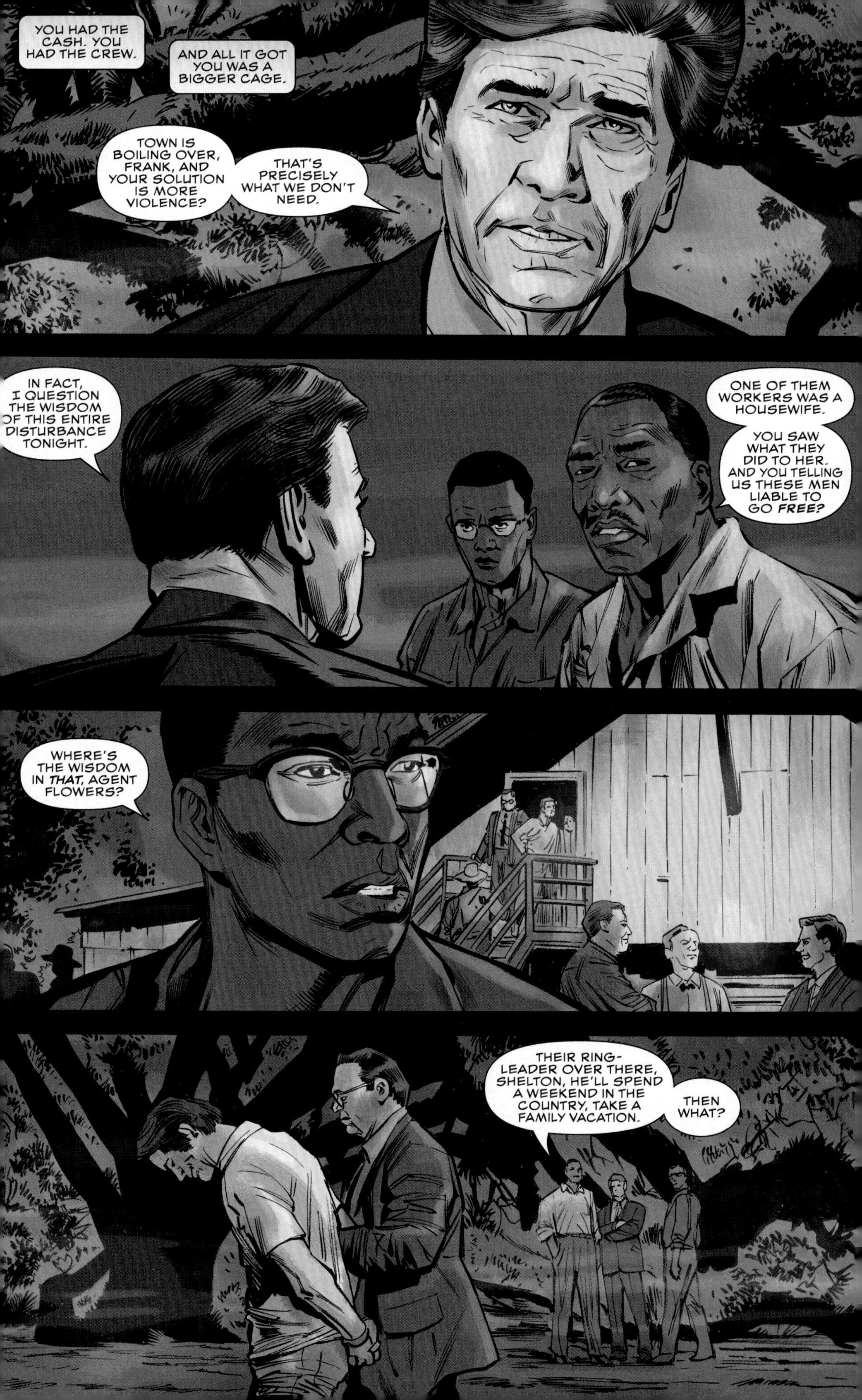
YOU HAD THE CASH. YOU HAD THE CREW.
AND ALL IT GOT YOU WAS A BIGGER CAGE.
TOWN IS BOILING OVER, FRANK, AND YOUR SOLUTION IS MORE VIOLENCE?
THAT'S PRECISELY WHAT WE DON'T NEED.
IN FACT, I QUESTION THE WISDOM OF THIS ENTIRE DISTURBANCE TONIGHT.
ONE OF THEM WORKERS WAS A HOUSEWIFE.
YOU SAW WHAT THEY DID TO HER. AND YOU TELLING US THESE MEN LIABLE TO GO *FREE?*
WHERE'S THE WISDOM IN *THAT,* AGENT FLOWERS?
THEIR RING-LEADER OVER THERE, SHELTON, HE'LL SPEND A WEEKEND IN THE COUNTRY, TAKE A FAMILY VACATION.
THEN WHAT?

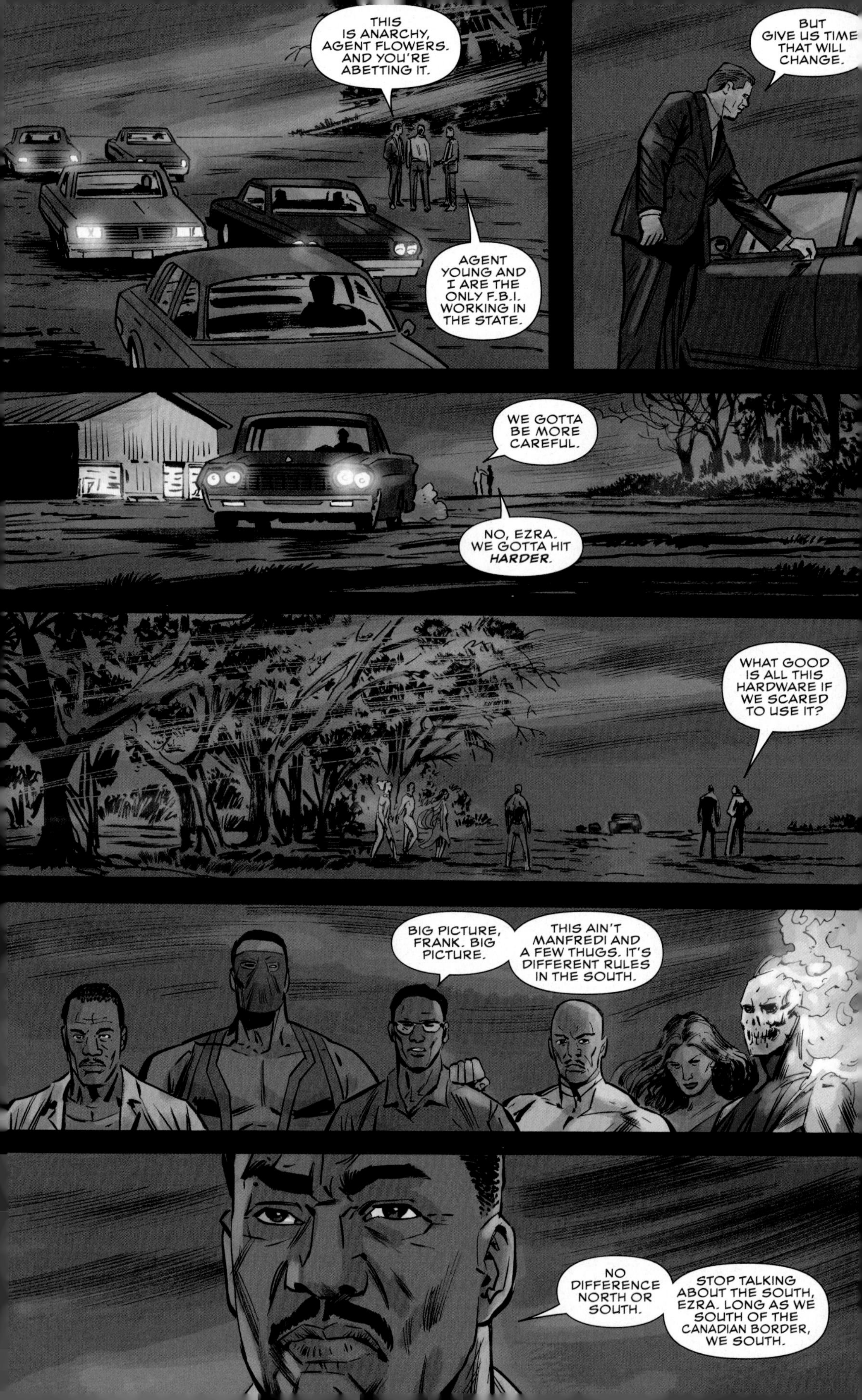
THIS IS ANARCHY, AGENT FLOWERS. AND YOU'RE ABETTING IT.
AGENT YOUNG AND I ARE THE ONLY F.B.I. WORKING IN THE STATE.
BUT GIVE US TIME THAT WILL CHANGE.
WE GOTTA BE MORE CAREFUL.
NO, EZRA. WE GOTTA HIT *HARDER*.
WHAT GOOD IS ALL THIS HARDWARE IF WE SCARED TO USE IT?
BIG PICTURE, FRANK. BIG PICTURE.
THIS AIN'T MANFREDI AND A FEW THUGS. IT'S DIFFERENT RULES IN THE SOUTH.
NO DIFFERENCE NORTH OR SOUTH.
STOP TALKING ABOUT THE SOUTH, EZRA. LONG AS WE SOUTH OF THE CANADIAN BORDER, WE SOUTH.

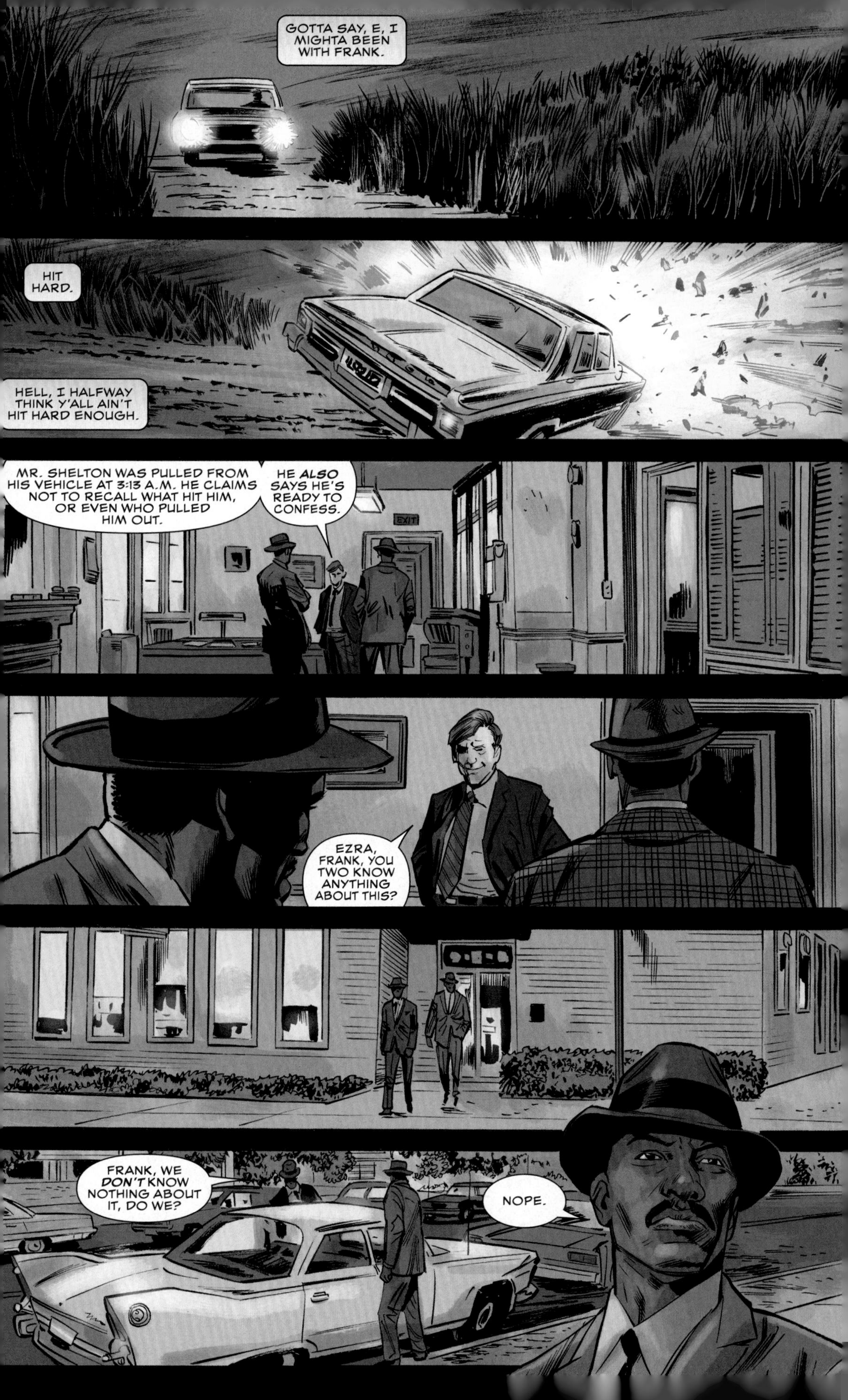
GOTTA SAY, E, I MIGHTA BEEN WITH FRANK.
HIT HARD.
HELL, I HALFWAY THINK Y'ALL AIN'T HIT HARD ENOUGH.
MR. SHELTON WAS PULLED FROM HIS VEHICLE AT 3:13 A.M. HE CLAIMS NOT TO RECALL WHAT HIT HIM, OR EVEN WHO PULLED HIM OUT.
HE *ALSO* SAYS HE'S READY TO CONFESS.
EXIT
EZRA, FRANK, YOU TWO KNOW ANYTHING ABOUT THIS?
FRANK, WE *DON'T* KNOW NOTHING ABOUT IT, DO WE?
NOPE.

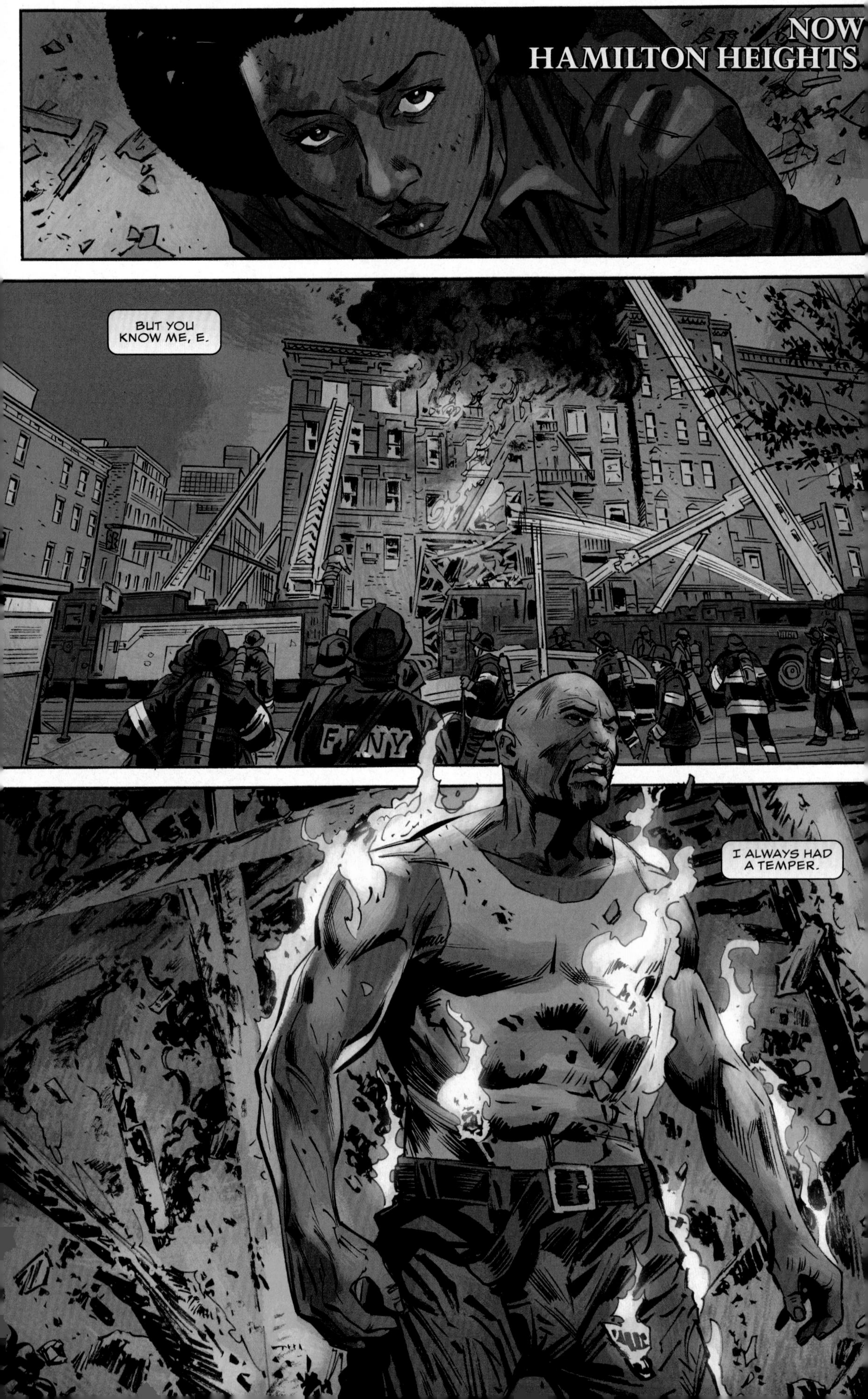
NOW
HAMILTON HEIGHTS
BUT YOU KNOW ME, E.
FDNY
I ALWAYS HAD A TEMPER.

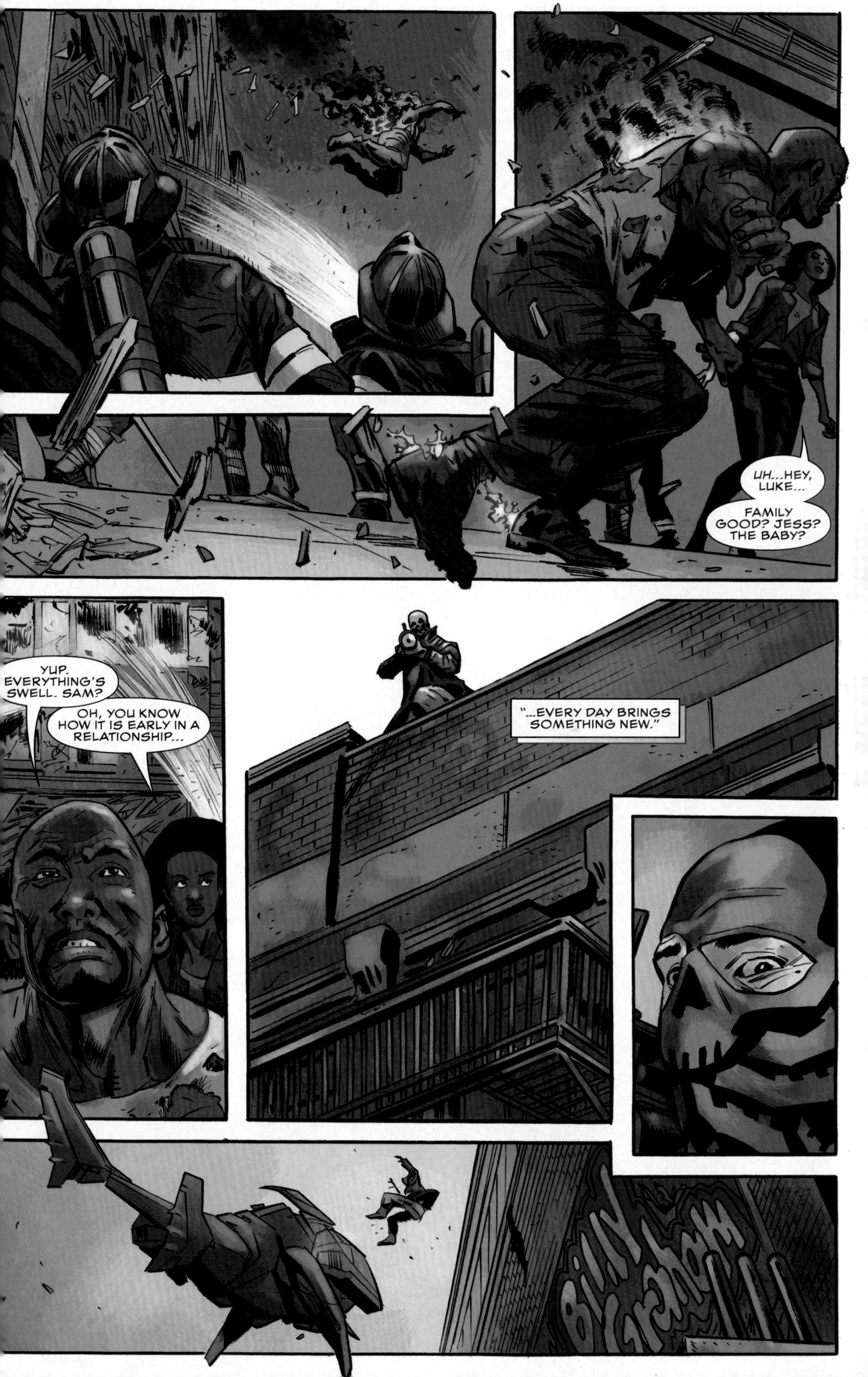
UH...HEY, LUKE...
FAMILY GOOD? JESS? THE BABY?
YUP. EVERYTHING'S SWELL. SAM?
OH, YOU KNOW HOW IT IS EARLY IN A RELATIONSHIP...
"...EVERY DAY BRINGS SOMETHING NEW."

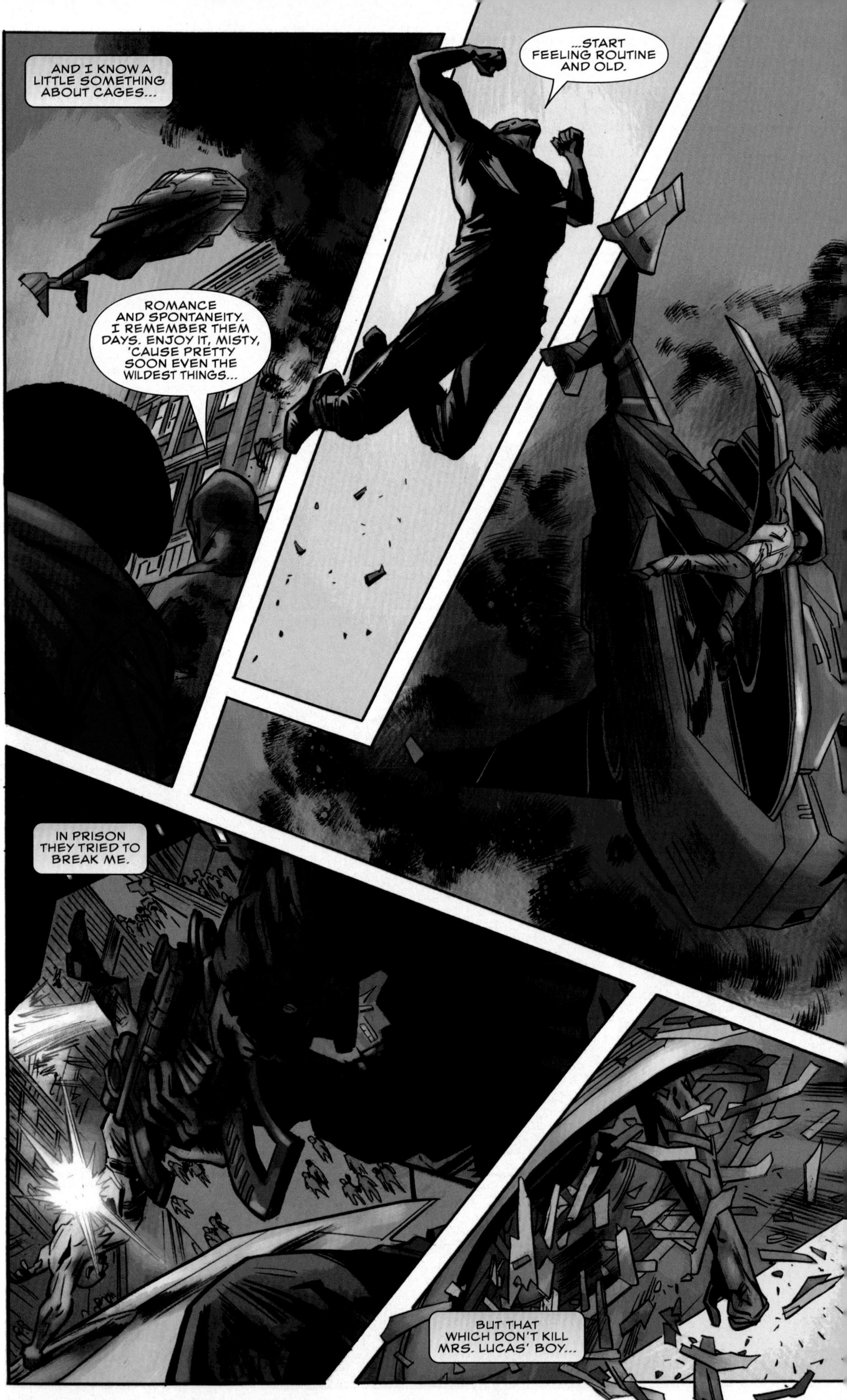
AND I KNOW A LITTLE SOMETHING ABOUT CAGES...
...START FEELING ROUTINE AND OLD.
ROMANCE AND SPONTANEITY. I REMEMBER THEM DAYS. ENJOY IT, MISTY, 'CAUSE PRETTY SOON EVEN THE WILDEST THINGS...
IN PRISON THEY TRIED TO BREAK ME.
BUT THAT WHICH DON'T KILL MRS. LUCAS' BOY...

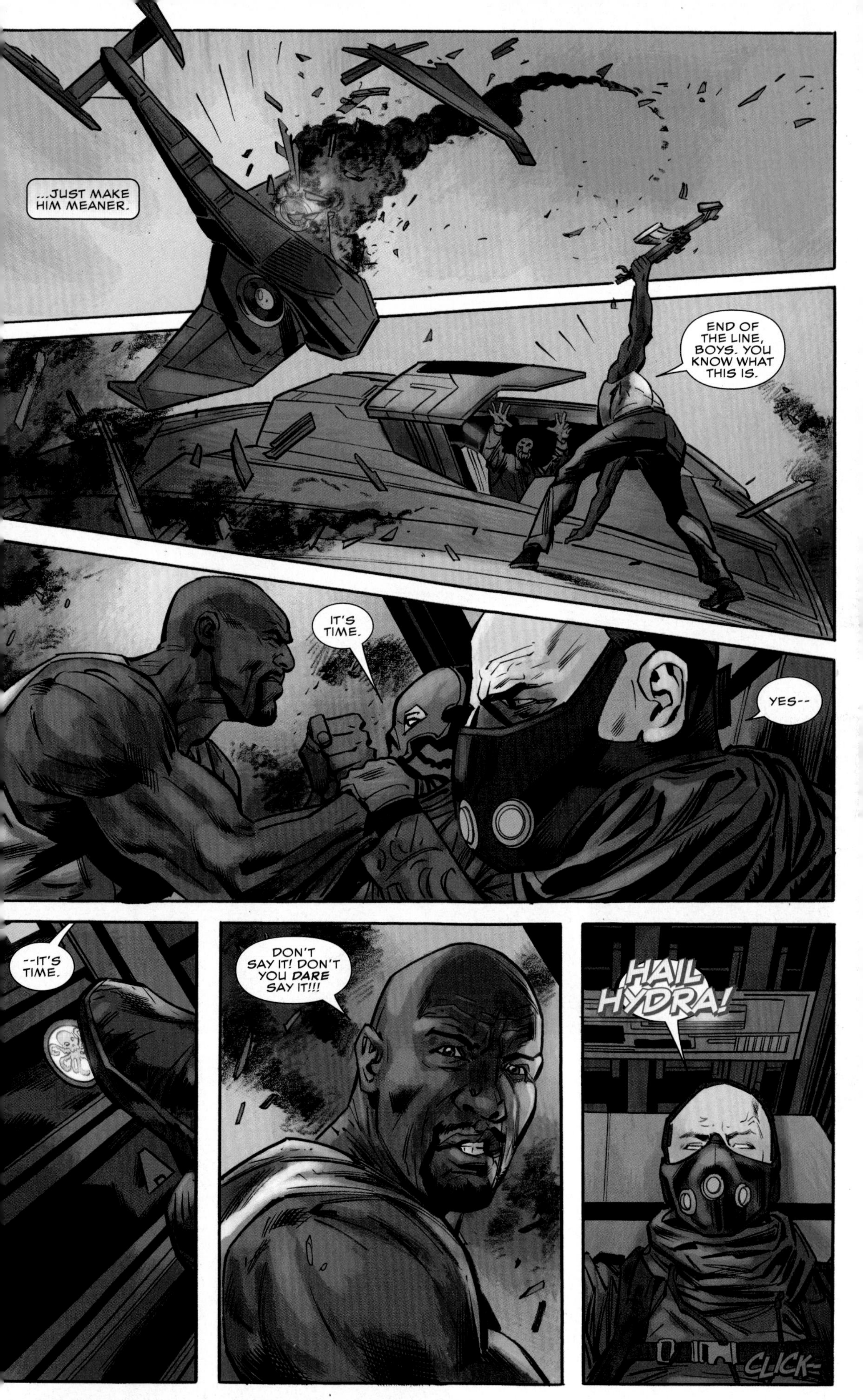
...JUST MAKE HIM MEANER.
END OF THE LINE, BOYS. YOU KNOW WHAT THIS IS.
IT'S TIME.
YES--
--IT'S TIME.
DON'T SAY IT! DON'T YOU DARE SAY IT!!!
HAIL HYDRA!
CLICK

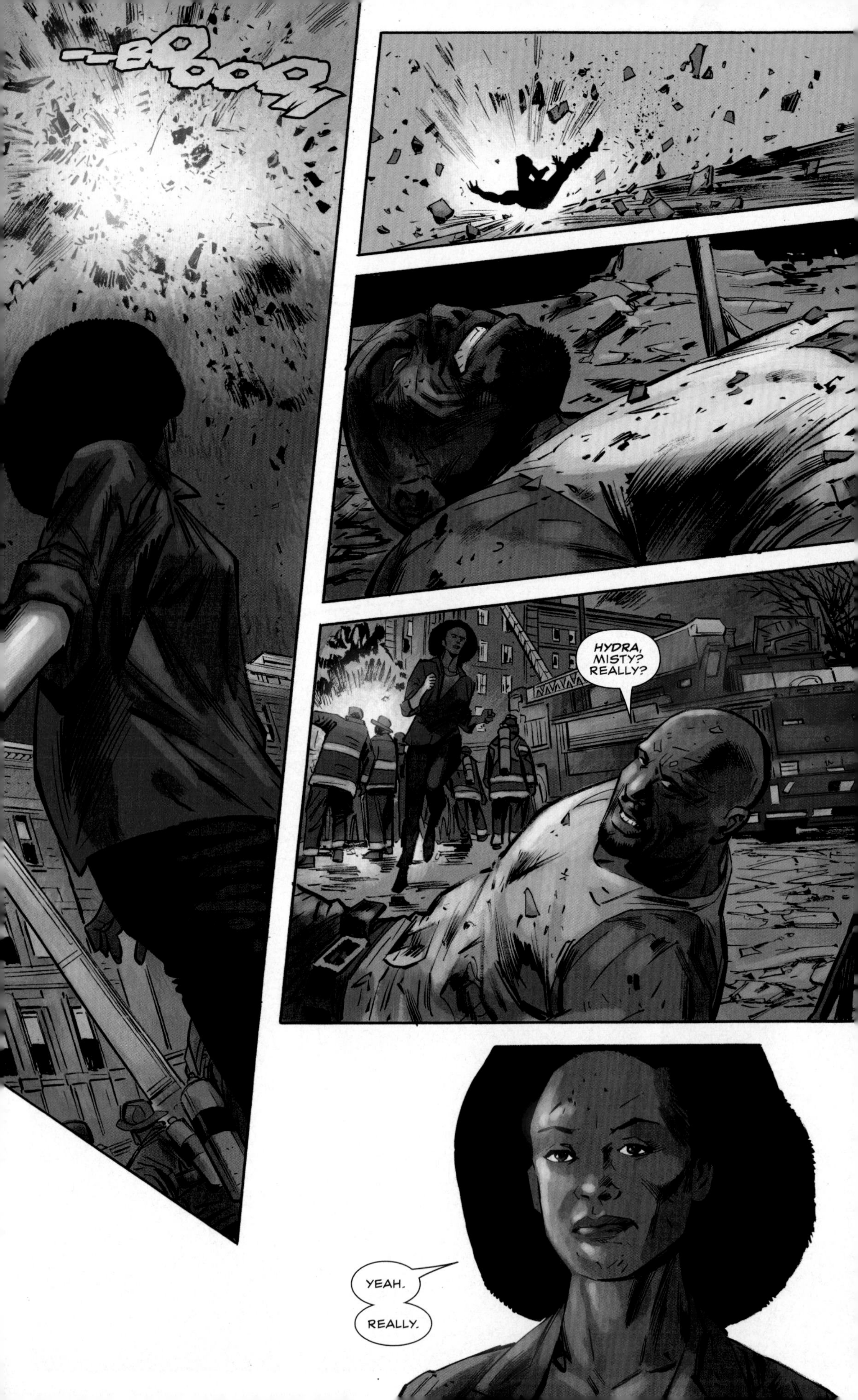
--BOOOM
HYDRA, MISTY? REALLY?
YEAH.
REALLY.

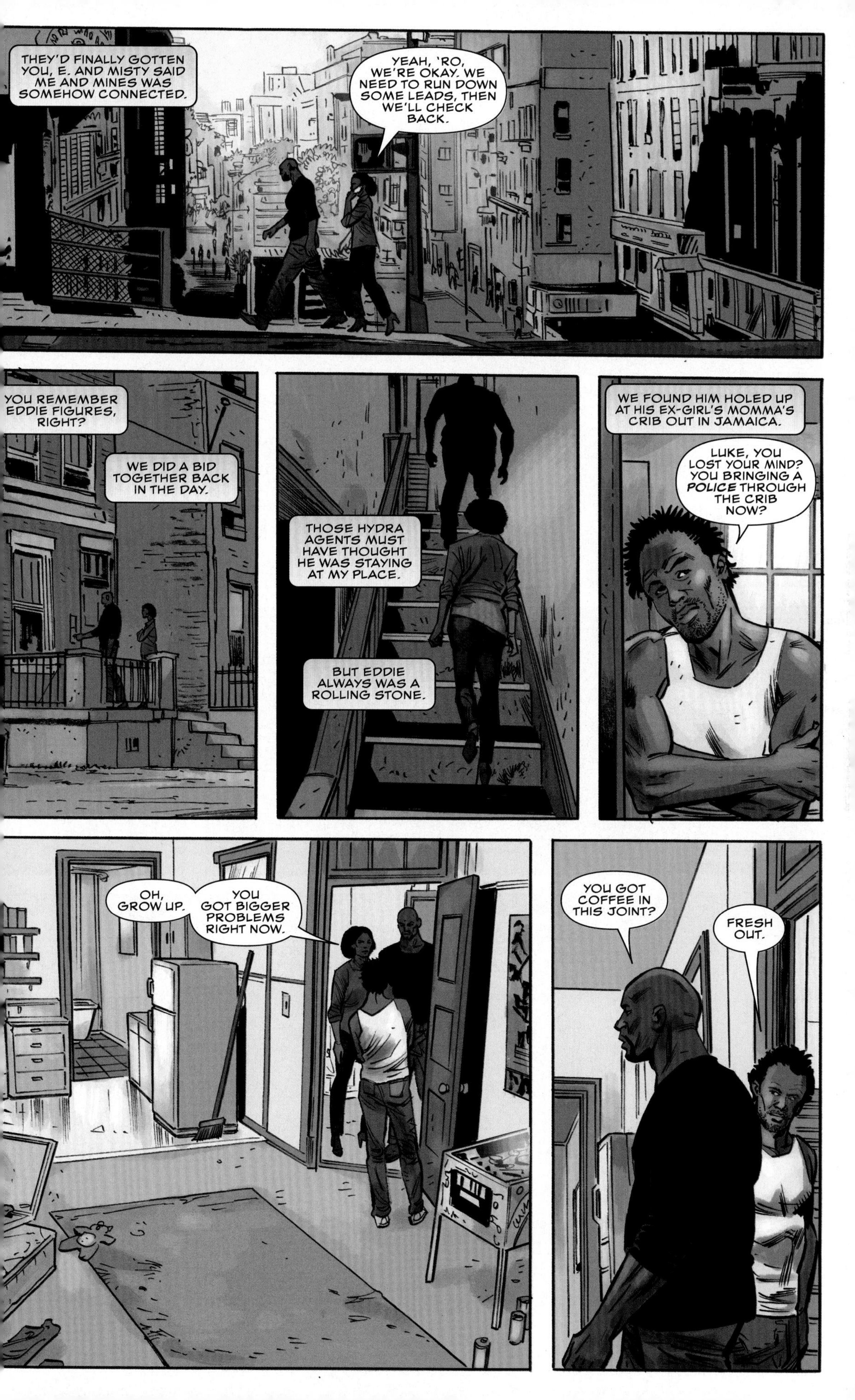

THEY'D FINALLY GOTTEN YOU, E. AND MISTY SAID ME AND MINES WAS SOMEHOW CONNECTED.
YEAH, 'RO, WE'RE OKAY. WE NEED TO RUN DOWN SOME LEADS, THEN WE'LL CHECK BACK.
YOU REMEMBER EDDIE FIGURES, RIGHT?
WE DID A BID TOGETHER BACK IN THE DAY.
THOSE HYDRA AGENTS MUST HAVE THOUGHT HE WAS STAYING AT MY PLACE.
BUT EDDIE ALWAYS WAS A ROLLING STONE.
WE FOUND HIM HOLED UP AT HIS EX-GIRL'S MOMMA'S CRIB OUT IN JAMAICA.
LUKE, YOU LOST YOUR MIND? YOU BRINGING A POLICE THROUGH THE CRIB NOW?
OH, GROW UP.
YOU GOT BIGGER PROBLEMS RIGHT NOW.
YOU GOT COFFEE IN THIS JOINT?
FRESH OUT.

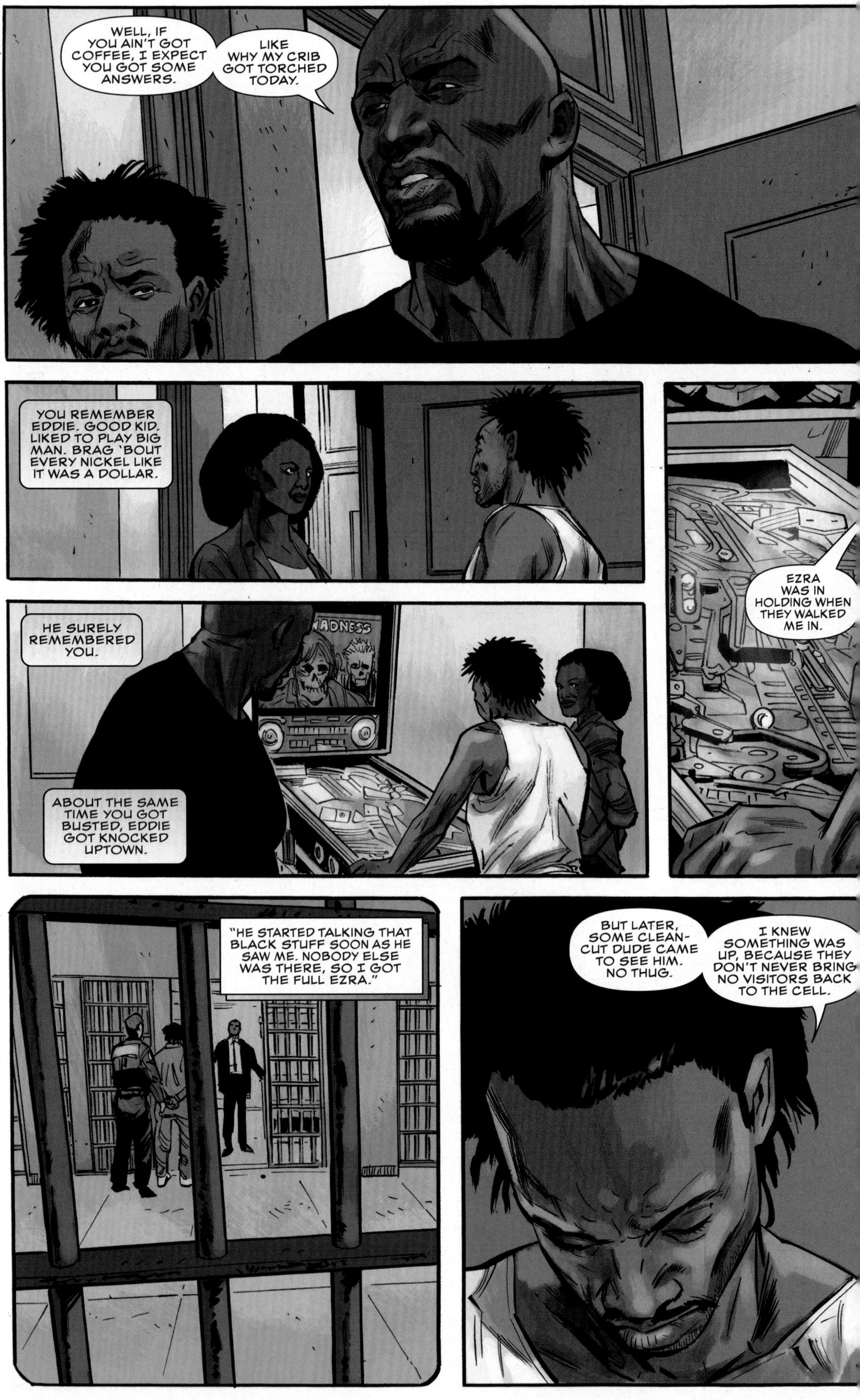
WELL, IF YOU AIN'T GOT COFFEE, I EXPECT YOU GOT SOME ANSWERS.
LIKE WHY MY CRIB GOT TORCHED TODAY.
YOU REMEMBER EDDIE. GOOD KID. LIKED TO PLAY BIG MAN. BRAG 'BOUT EVERY NICKEL LIKE IT WAS A DOLLAR.
HE SURELY REMEMBERED YOU.
ABOUT THE SAME TIME YOU GOT BUSTED, EDDIE GOT KNOCKED UPTOWN.
MADNESS
EZRA WAS IN HOLDING WHEN THEY WALKED ME IN.
"HE STARTED TALKING THAT BLACK STUFF SOON AS HE SAW ME. NOBODY ELSE WAS THERE, SO I GOT THE FULL EZRA."
BUT LATER, SOME CLEAN-CUT DUDE CAME TO SEE HIM. NO THUG.
I KNEW SOMETHING WAS UP, BECAUSE THEY DON'T NEVER BRING NO VISITORS BACK TO THE CELL.

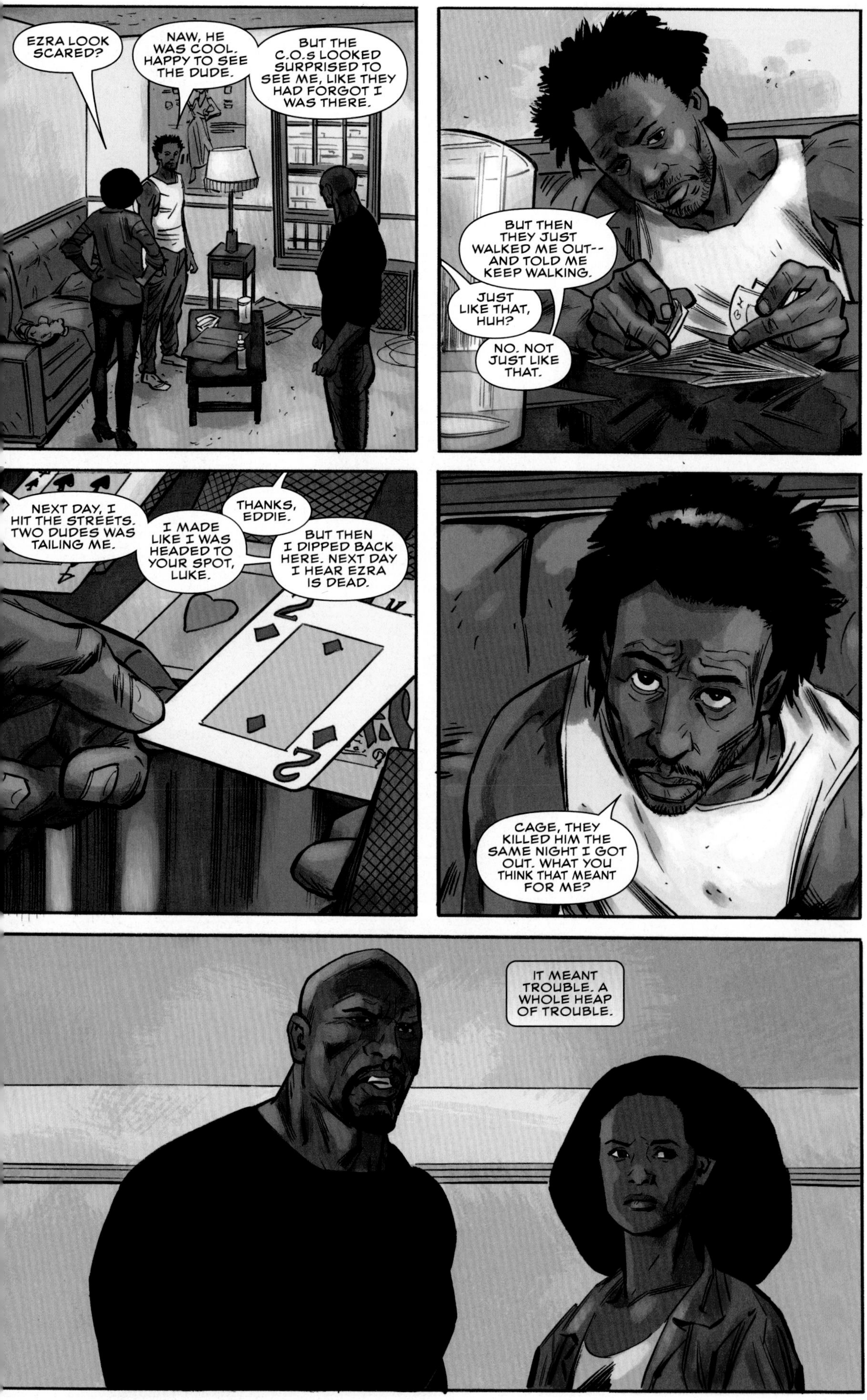
EZRA LOOK SCARED?
NAW, HE WAS COOL. HAPPY TO SEE THE DUDE.
BUT THE C.O.s LOOKED SURPRISED TO SEE ME, LIKE THEY HAD FORGOT I WAS THERE.
BUT THEN THEY JUST WALKED ME OUT-- AND TOLD ME KEEP WALKING.
JUST LIKE THAT, HUH?
NO. NOT JUST LIKE THAT.
NEXT DAY, I HIT THE STREETS. TWO DUDES WAS TAILING ME.
I MADE LIKE I WAS HEADED TO YOUR SPOT, LUKE.
THANKS, EDDIE.
BUT THEN I DIPPED BACK HERE. NEXT DAY I HEAR EZRA IS DEAD.
CAGE, THEY KILLED HIM THE SAME NIGHT I GOT OUT. WHAT YOU THINK THAT MEANT FOR ME?
IT MEANT TROUBLE. A WHOLE HEAP OF TROUBLE.

ONE OTHER THREAD TO TIE UP--PARAGON INDUSTRIES.

SAME FOOLS RESPONSIBLE FOR THE AMERICOPS.

SAME FOOLS RESPONSIBLE FOR MISTY GETTING RUSHED IN THE PARK.

PAUL KEANE. BIGWIG AT PARAGON. THE MAN BEHIND THE AMERICOPS. YOU'D THINK HE'D WANT TO KEEP HYDRA OUT OF HARLEM.

MS. KNIGHT. A PLEASURE TO MEET YOU IN PERSON.

I HOPE YOU RECEIVED OUR APOLOGY FOR THAT UNFORTUNATE INCIDENT? STILL WORKING OUT SOME KINKS, YOU SEE...

TURNS OUT HIS MOTIVES WERE A BIT MORE MIXED.

DON'T WORRY, MR. KEANE. NO LAWSUIT. NO CHARGES.

THE LAW IS ALL THAT STANDS BETWEEN US AND SAVAGERY.

PARAGON INDUSTRIES PRESENTS: AMERICOPS

EVEN IF THE LAW IS JUST A MACHINE.

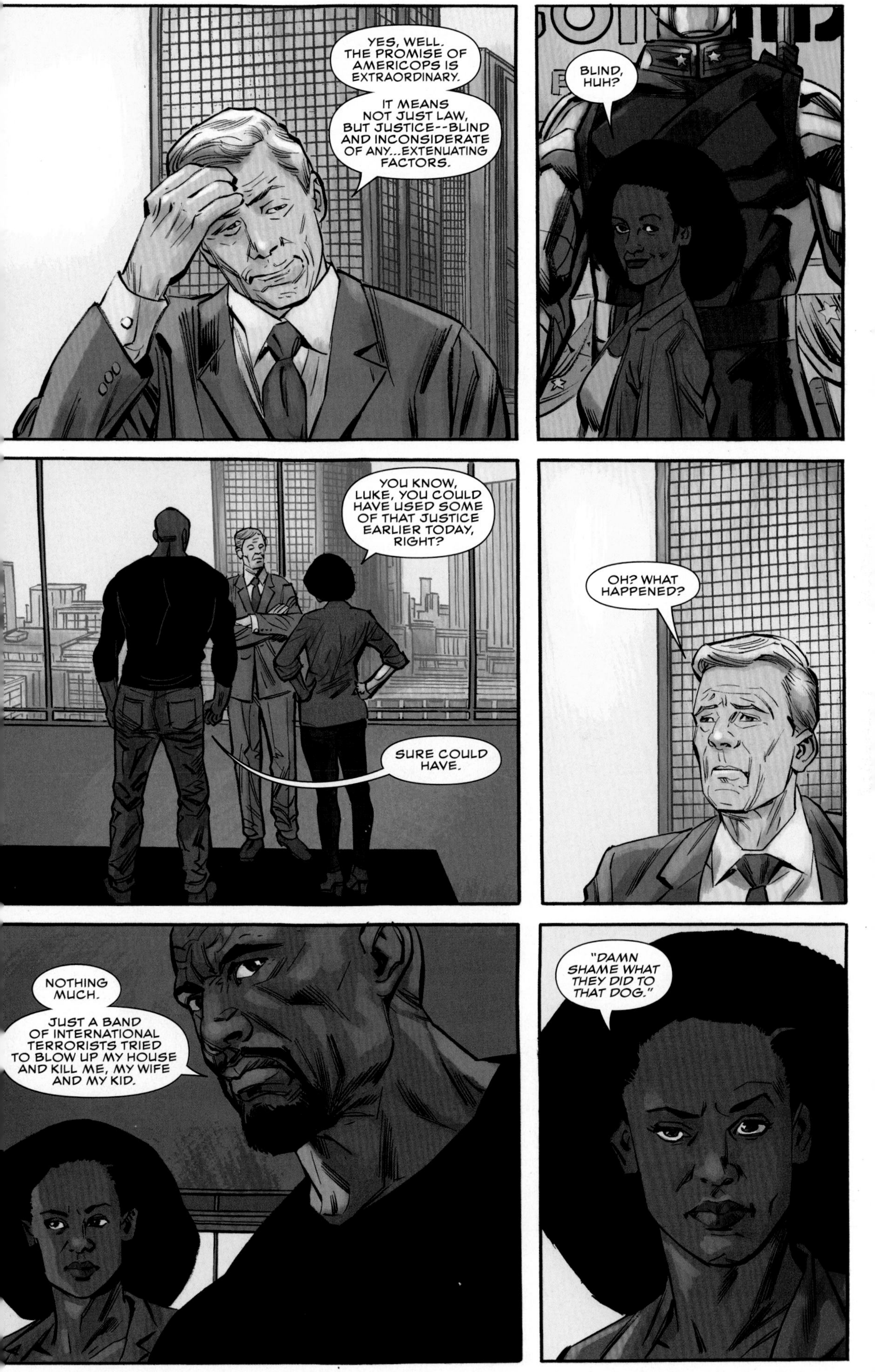
YES, WELL. THE PROMISE OF AMERICOPS IS EXTRAORDINARY.
IT MEANS NOT JUST LAW, BUT JUSTICE--BLIND AND INCONSIDERATE OF ANY...EXTENUATING FACTORS.
BLIND, HUH?
YOU KNOW, LUKE, YOU COULD HAVE USED SOME OF THAT JUSTICE EARLIER TODAY, RIGHT?
SURE COULD HAVE.
OH? WHAT HAPPENED?
NOTHING MUCH.
JUST A BAND OF INTERNATIONAL TERRORISTS TRIED TO BLOW UP MY HOUSE AND KILL ME, MY WIFE AND MY KID.
"DAMN SHAME WHAT THEY DID TO THAT DOG."

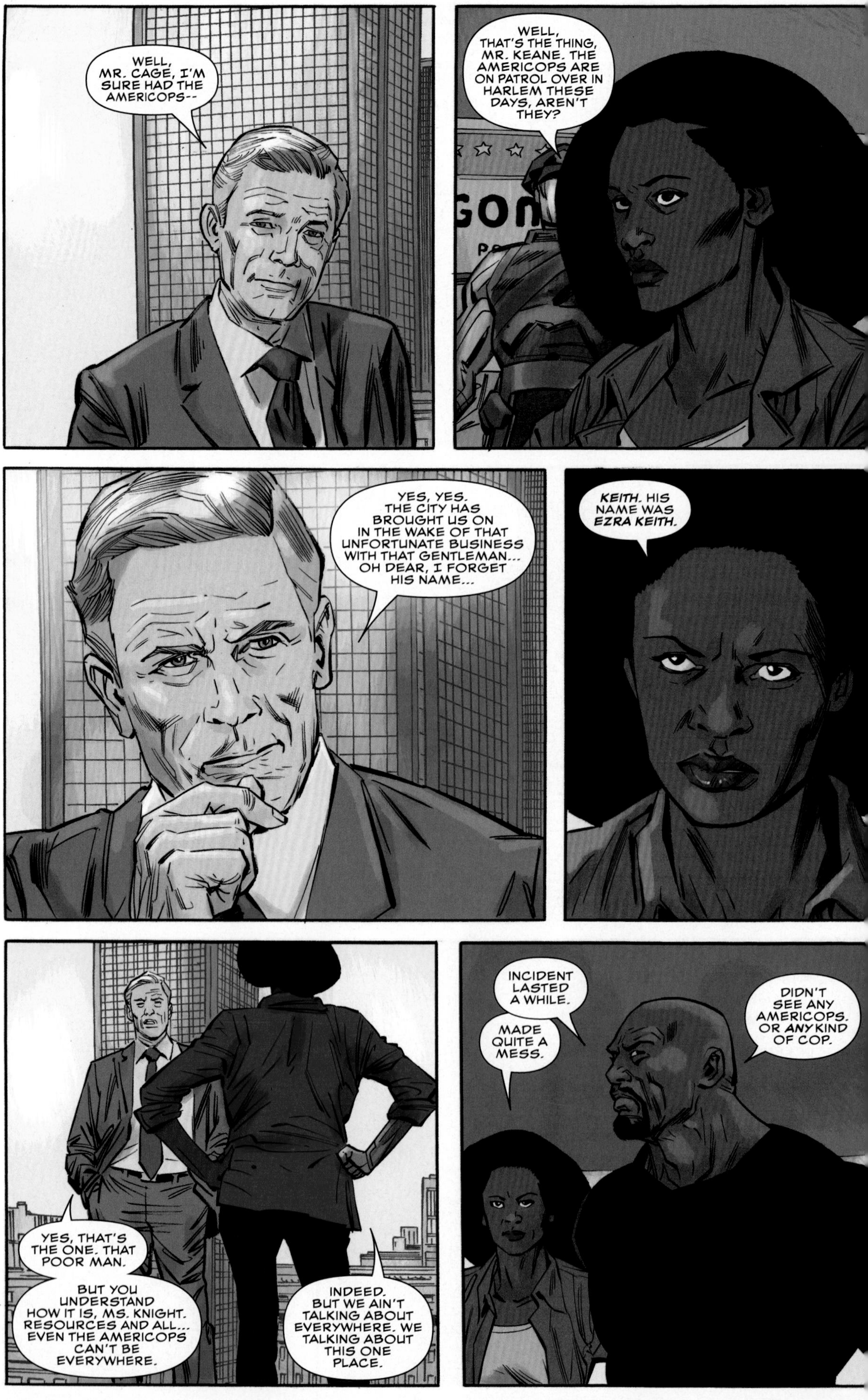
WELL, MR. CAGE, I'M SURE HAD THE AMERICOPS--
WELL, THAT'S THE THING, MR. KEANE. THE AMERICOPS ARE ON PATROL OVER IN HARLEM THESE DAYS, AREN'T THEY?
YES, YES. THE CITY HAS BROUGHT US ON IN THE WAKE OF THAT UNFORTUNATE BUSINESS WITH THAT GENTLEMAN... OH DEAR, I FORGET HIS NAME...
KEITH. HIS NAME WAS EZRA KEITH.
YES, THAT'S THE ONE. THAT POOR MAN.
BUT YOU UNDERSTAND HOW IT IS, MS. KNIGHT. RESOURCES AND ALL... EVEN THE AMERICOPS CAN'T BE EVERYWHERE.
INDEED. BUT WE AIN'T TALKING ABOUT EVERYWHERE. WE TALKING ABOUT THIS ONE PLACE.
INCIDENT LASTED A WHILE.
MADE QUITE A MESS.
DIDN'T SEE ANY AMERICOPS. OR ANY KIND OF COP.

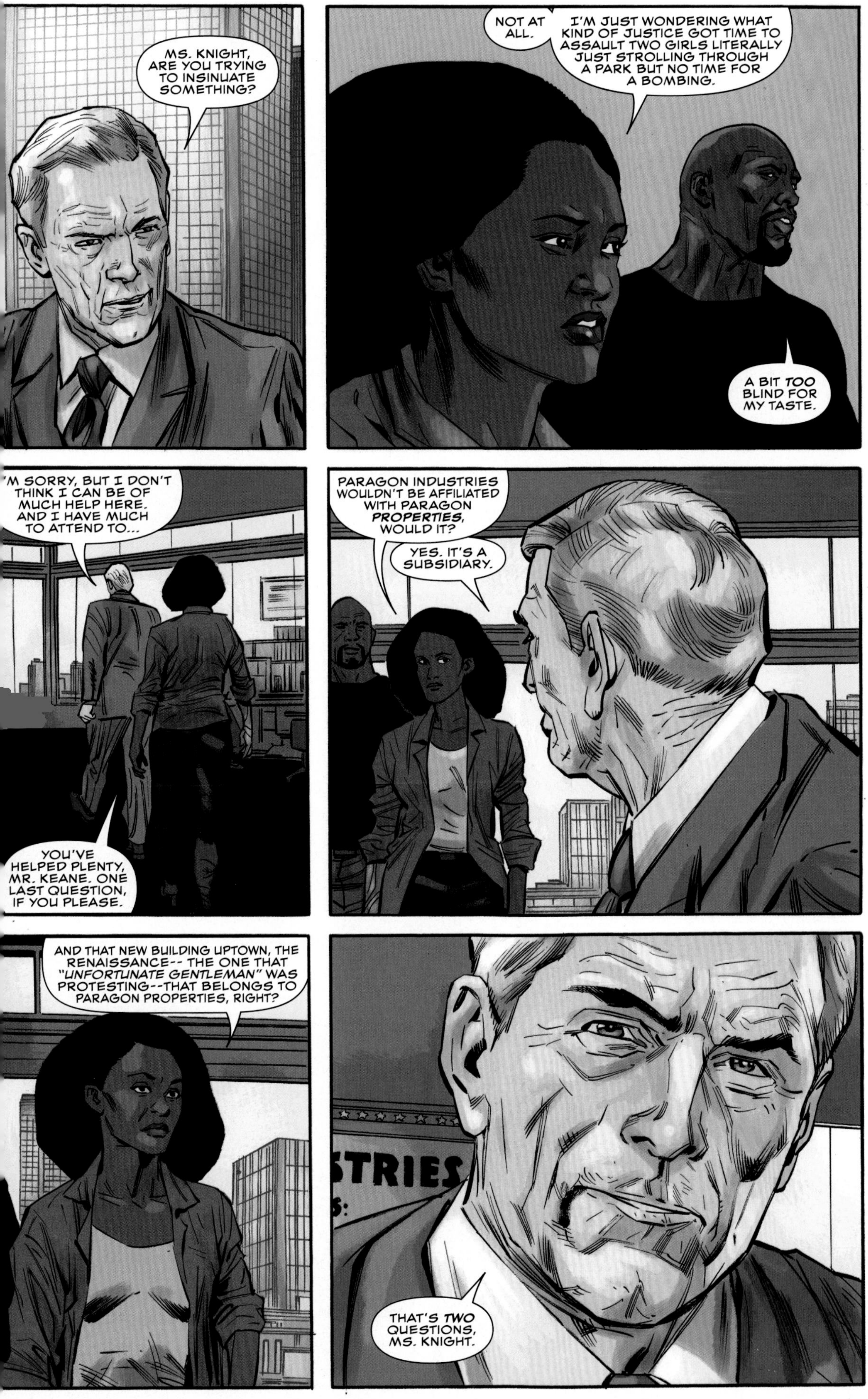
MS. KNIGHT, ARE YOU TRYING TO INSINUATE SOMETHING?
NOT AT ALL.
I'M JUST WONDERING WHAT KIND OF JUSTICE GOT TIME TO ASSAULT TWO GIRLS LITERALLY JUST STROLLING THROUGH A PARK BUT NO TIME FOR A BOMBING.
A BIT TOO BLIND FOR MY TASTE.
'M SORRY, BUT I DON'T THINK I CAN BE OF MUCH HELP HERE. AND I HAVE MUCH TO ATTEND TO...
YOU'VE HELPED PLENTY, MR. KEANE. ONE LAST QUESTION, IF YOU PLEASE.
PARAGON INDUSTRIES WOULDN'T BE AFFILIATED WITH PARAGON PROPERTIES, WOULD IT?
YES. IT'S A SUBSIDIARY.
AND THAT NEW BUILDING UPTOWN, THE RENAISSANCE-- THE ONE THAT "UNFORTUNATE GENTLEMAN" WAS PROTESTING--THAT BELONGS TO PARAGON PROPERTIES, RIGHT?
STRIES
THAT'S TWO QUESTIONS, MS. KNIGHT.

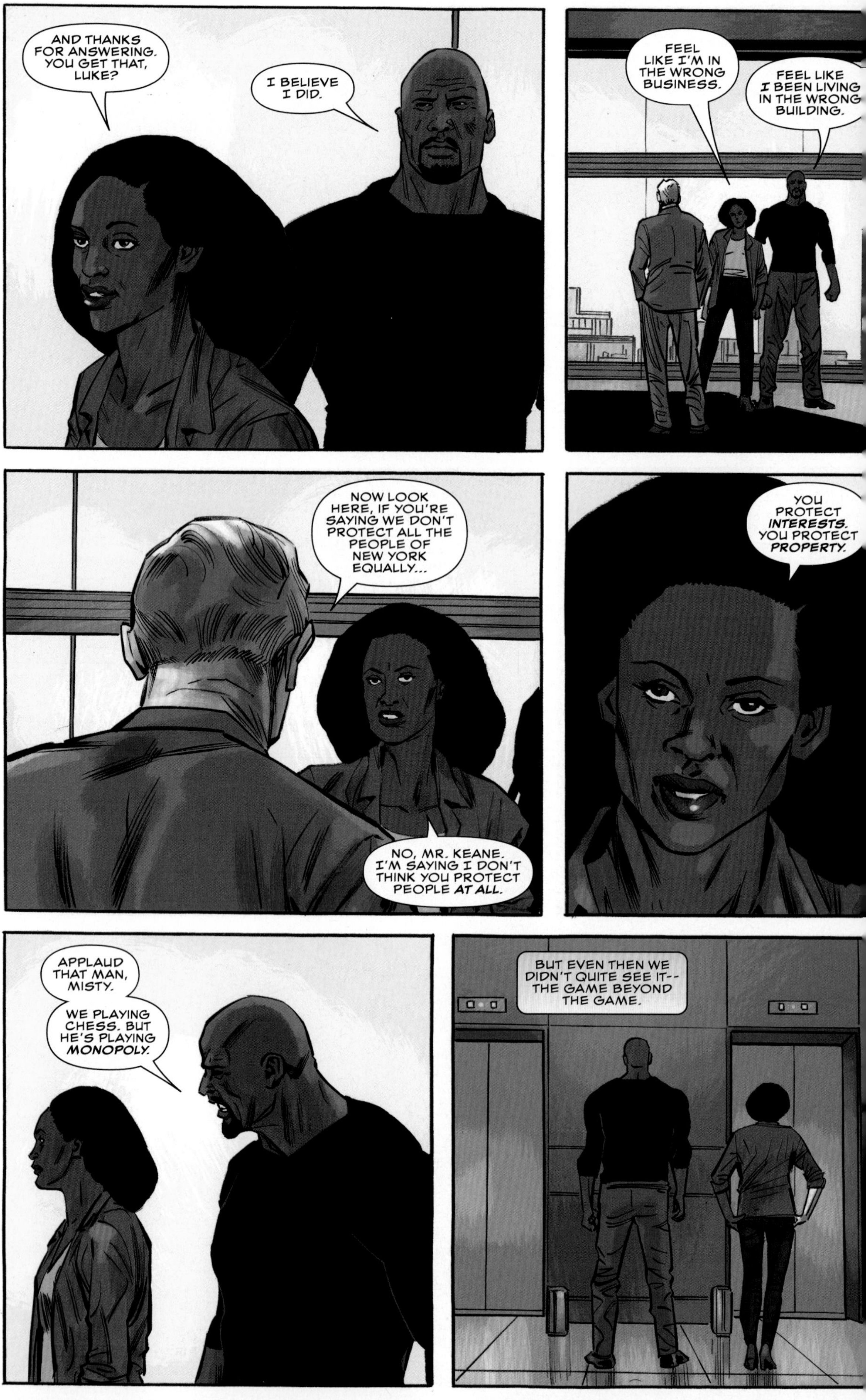
AND THANKS FOR ANSWERING. YOU GET THAT, LUKE?
I BELIEVE I DID.
FEEL LIKE I'M IN THE WRONG BUSINESS.
FEEL LIKE I BEEN LIVING IN THE WRONG BUILDING.
NOW LOOK HERE, IF YOU'RE SAYING WE DON'T PROTECT ALL THE PEOPLE OF NEW YORK EQUALLY...
NO, MR. KEANE. I'M SAYING I DON'T THINK YOU PROTECT PEOPLE AT ALL.
YOU PROTECT INTERESTS. YOU PROTECT PROPERTY.
APPLAUD THAT MAN, MISTY.
WE PLAYING CHESS. BUT HE'S PLAYING MONOPOLY.
BUT EVEN THEN WE DIDN'T QUITE SEE IT-- THE GAME BEYOND THE GAME.

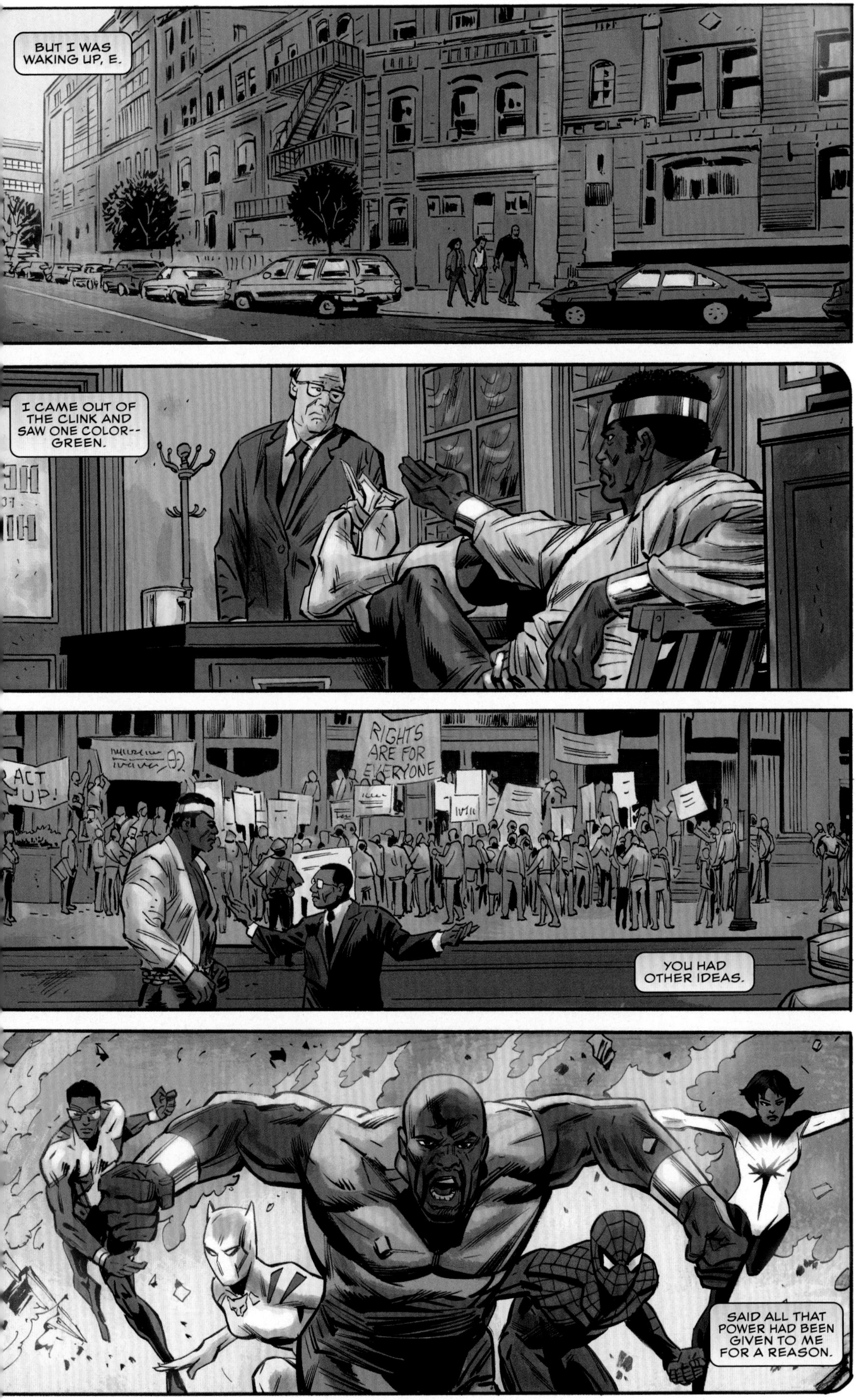
BUT I WAS WAKING UP, E.
I CAME OUT OF THE CLINK AND SAW ONE COLOR-- GREEN.
ACT UP!
RIGHTS ARE FOR EVERYONE
YOU HAD OTHER IDEAS.
SAID ALL THAT POWER HAD BEEN GIVEN TO ME FOR A REASON.

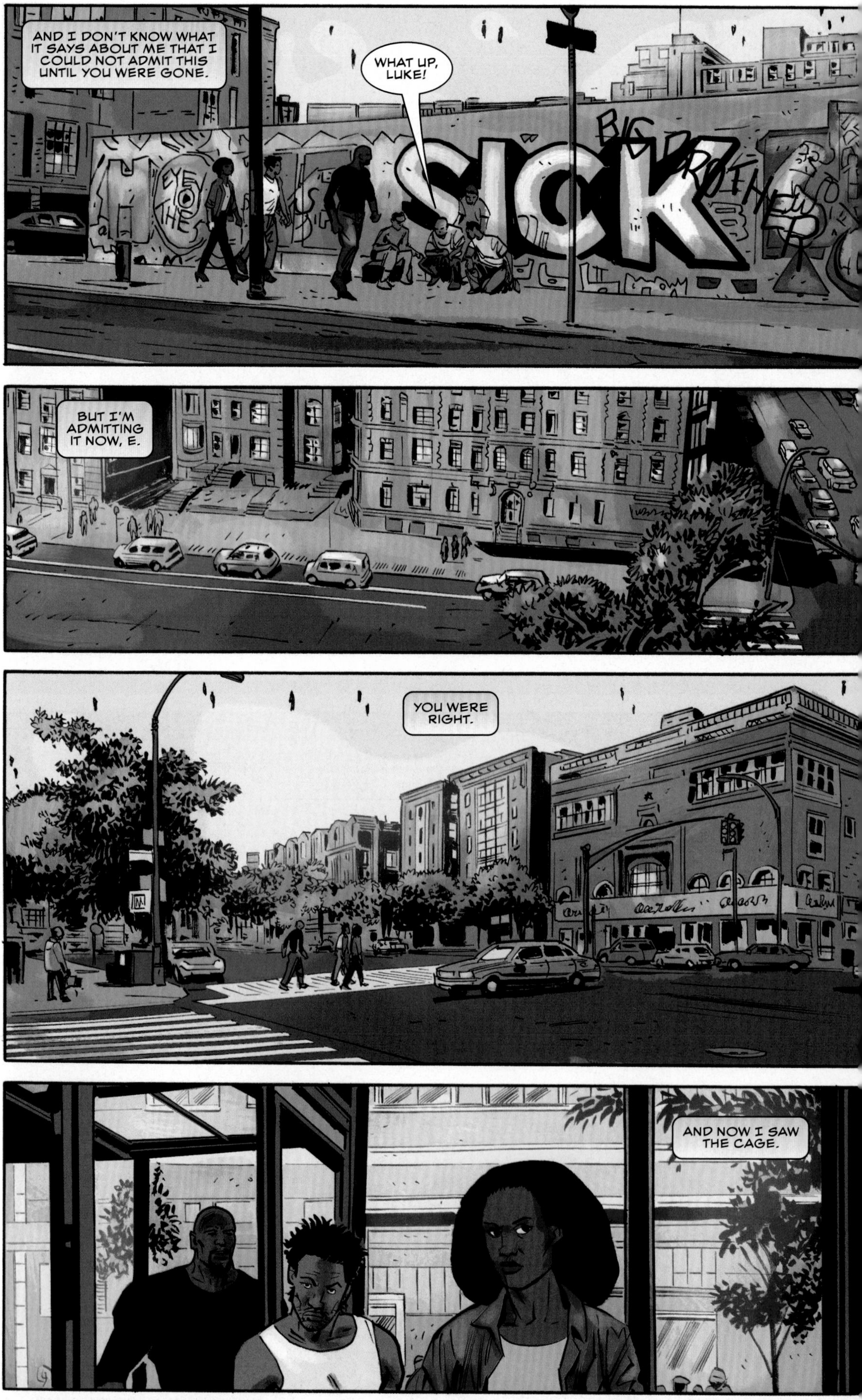
AND I DON'T KNOW WHAT IT SAYS ABOUT ME THAT I COULD NOT ADMIT THIS UNTIL YOU WERE GONE.
WHAT UP, LUKE!
BUT I'M ADMITTING IT NOW, E.
YOU WERE RIGHT.
AND NOW I SAW THE CAGE.

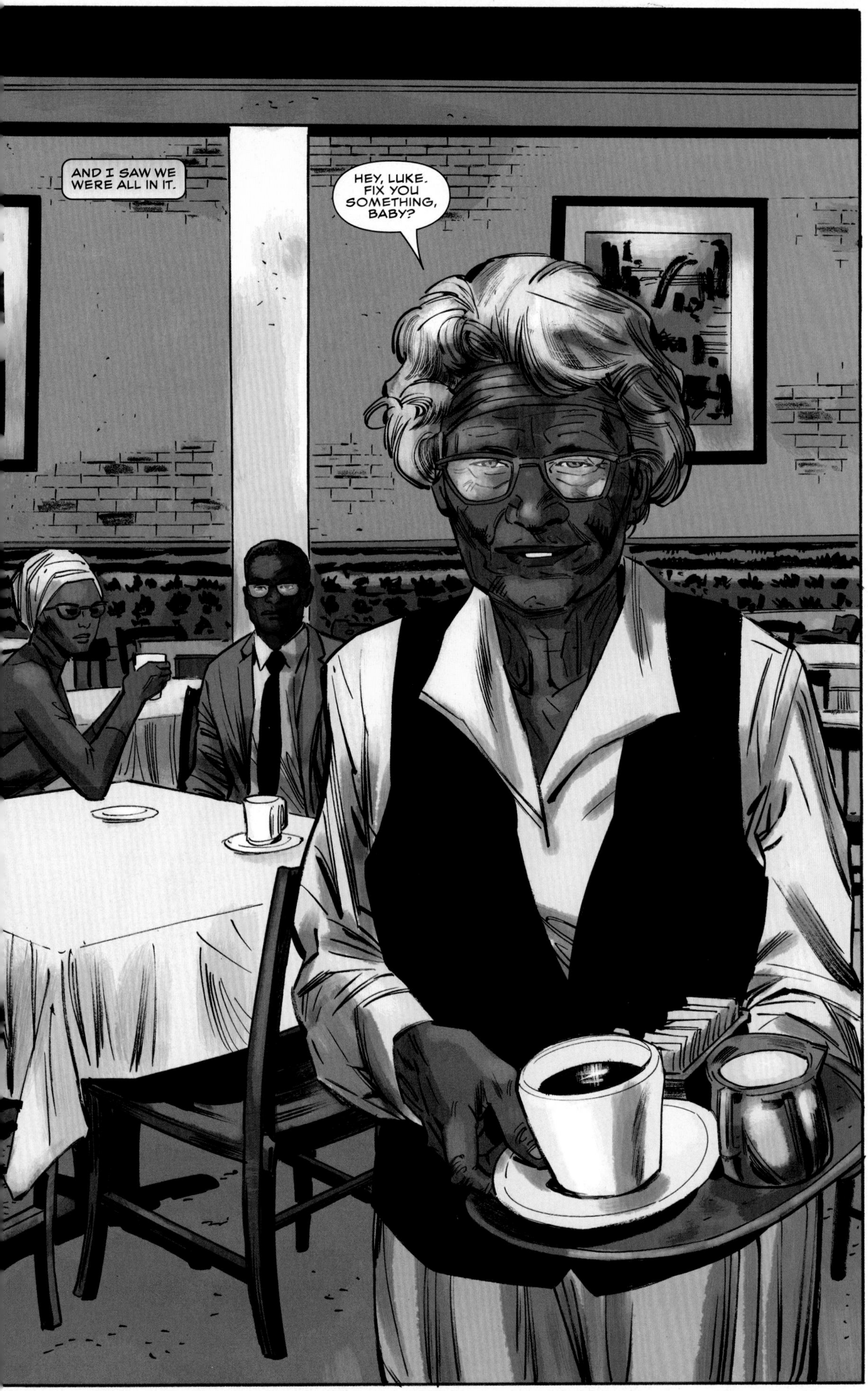
AND I SAW WE WERE ALL IN IT.
HEY, LUKE. FIX YOU SOMETHING, BABY?

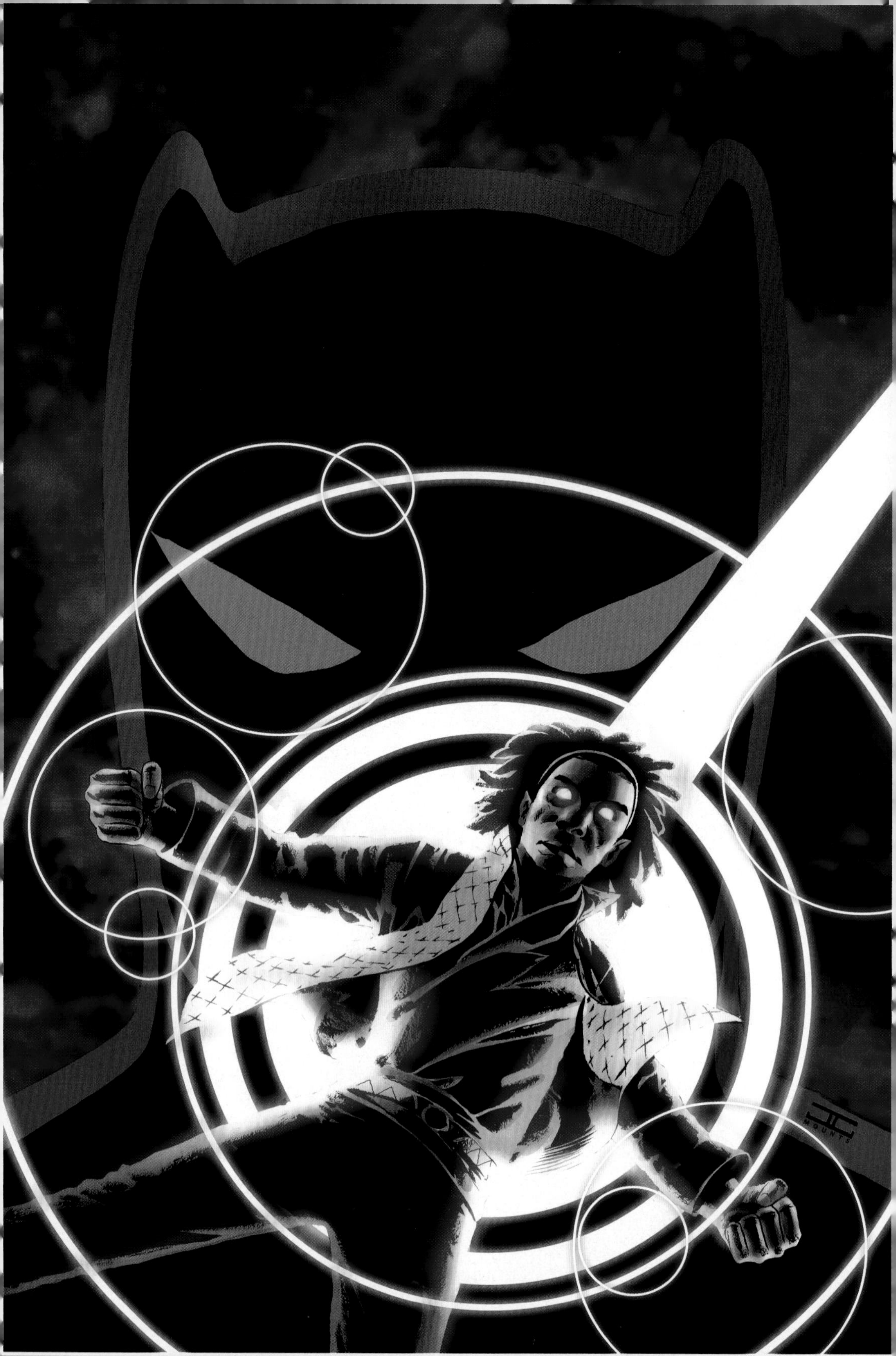

PART 5 DOWN THESE MEAN STREETS

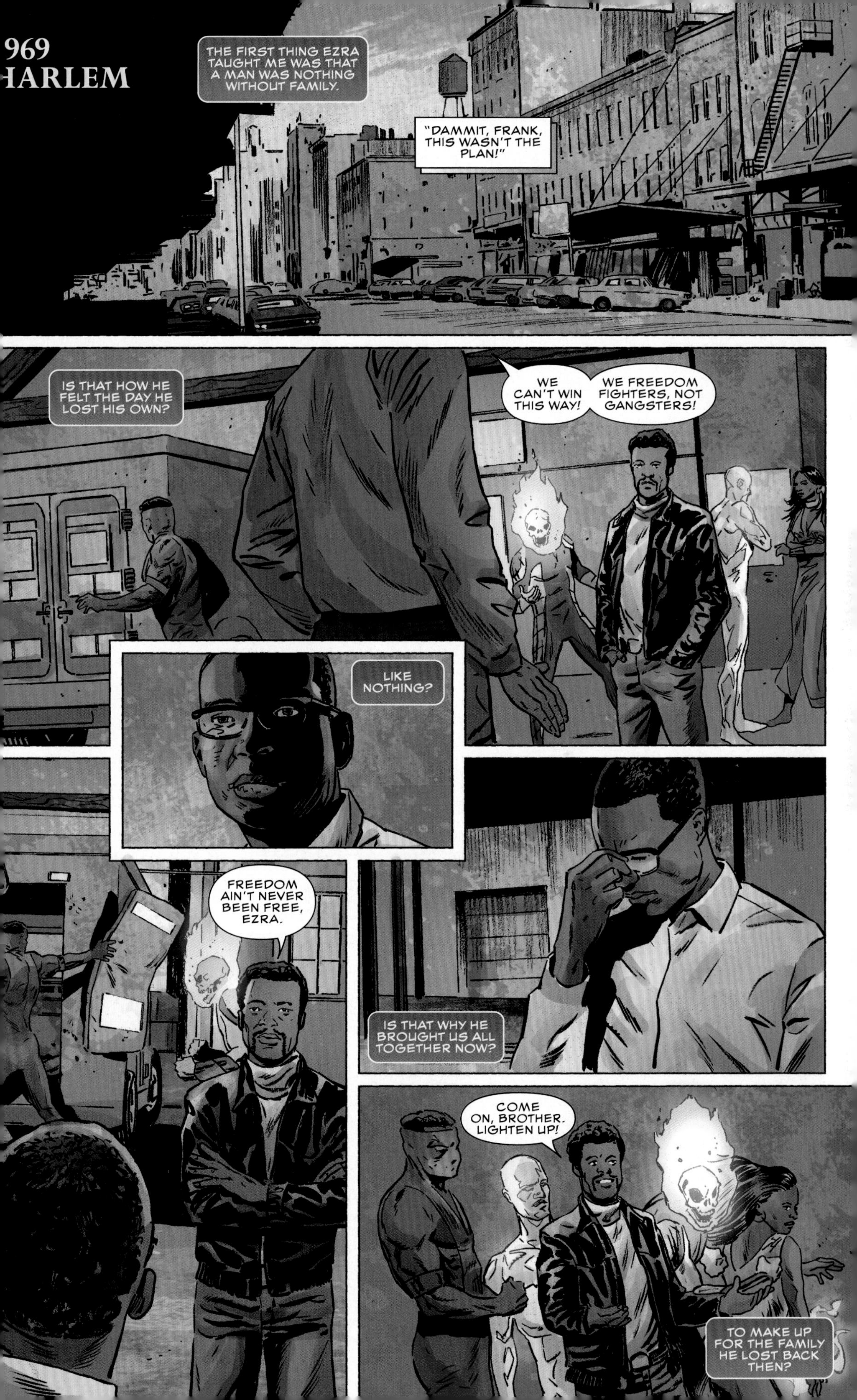
969
HARLEM
THE FIRST THING EZRA TAUGHT ME WAS THAT A MAN WAS NOTHING WITHOUT FAMILY.
"DAMMIT, FRANK, THIS WASN'T THE PLAN!"
IS THAT HOW HE FELT THE DAY HE LOST HIS OWN?
WE CAN'T WIN THIS WAY!
WE FREEDOM FIGHTERS, NOT GANGSTERS!
LIKE NOTHING?
FREEDOM AIN'T NEVER BEEN FREE, EZRA.
IS THAT WHY HE BROUGHT US ALL TOGETHER NOW?
COME ON, BROTHER. LIGHTEN UP!
TO MAKE UP FOR THE FAMILY HE LOST BACK THEN?

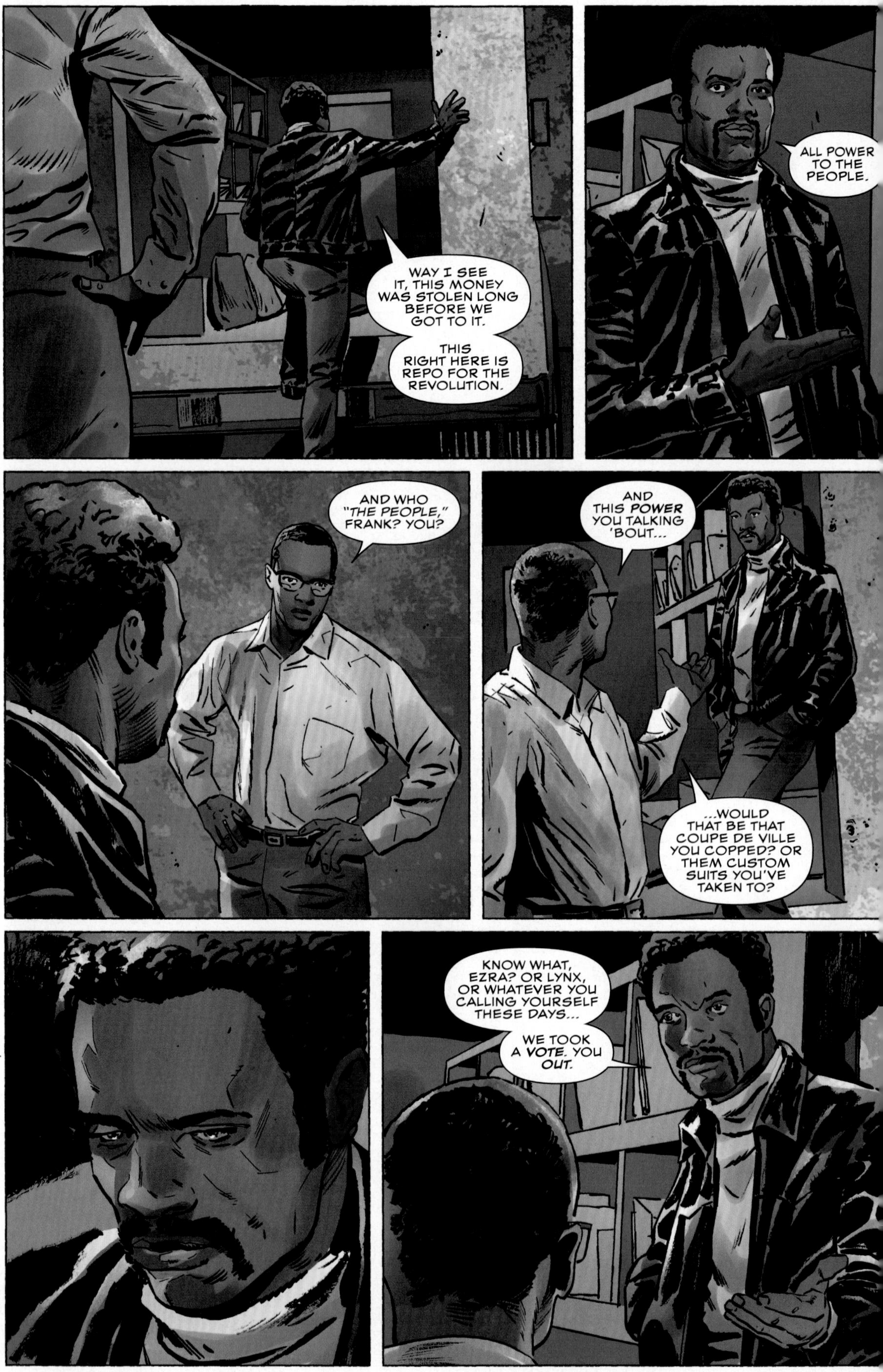
WAY I SEE IT, THIS MONEY WAS STOLEN LONG BEFORE WE GOT TO IT.
THIS RIGHT HERE IS REPO FOR THE REVOLUTION.
ALL POWER TO THE PEOPLE.
AND WHO "THE PEOPLE," FRANK? YOU?
AND THIS POWER YOU TALKING 'BOUT...
...WOULD THAT BE THAT COUPE DE VILLE YOU COPPED? OR THEM CUSTOM SUITS YOU'VE TAKEN TO?
KNOW WHAT, EZRA? OR LYNX, OR WHATEVER YOU CALLING YOURSELF THESE DAYS...
WE TOOK A VOTE. YOU OUT.

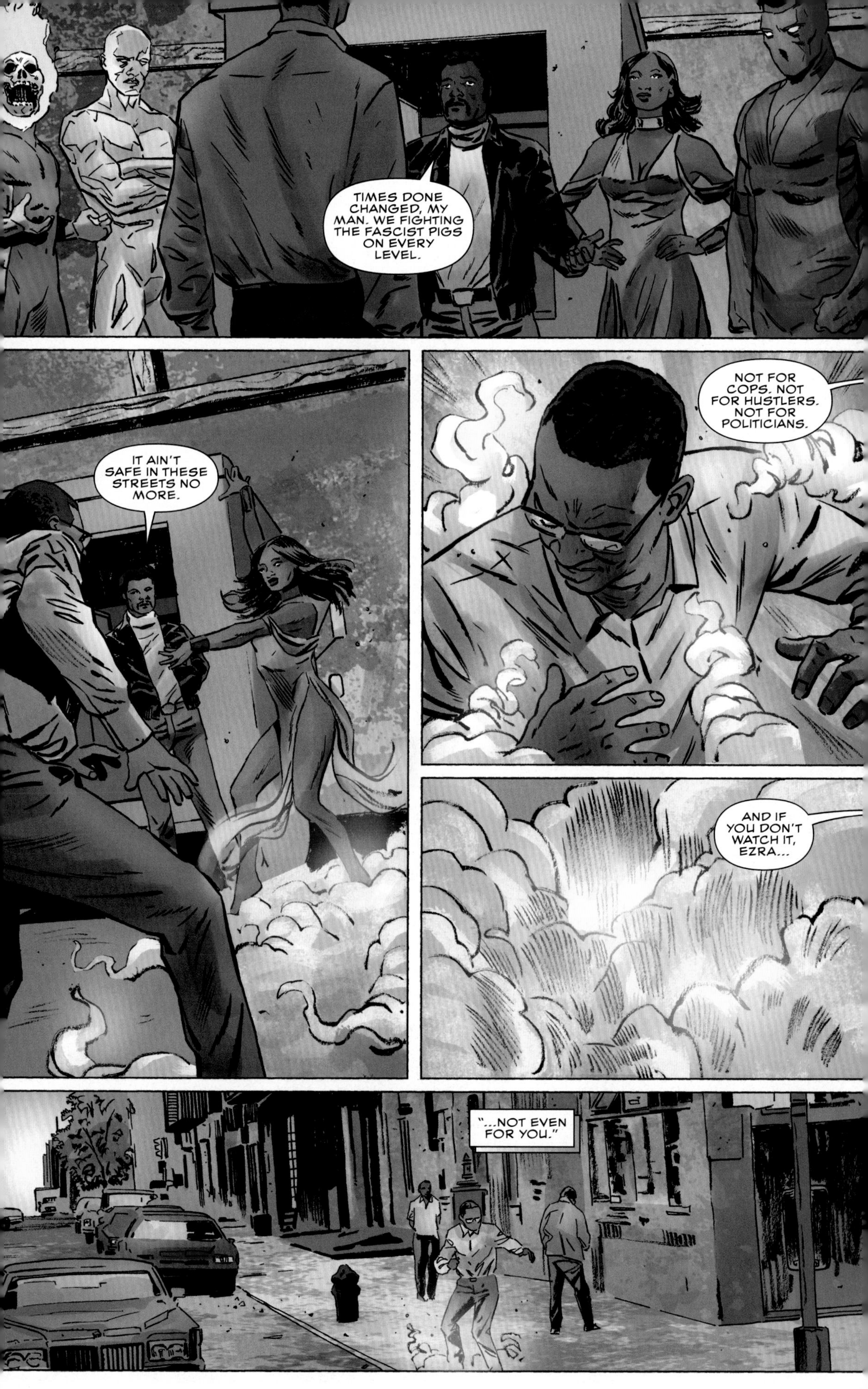
TIMES DONE CHANGED, MY MAN. WE FIGHTING THE FASCIST PIGS ON EVERY LEVEL.
IT AIN'T SAFE IN THESE STREETS NO MORE.
NOT FOR COPS. NOT FOR HUSTLERS. NOT FOR POLITICIANS.
AND IF YOU DON'T WATCH IT, EZRA...
"...NOT EVEN FOR YOU."

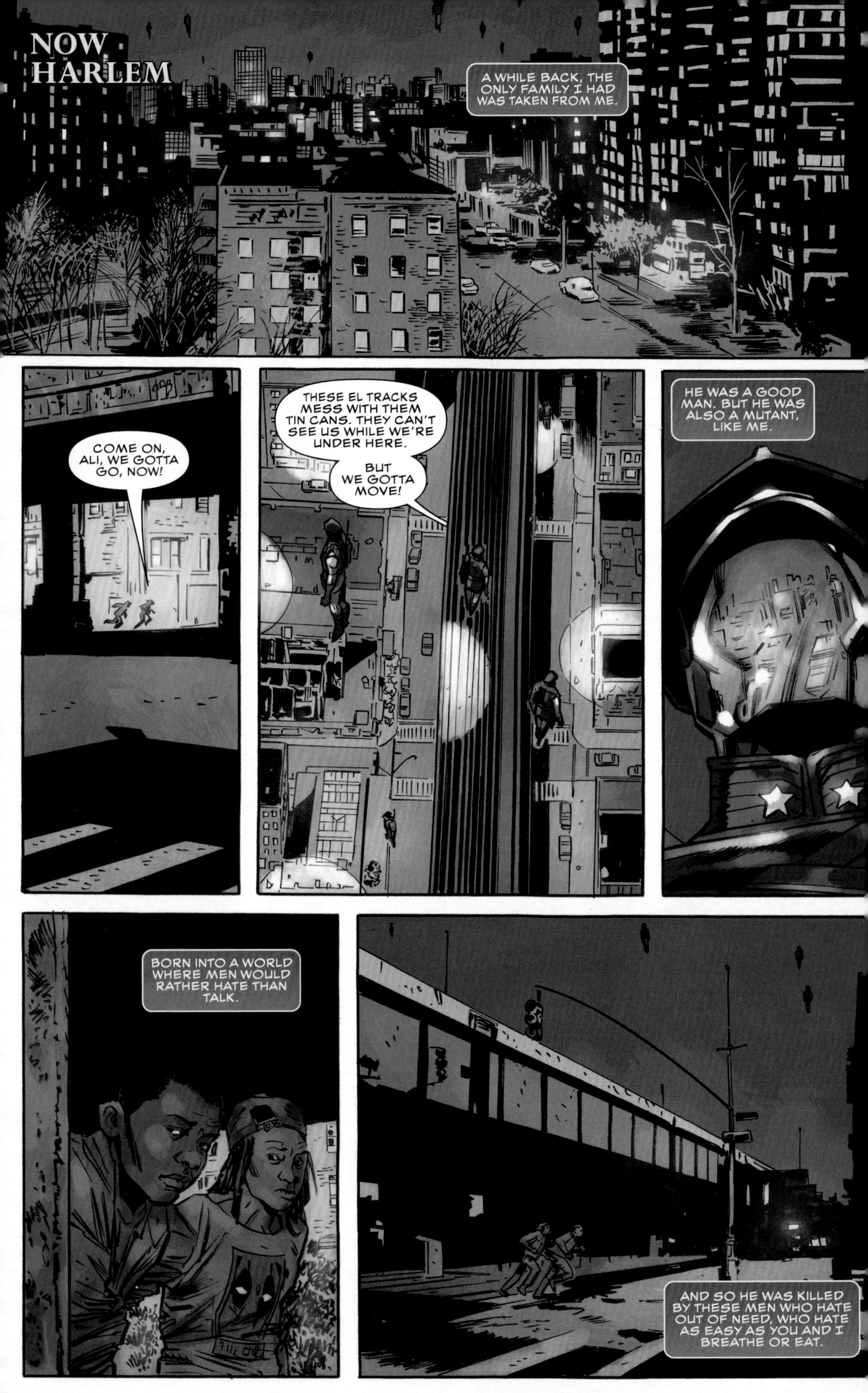
NOW
HARLEM
A WHILE BACK, THE ONLY FAMILY I HAD WAS TAKEN FROM ME.
COME ON, ALI, WE GOTTA GO, NOW!
THESE EL TRACKS MESS WITH THEM TIN CANS. THEY CAN'T SEE US WHILE WE'RE UNDER HERE.
BUT WE GOTTA MOVE!
HE WAS A GOOD MAN. BUT HE WAS ALSO A MUTANT, LIKE ME.
BORN INTO A WORLD WHERE MEN WOULD RATHER HATE THAN TALK.
AND SO HE WAS KILLED BY THESE MEN WHO HATE OUT OF NEED, WHO HATE AS EASY AS YOU AND I BREATHE OR EAT.

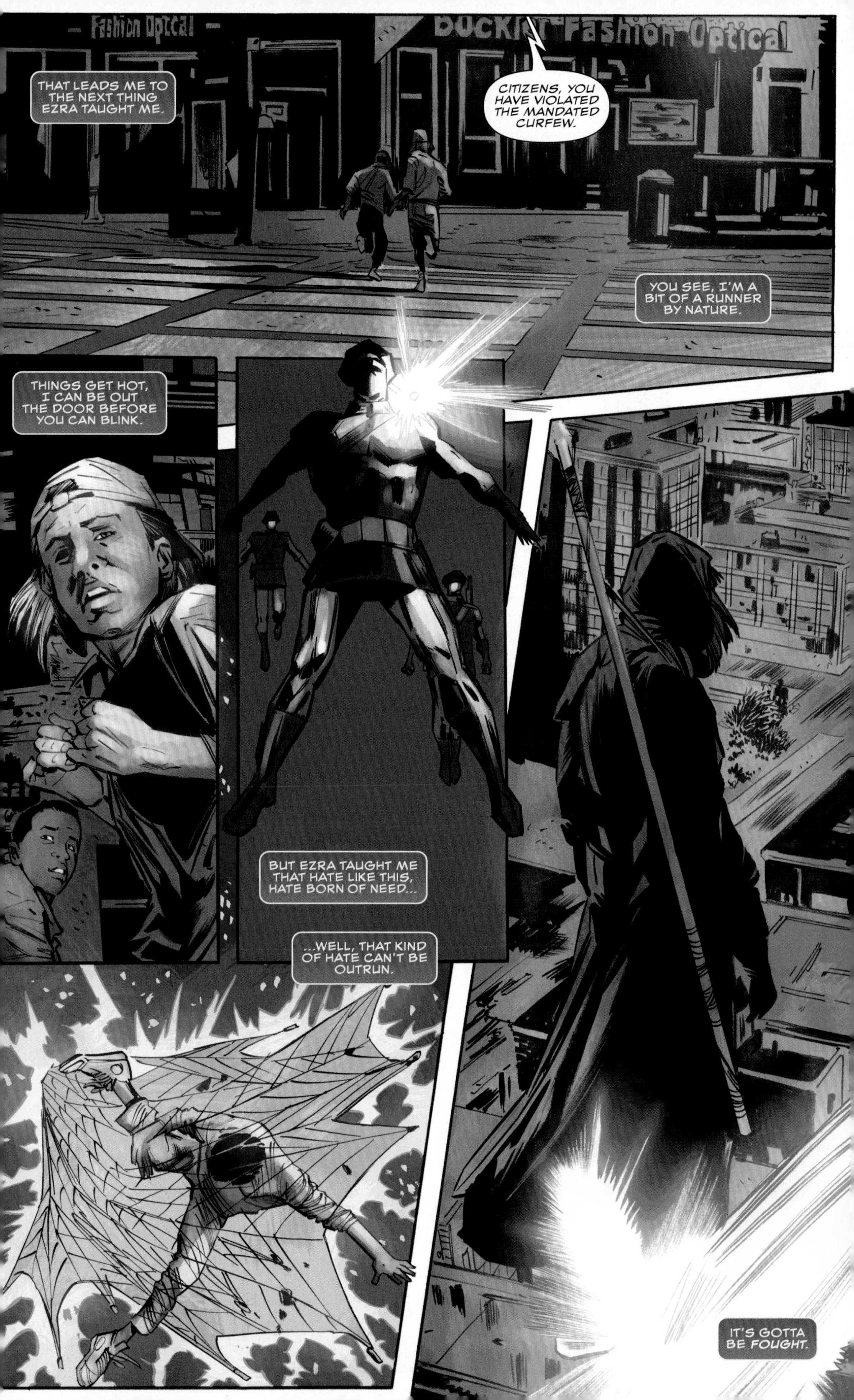
Fashion Optical
Buckler Fashion Optical
THAT LEADS ME TO THE NEXT THING EZRA TAUGHT ME.
CITIZENS, YOU HAVE VIOLATED THE MANDATED CURFEW.
YOU SEE, I'M A BIT OF A RUNNER BY NATURE.
THINGS GET HOT, I CAN BE OUT THE DOOR BEFORE YOU CAN BLINK.
BUT EZRA TAUGHT ME THAT HATE LIKE THIS, HATE BORN OF NEED...
...WELL, THAT KIND OF HATE CAN'T BE OUTRUN.
IT'S GOTTA BE FOUGHT.

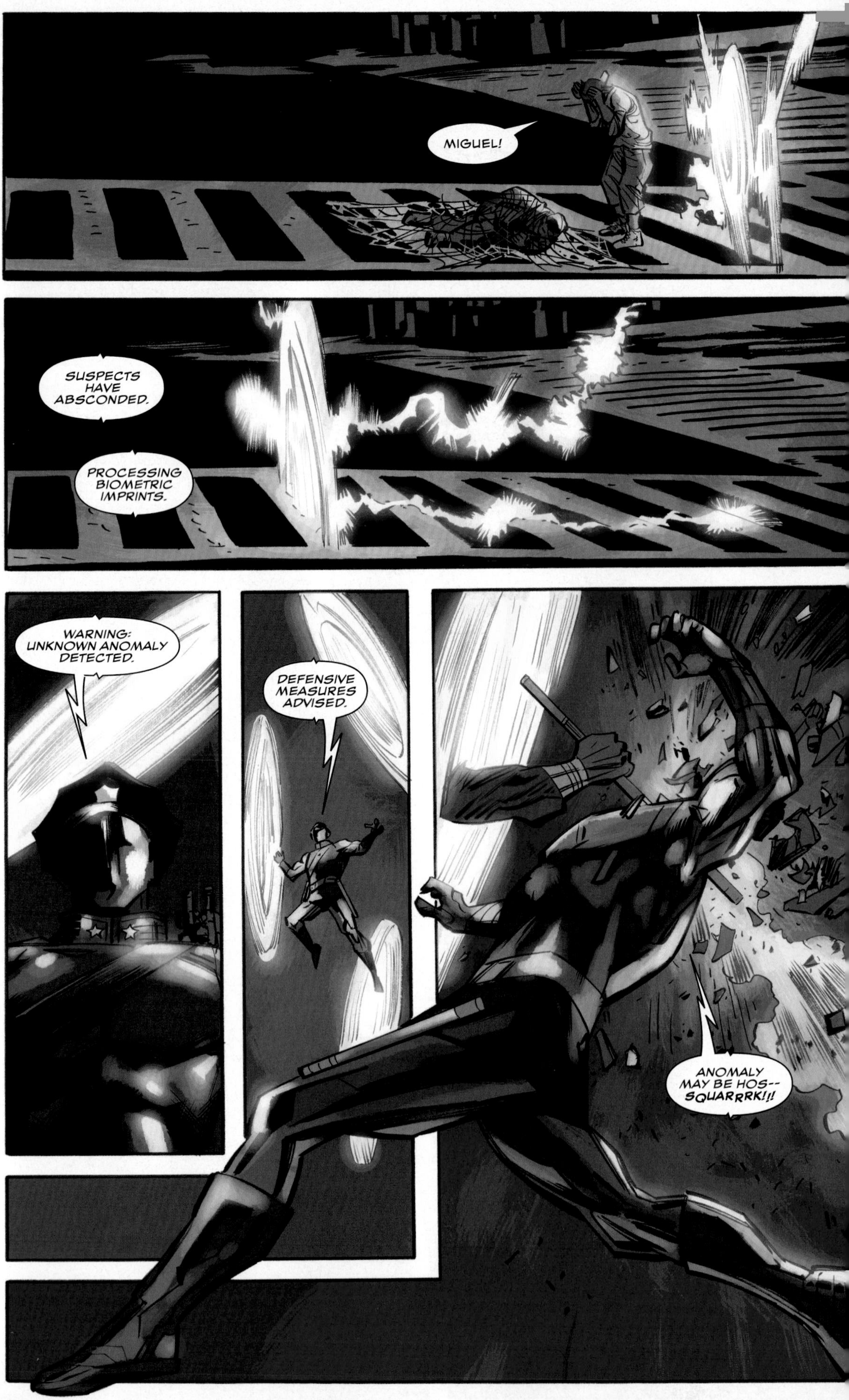
MIGUEL!
SUSPECTS HAVE ABSCONDED.
PROCESSING BIOMETRIC IMPRINTS.
WARNING: UNKNOWN ANOMALY DETECTED.
DEFENSIVE MEASURES ADVISED.
ANOMALY MAY BE HOS-- SQUARRRK!!!

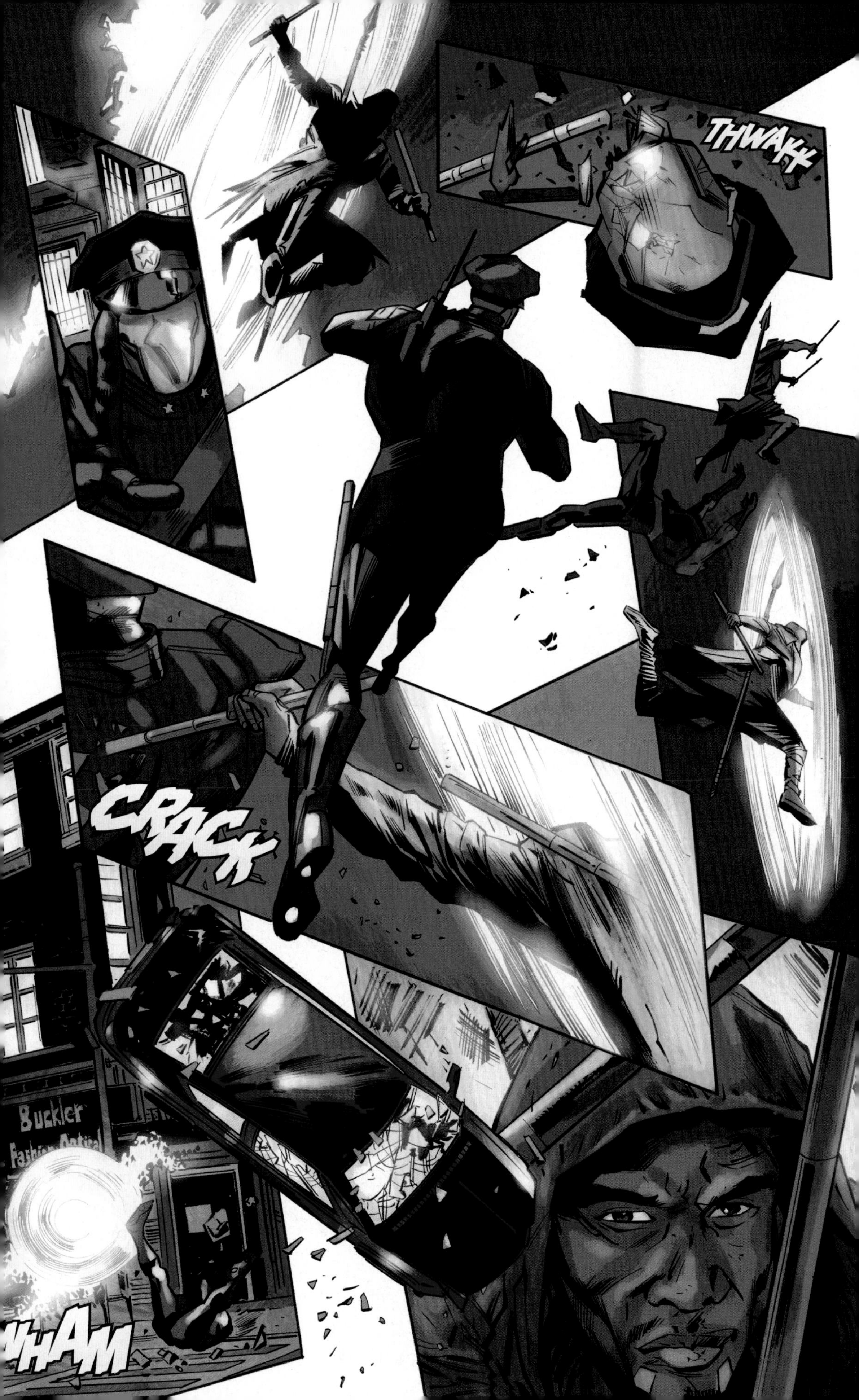
THWAKK
CRACK
Buckler

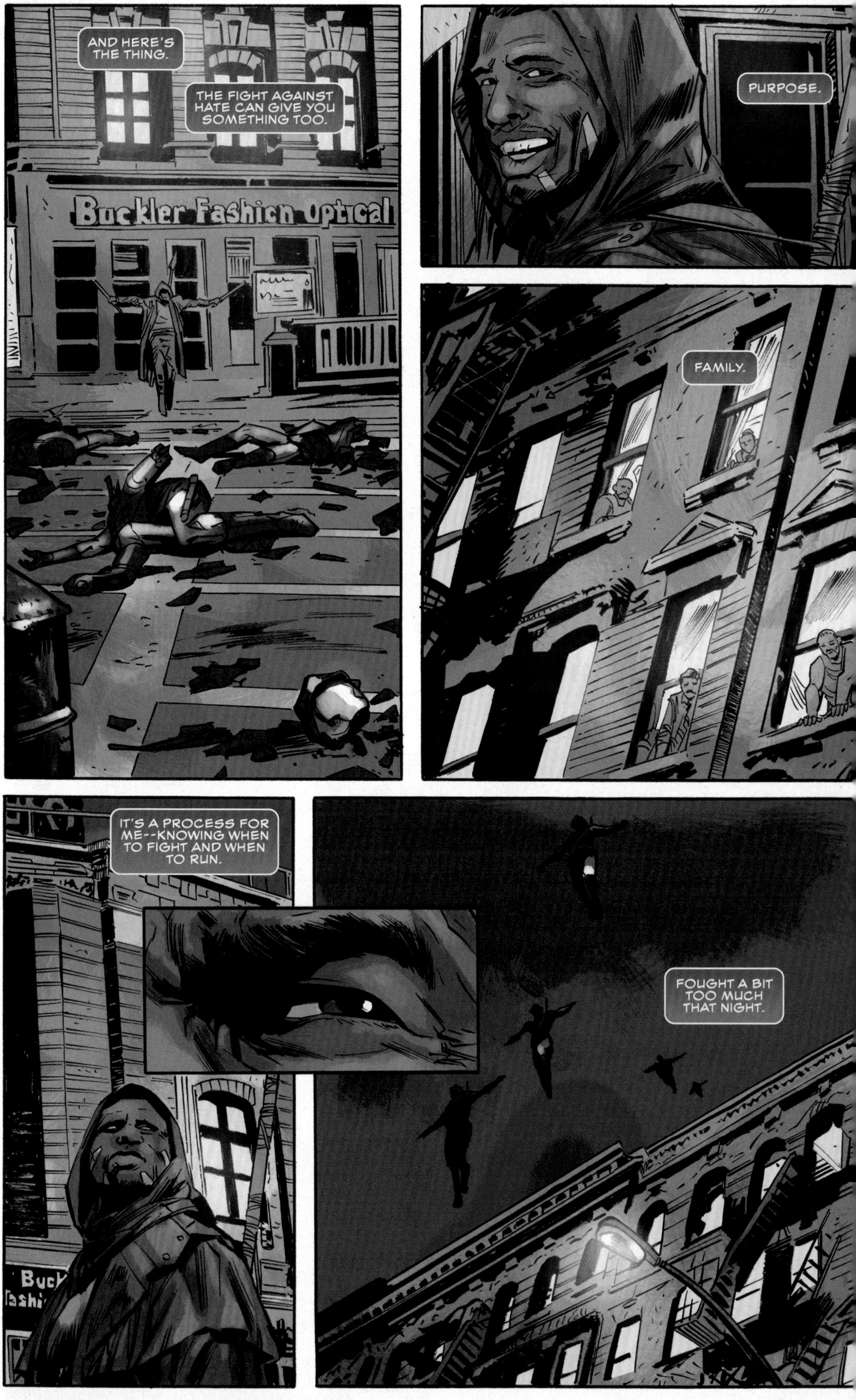

AND HERE'S THE THING.
THE FIGHT AGAINST HATE CAN GIVE YOU SOMETHING TOO.
Buckler Fashion Optical
PURPOSE.
FAMILY.
IT'S A PROCESS FOR ME--KNOWING WHEN TO FIGHT AND WHEN TO RUN.
FOUGHT A BIT TOO MUCH THAT NIGHT.

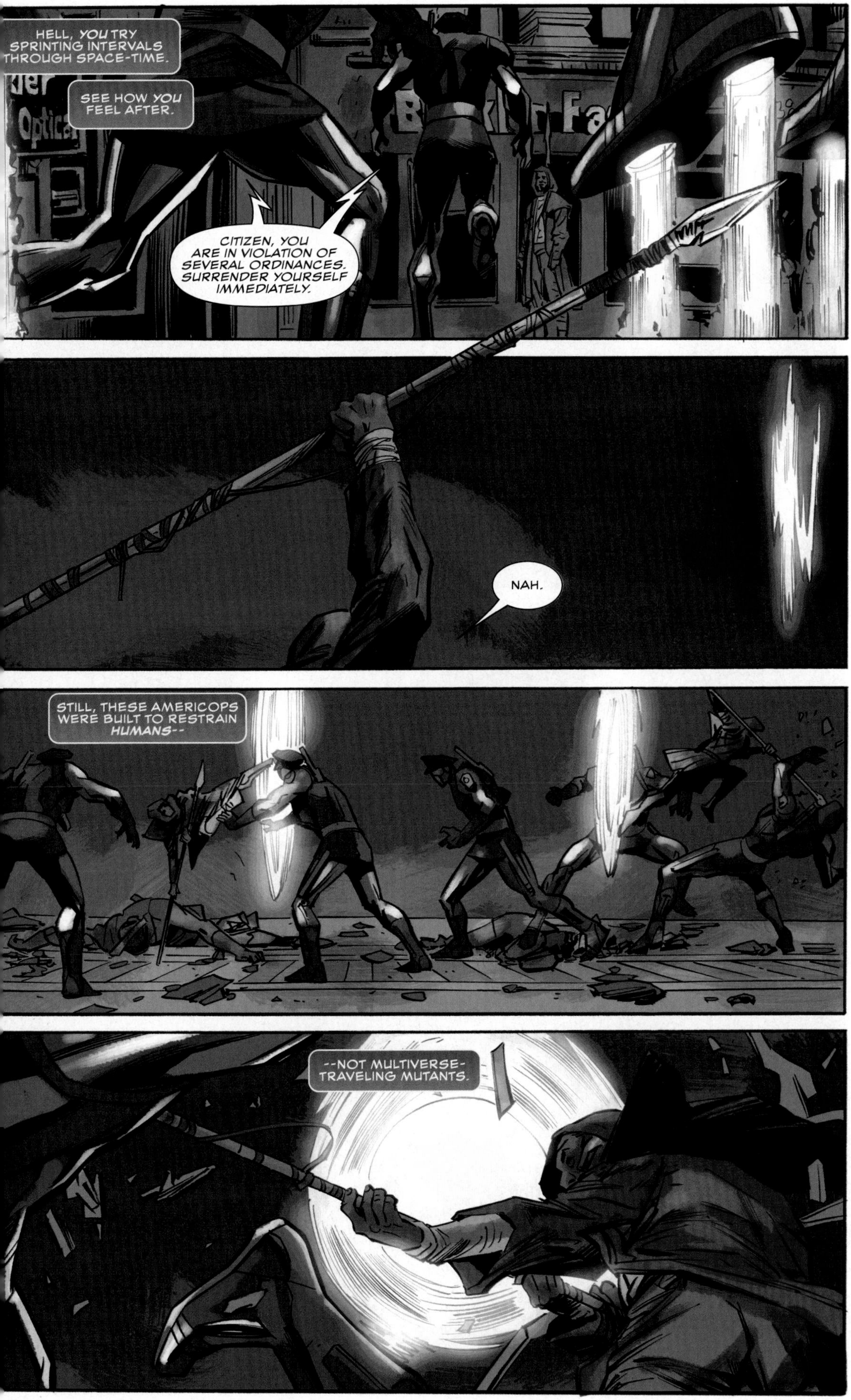
HELL, YOU TRY SPRINTING INTERVALS THROUGH SPACE-TIME.
SEE HOW YOU FEEL AFTER.
CITIZEN, YOU ARE IN VIOLATION OF SEVERAL ORDINANCES. SURRENDER YOURSELF IMMEDIATELY.
NAH.
STILL, THESE AMERICOPS WERE BUILT TO RESTRAIN HUMANS--
--NOT MULTIVERSE-TRAVELING MUTANTS.

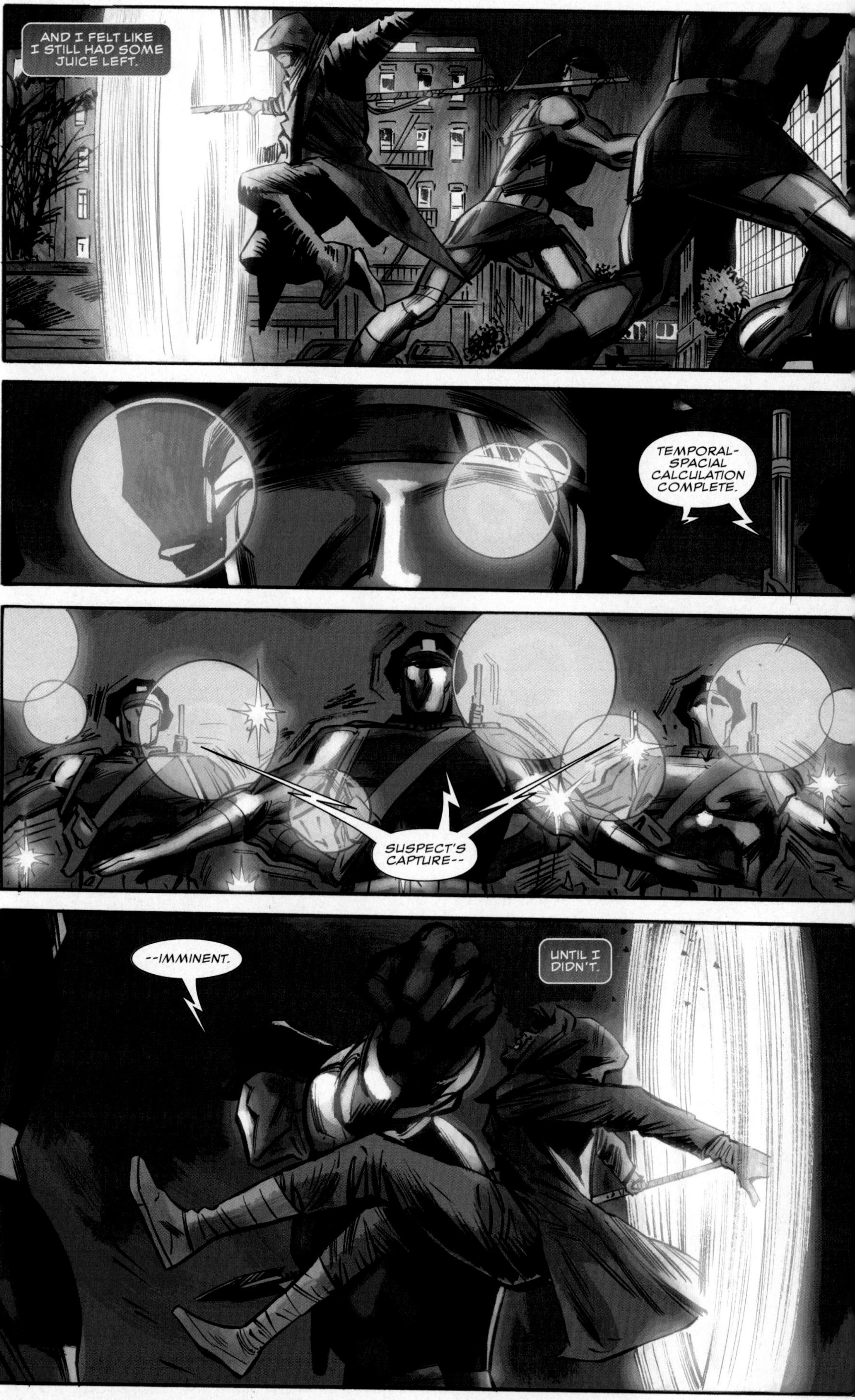
AND I FELT LIKE I STILL HAD SOME JUICE LEFT.
TEMPORAL-SPACIAL CALCULATION COMPLETE.
SUSPECT'S CAPTURE--
--IMMINENT.
UNTIL I DIDN'T.

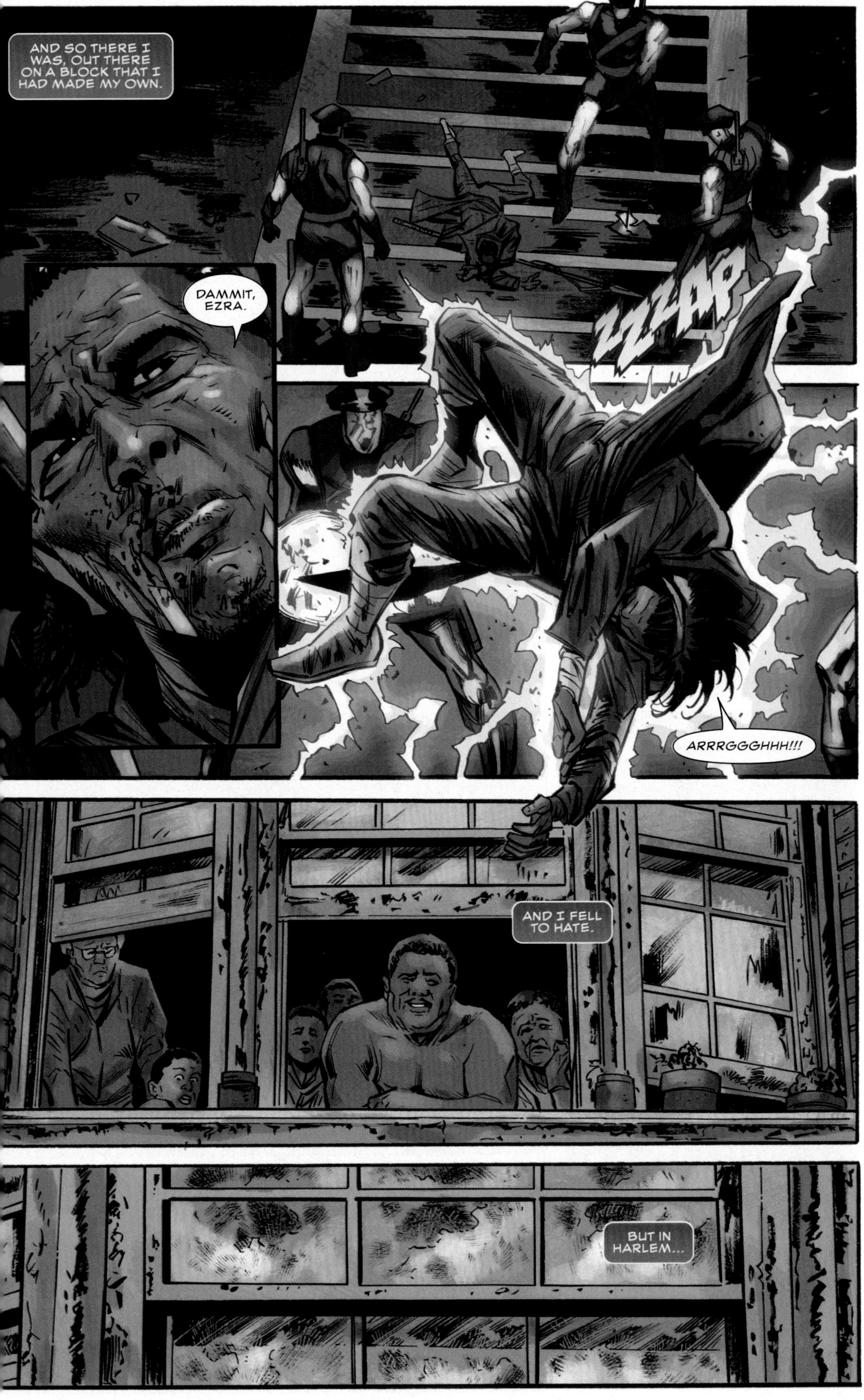
AND SO THERE I WAS, OUT THERE ON A BLOCK THAT I HAD MADE MY OWN.
DAMMIT, EZRA.
ZZZAP
ARRRGGGHHH!!!
AND I FELL TO HATE.
BUT IN HARLEM...

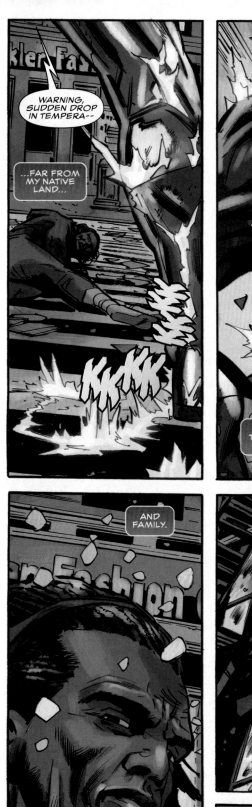

WARNING, SUDDEN DROP IN TEMPERA--

...FAR FROM MY NATIVE LAND...

...I ROSE ON THE STRENGTH OF PURPOSE.

AND FAMILY.

ON THE STRENGTH OF *CREW*.

AND AFTER I FOUND THAT...

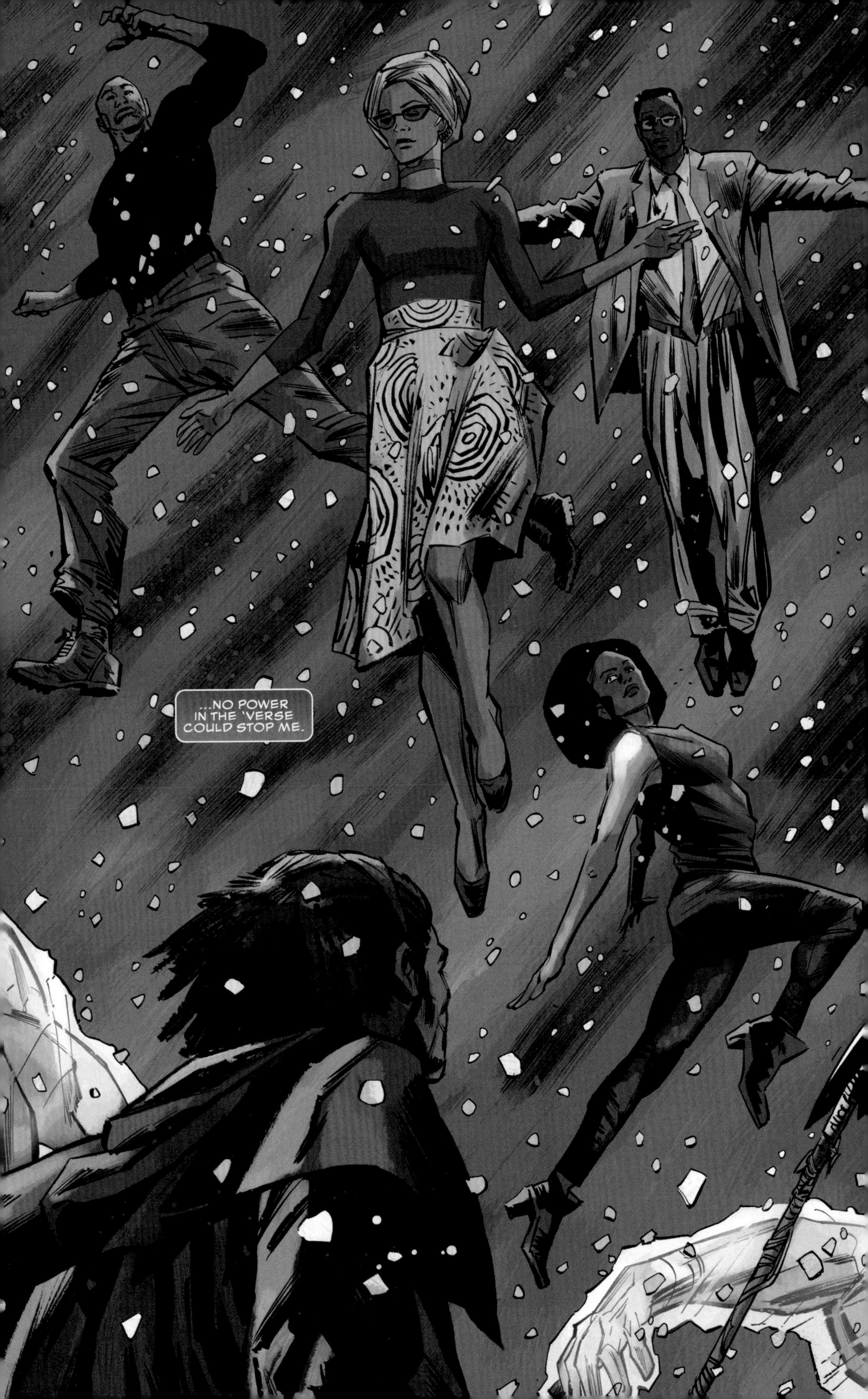
...NO POWER IN THE 'VERSE COULD STOP ME.

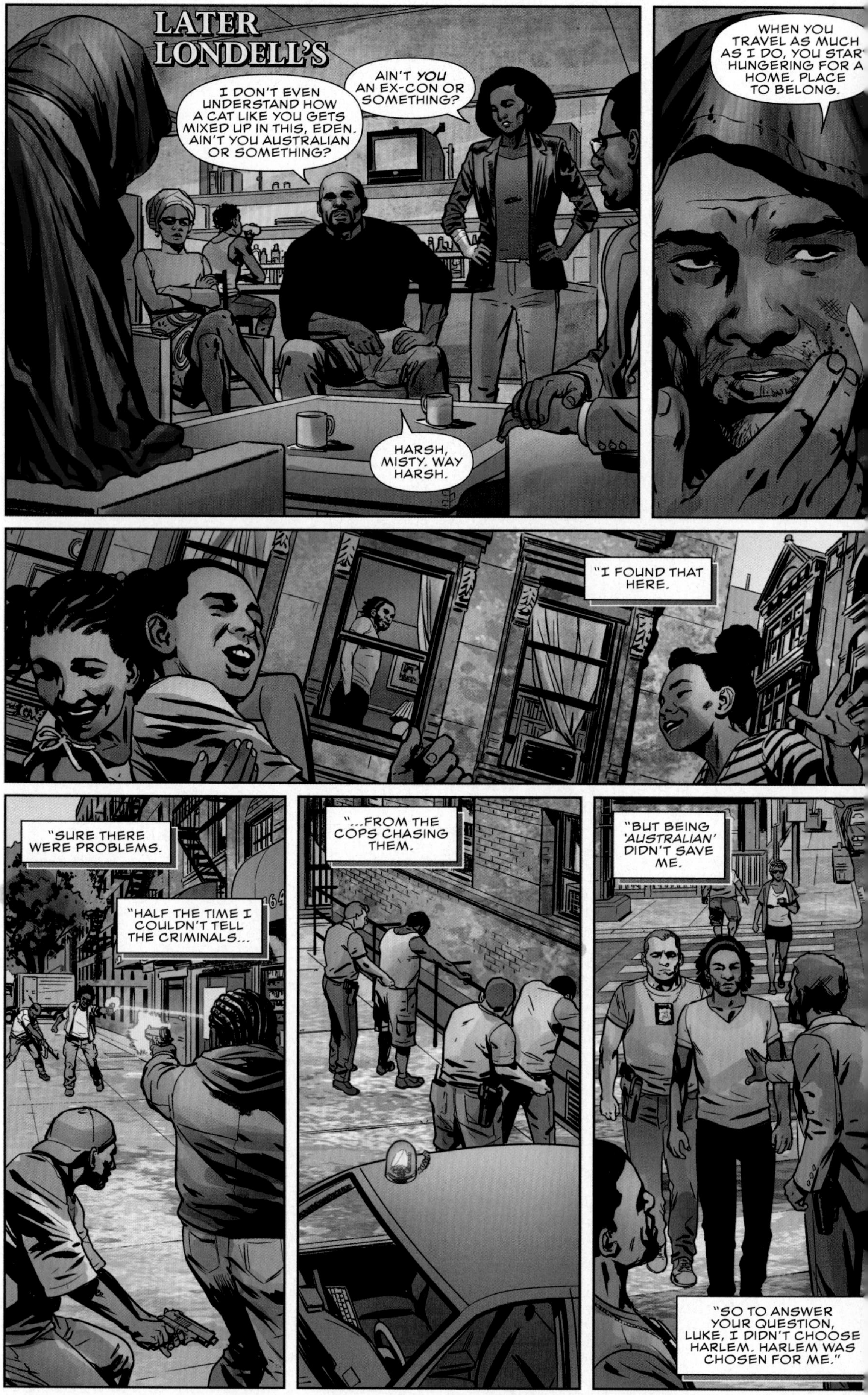
LATER LONDELL'S
I DON'T EVEN UNDERSTAND HOW A CAT LIKE YOU GETS MIXED UP IN THIS, EDEN. AIN'T YOU AUSTRALIAN OR SOMETHING?
AIN'T YOU AN EX-CON OR SOMETHING?
HARSH, MISTY. WAY HARSH.
WHEN YOU TRAVEL AS MUCH AS I DO, YOU STAR HUNGERING FOR A HOME. PLACE TO BELONG.
"I FOUND THAT HERE.
"SURE THERE WERE PROBLEMS.
"HALF THE TIME I COULDN'T TELL THE CRIMINALS...
"...FROM THE COPS CHASING THEM.
"BUT BEING 'AUSTRALIAN' DIDN'T SAVE ME.
"SO TO ANSWER YOUR QUESTION, LUKE, I DIDN'T CHOOSE HARLEM. HARLEM WAS CHOSEN FOR ME."

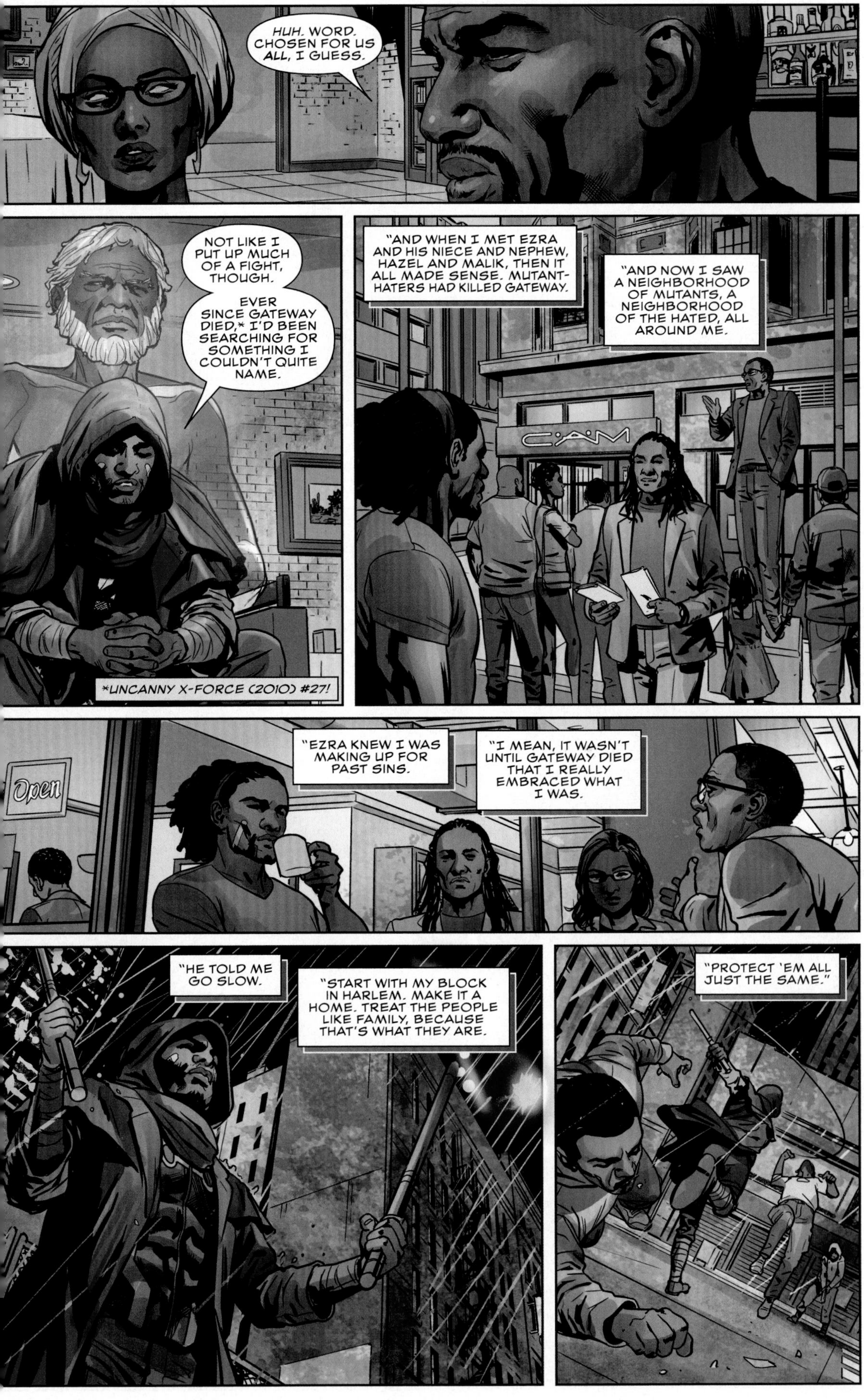
HUH. WORD. CHOSEN FOR US ALL, I GUESS.
NOT LIKE I PUT UP MUCH OF A FIGHT, THOUGH.
EVER SINCE GATEWAY DIED,* I'D BEEN SEARCHING FOR SOMETHING I COULDN'T QUITE NAME.
*UNCANNY X-FORCE (2010) #27!
"AND WHEN I MET EZRA AND HIS NIECE AND NEPHEW, HAZEL AND MALIK, THEN IT ALL MADE SENSE. MUTANT-HATERS HAD KILLED GATEWAY.
"AND NOW I SAW A NEIGHBORHOOD OF MUTANTS, A NEIGHBORHOOD OF THE HATED, ALL AROUND ME.
CAM
Open
"EZRA KNEW I WAS MAKING UP FOR PAST SINS.
"I MEAN, IT WASN'T UNTIL GATEWAY DIED THAT I REALLY EMBRACED WHAT I WAS.
"HE TOLD ME GO SLOW.
"START WITH MY BLOCK IN HARLEM. MAKE IT A HOME. TREAT THE PEOPLE LIKE FAMILY, BECAUSE THAT'S WHAT THEY ARE.
"PROTECT 'EM ALL JUST THE SAME."

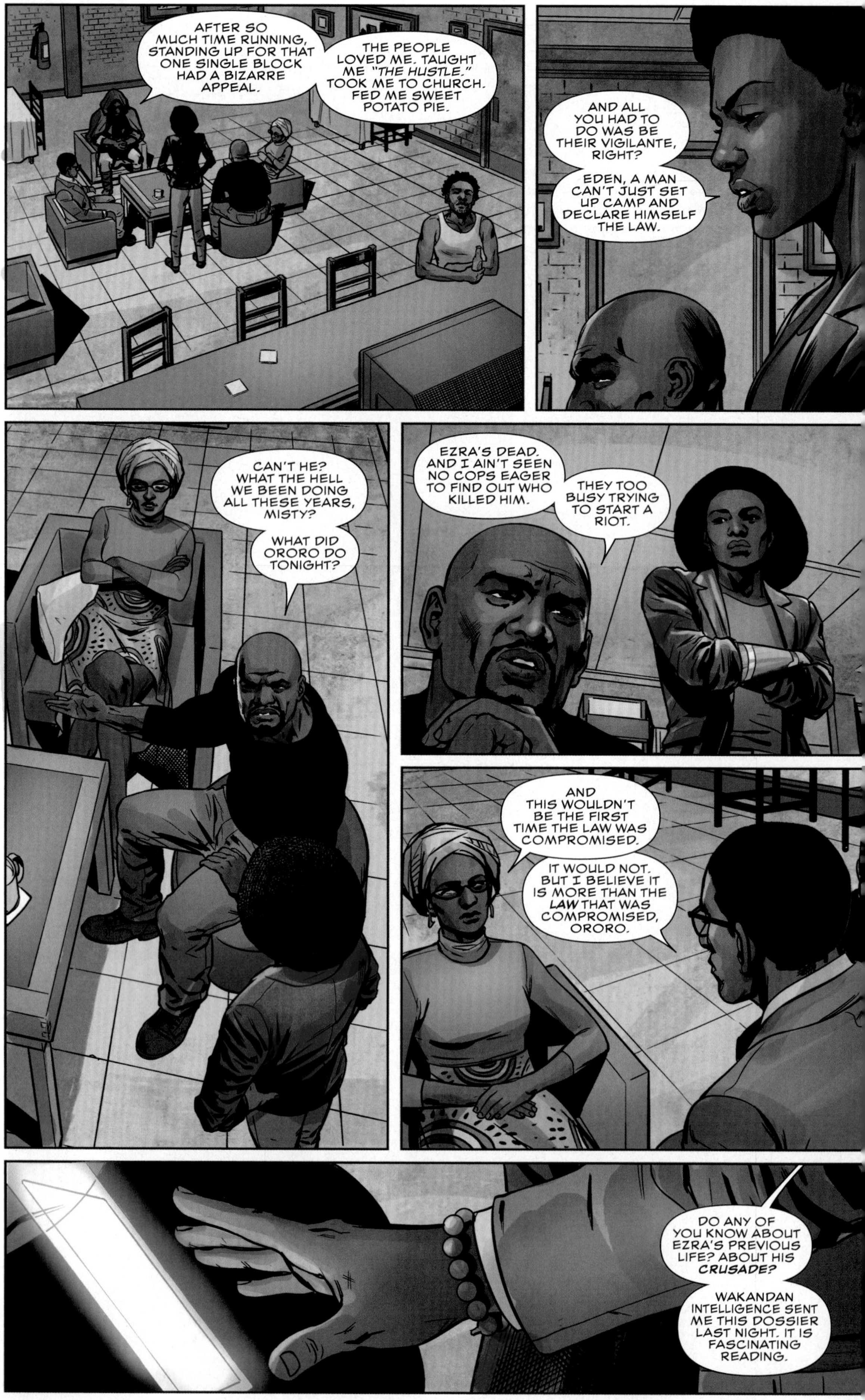
AFTER SO MUCH TIME RUNNING, STANDING UP FOR THAT ONE SINGLE BLOCK HAD A BIZARRE APPEAL.
THE PEOPLE LOVED ME. TAUGHT ME "THE HUSTLE." TOOK ME TO CHURCH. FED ME SWEET POTATO PIE.
AND ALL YOU HAD TO DO WAS BE THEIR VIGILANTE, RIGHT?
EDEN, A MAN CAN'T JUST SET UP CAMP AND DECLARE HIMSELF THE LAW.
CAN'T HE? WHAT THE HELL WE BEEN DOING ALL THESE YEARS, MISTY?
WHAT DID ORORO DO TONIGHT?
EZRA'S DEAD. AND I AIN'T SEEN NO COPS EAGER TO FIND OUT WHO KILLED HIM.
THEY TOO BUSY TRYING TO START A RIOT.
AND THIS WOULDN'T BE THE FIRST TIME THE LAW WAS COMPROMISED.
IT WOULD NOT. BUT I BELIEVE IT IS MORE THAN THE LAW THAT WAS COMPROMISED, ORORO.
DO ANY OF YOU KNOW ABOUT EZRA'S PREVIOUS LIFE? ABOUT HIS CRUSADE?
WAKANDAN INTELLIGENCE SENT ME THIS DOSSIER LAST NIGHT. IT IS FASCINATING READING.

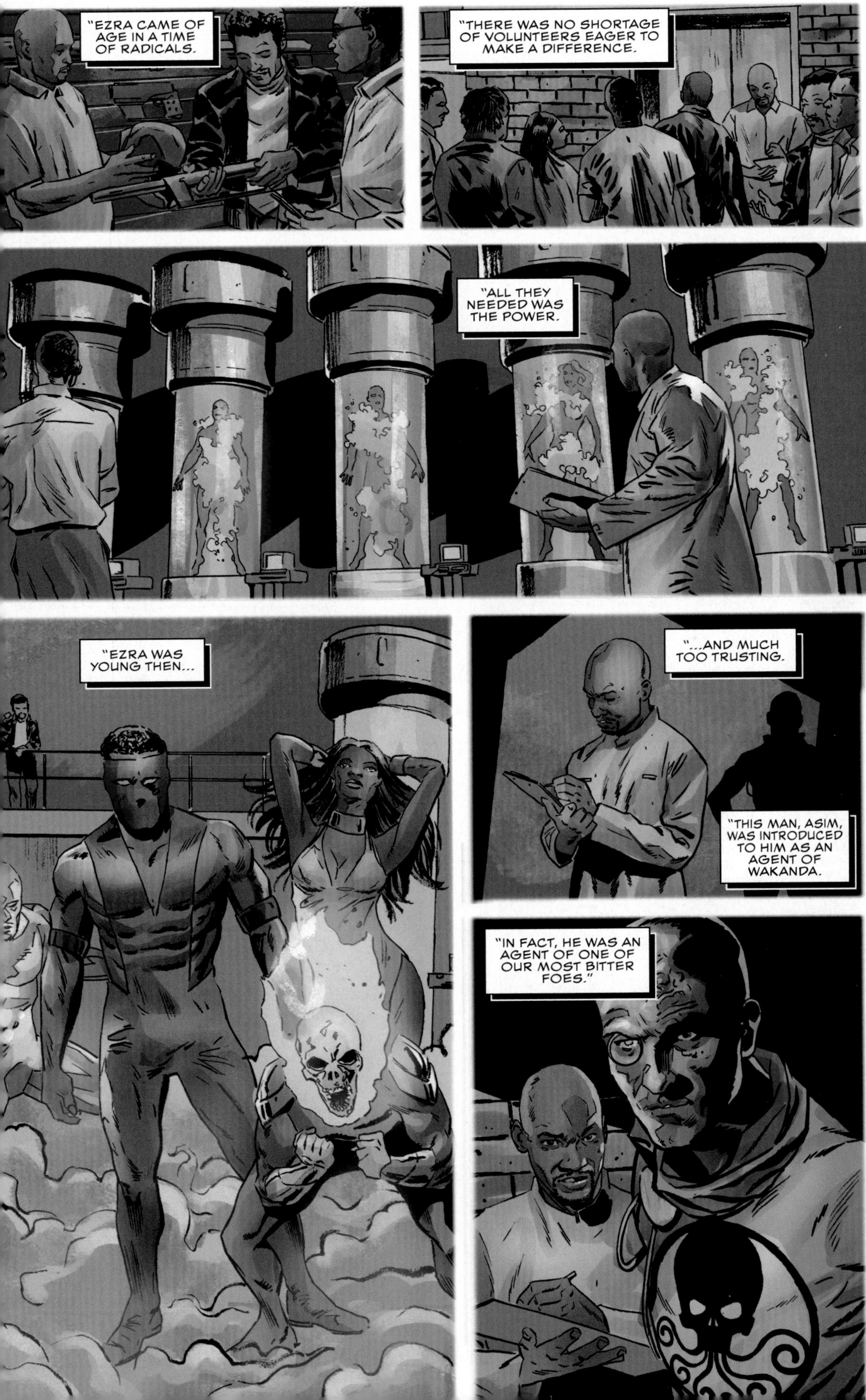
"EZRA CAME OF AGE IN A TIME OF RADICALS.
"THERE WAS NO SHORTAGE OF VOLUNTEERS EAGER TO MAKE A DIFFERENCE.
"ALL THEY NEEDED WAS THE POWER.
"EZRA WAS YOUNG THEN...
"...AND MUCH TOO TRUSTING.
"THIS MAN, ASIM, WAS INTRODUCED TO HIM AS AN AGENT OF WAKANDA.
"IN FACT, HE WAS AN AGENT OF ONE OF OUR MOST BITTER FOES."

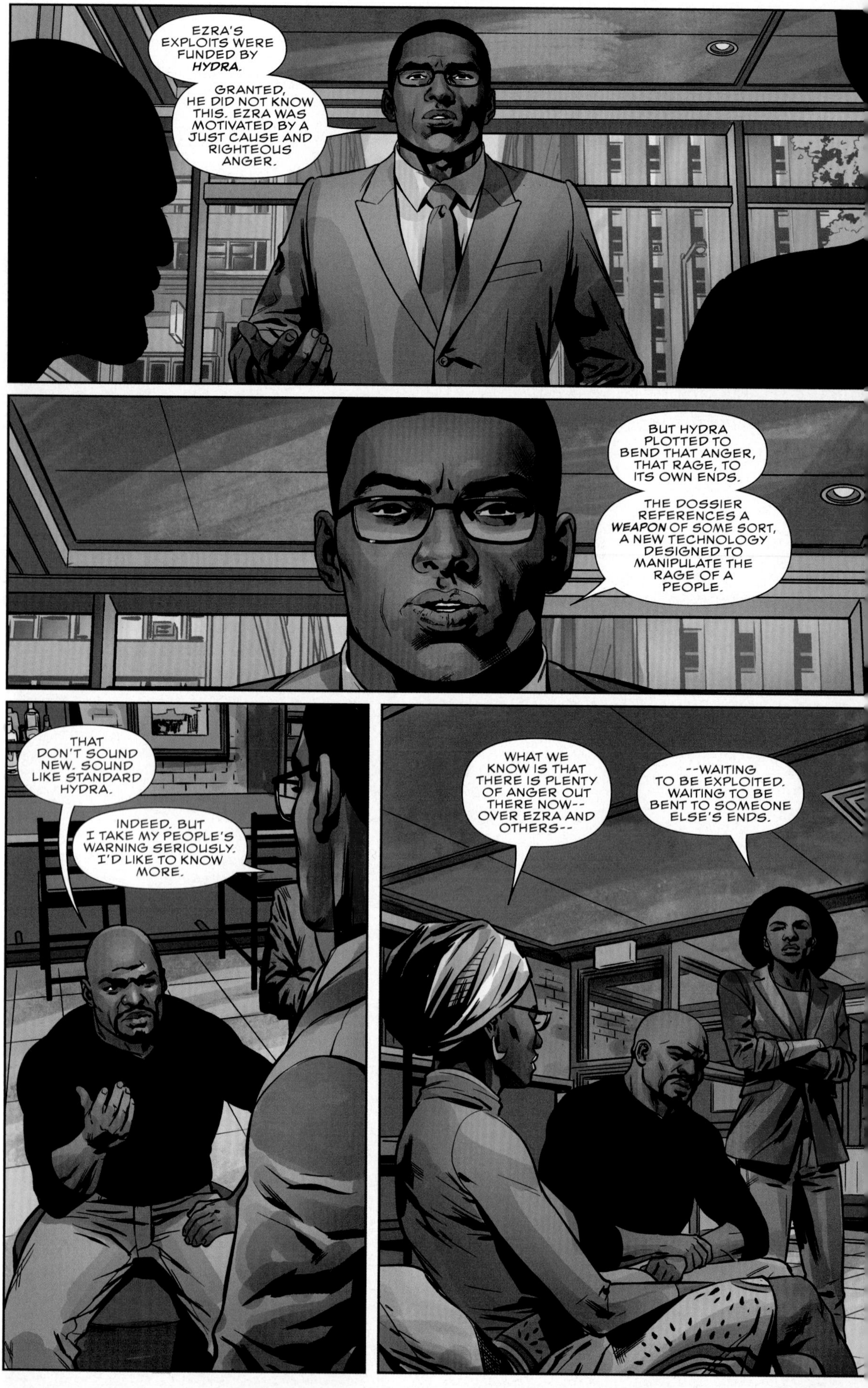
EZRA'S EXPLOITS WERE FUNDED BY HYDRA.
GRANTED, HE DID NOT KNOW THIS. EZRA WAS MOTIVATED BY A JUST CAUSE AND RIGHTEOUS ANGER.
BUT HYDRA PLOTTED TO BEND THAT ANGER, THAT RAGE, TO ITS OWN ENDS.
THE DOSSIER REFERENCES A WEAPON OF SOME SORT, A NEW TECHNOLOGY DESIGNED TO MANIPULATE THE RAGE OF A PEOPLE.
THAT DON'T SOUND NEW. SOUND LIKE STANDARD HYDRA.
INDEED. BUT I TAKE MY PEOPLE'S WARNING SERIOUSLY. I'D LIKE TO KNOW MORE.
WHAT WE KNOW IS THAT THERE IS PLENTY OF ANGER OUT THERE NOW-- OVER EZRA AND OTHERS--
--WAITING TO BE EXPLOITED. WAITING TO BE BENT TO SOMEONE ELSE'S ENDS.

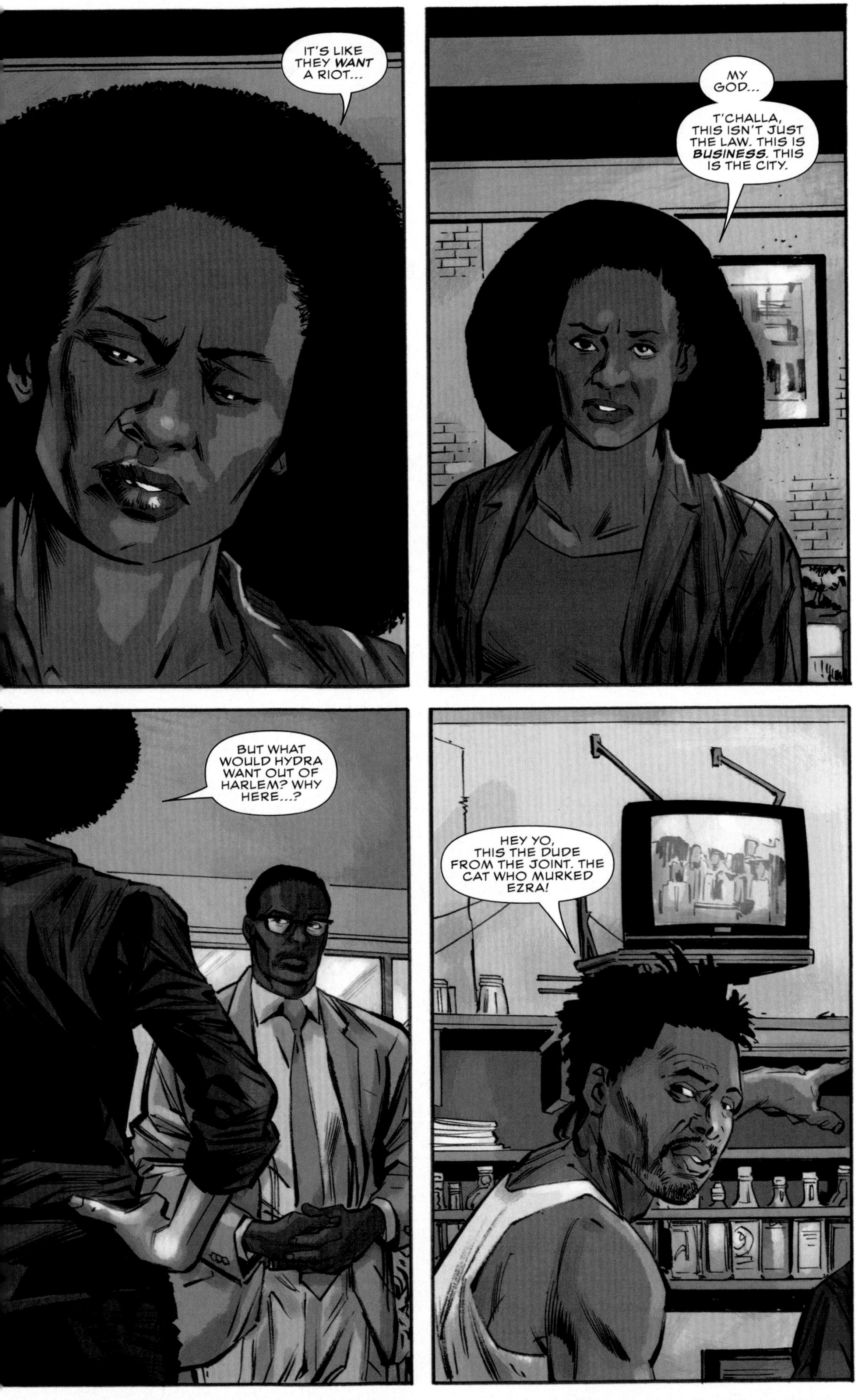
IT'S LIKE THEY *WANT* A RIOT...
MY GOD...
T'CHALLA, THIS ISN'T JUST THE LAW. THIS IS *BUSINESS*. THIS IS THE CITY.
BUT WHAT WOULD HYDRA WANT OUT OF HARLEM? WHY HERE...?
HEY YO, THIS THE DUDE FROM THE JOINT. THE CAT WHO MURKED EZRA!

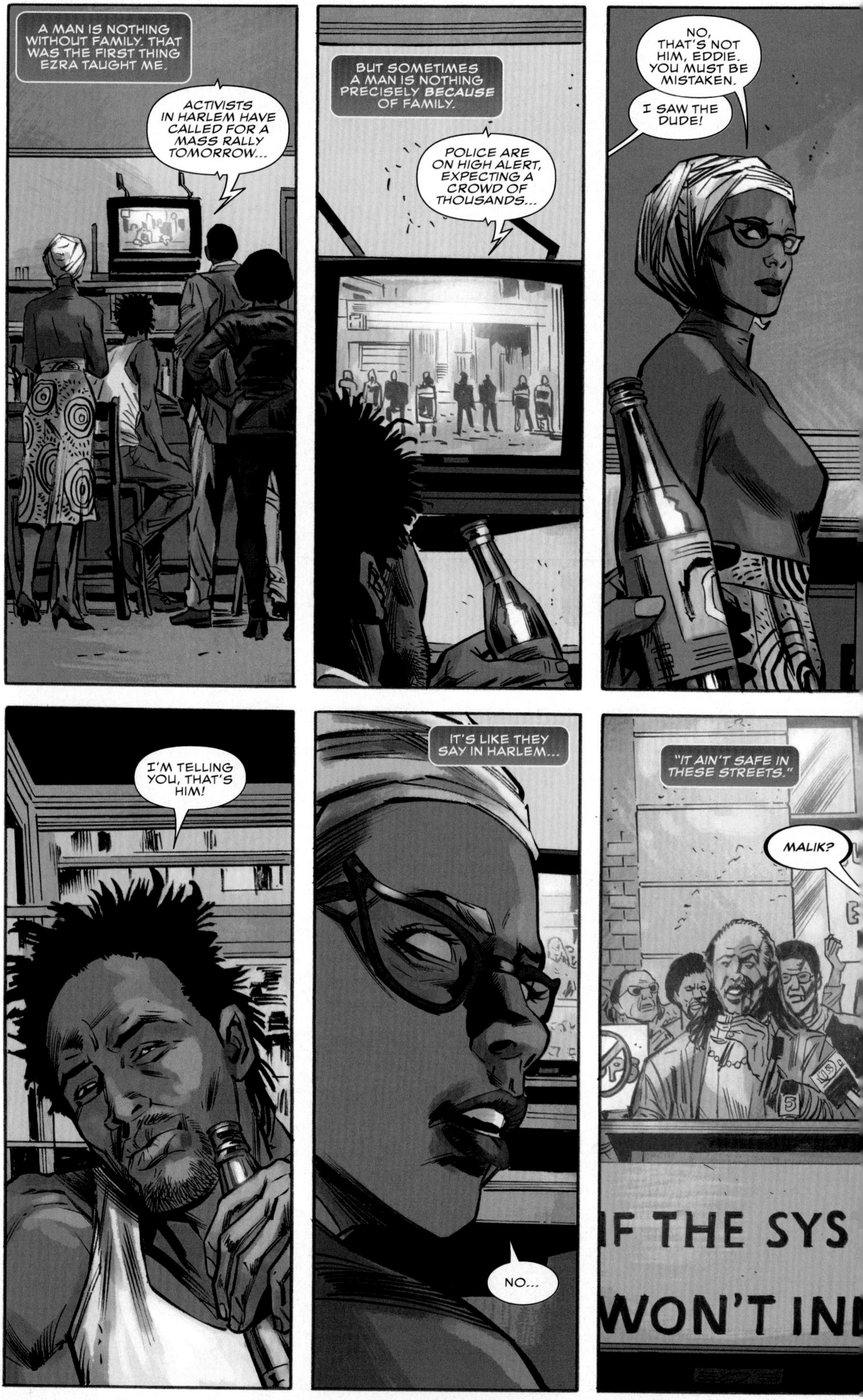
A MAN IS NOTHING WITHOUT FAMILY. THAT WAS THE FIRST THING EZRA TAUGHT ME.
ACTIVISTS IN HARLEM HAVE CALLED FOR A MASS RALLY TOMORROW...
BUT SOMETIMES A MAN IS NOTHING PRECISELY BECAUSE OF FAMILY.
POLICE ARE ON HIGH ALERT, EXPECTING A CROWD OF THOUSANDS...
NO, THAT'S NOT HIM, EDDIE. YOU MUST BE MISTAKEN.
I SAW THE DUDE!
I'M TELLING YOU, THAT'S HIM!
IT'S LIKE THEY SAY IN HARLEM...
NO...
"IT AIN'T SAFE IN THESE STREETS."
MALIK?
IF THE SYS
WON'T IN

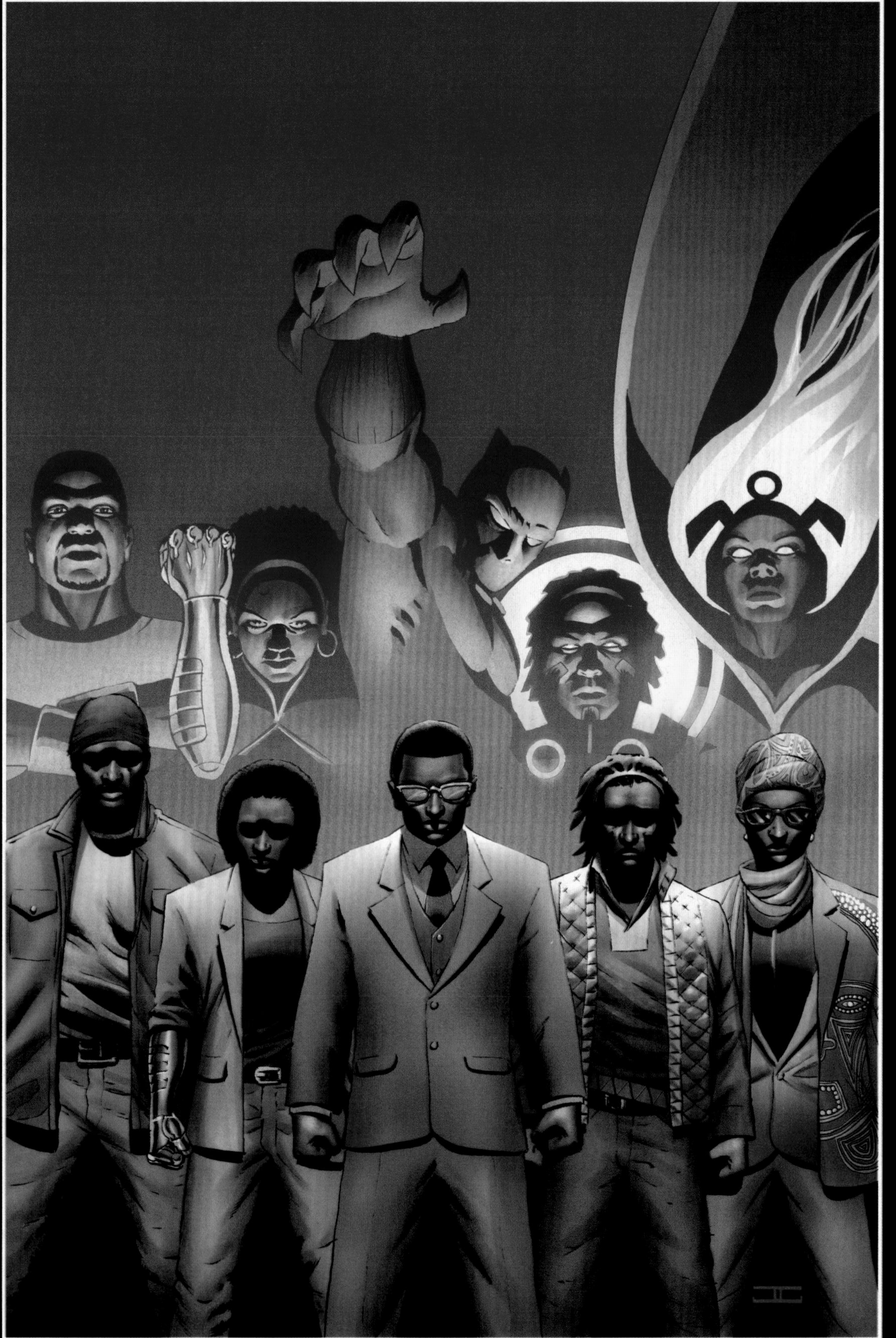

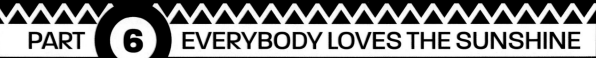

PART 6 EVERYBODY LOVES THE SUNSHINE

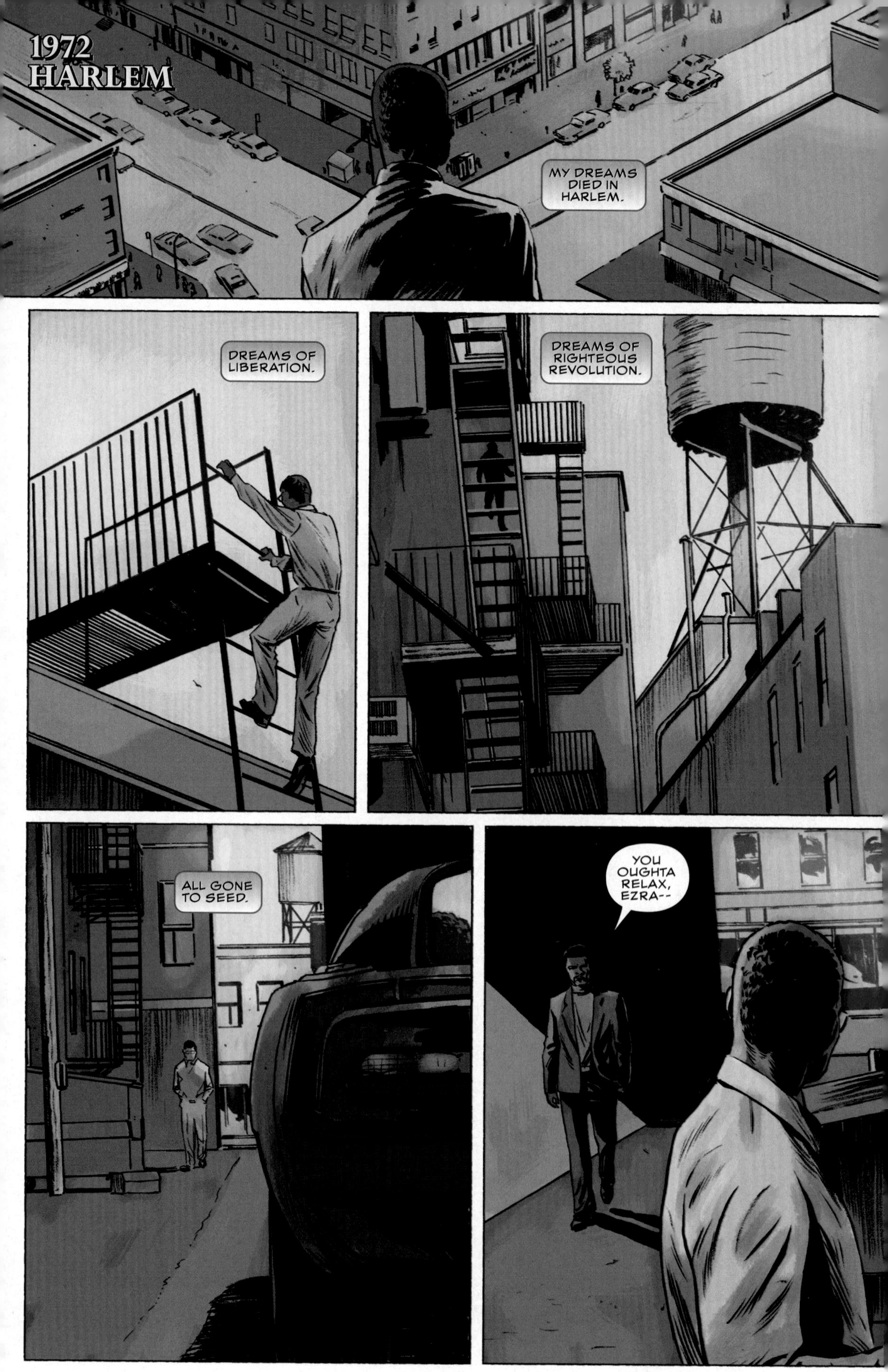
1972
HARLEM
MY DREAMS DIED IN HARLEM.
DREAMS OF LIBERATION.
DREAMS OF RIGHTEOUS REVOLUTION.
ALL GONE TO SEED.
YOU OUGHTA RELAX, EZRA--

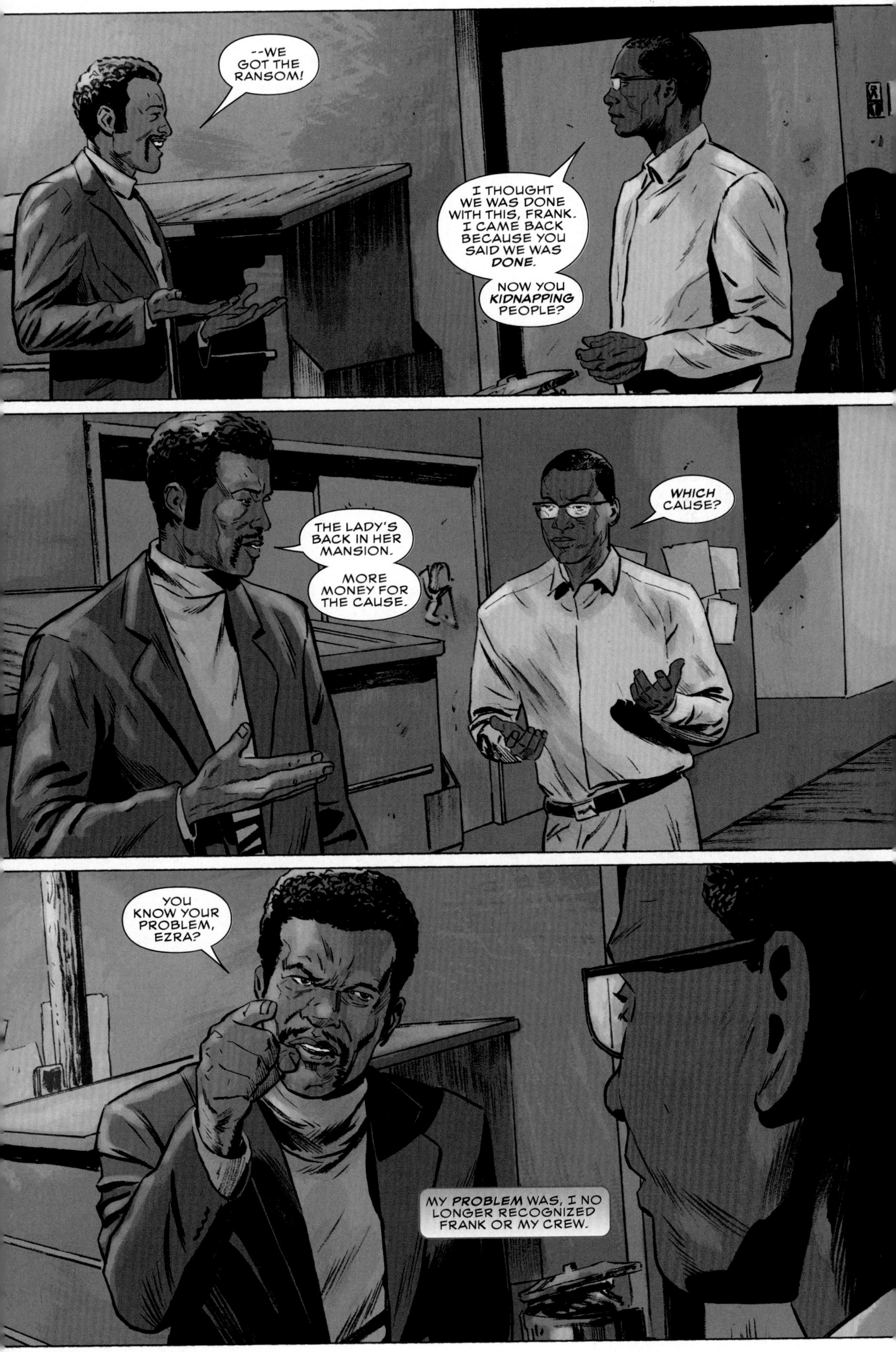
--WE GOT THE RANSOM!
I THOUGHT WE WAS DONE WITH THIS, FRANK. I CAME BACK BECAUSE YOU SAID WE WAS *DONE.*
NOW YOU *KIDNAPPING* PEOPLE?
THE LADY'S BACK IN HER MANSION.
MORE MONEY FOR THE CAUSE.
WHICH CAUSE?
YOU KNOW YOUR PROBLEM, EZRA?
MY *PROBLEM* WAS, I NO LONGER RECOGNIZED FRANK OR MY CREW.

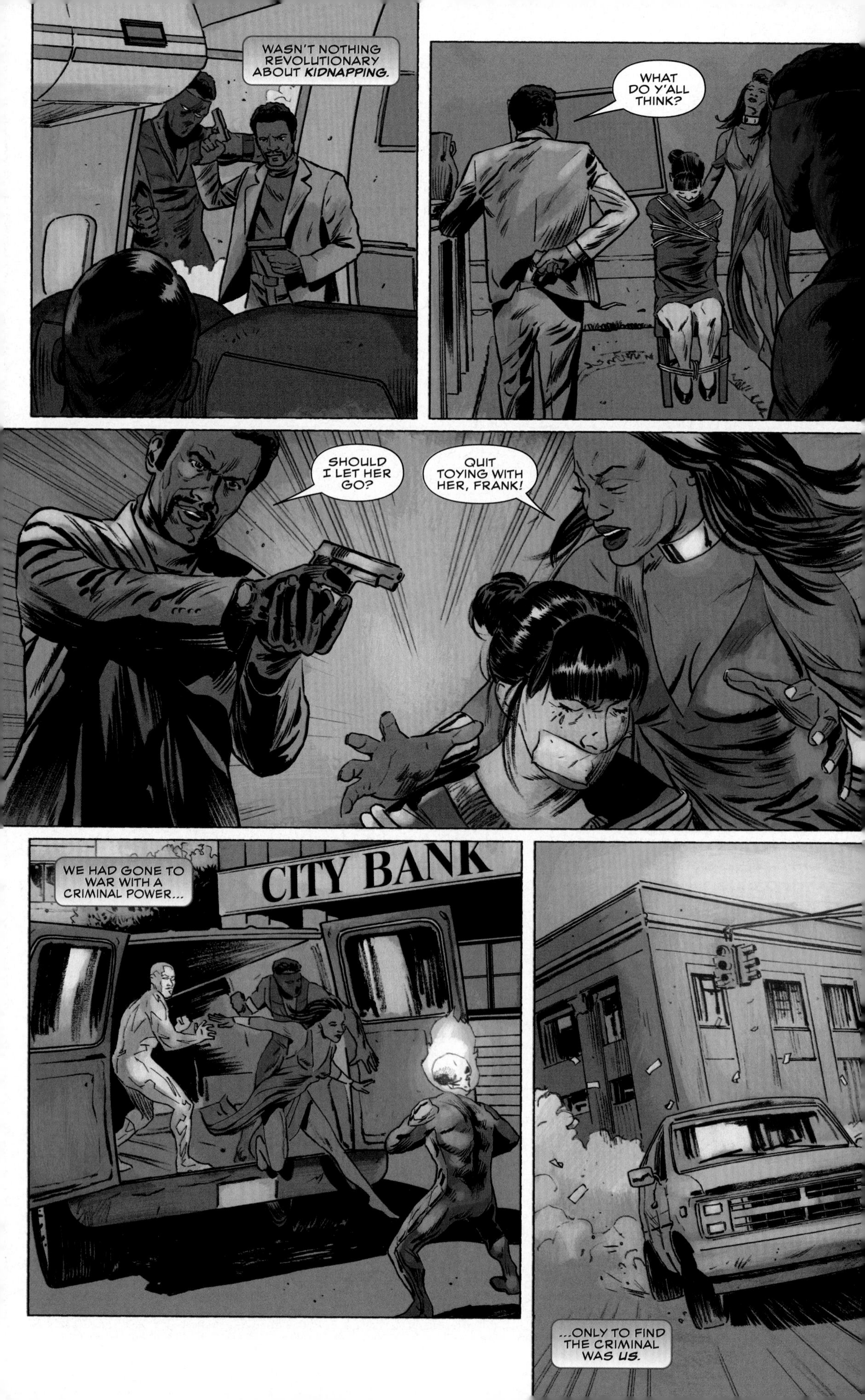
WASN'T NOTHING REVOLUTIONARY ABOUT *KIDNAPPING*.
WHAT DO Y'ALL THINK?
SHOULD I LET HER GO?
QUIT TOYING WITH HER, FRANK!
WE HAD GONE TO WAR WITH A CRIMINAL POWER...
CITY BANK
...ONLY TO FIND THE CRIMINAL WAS *US*.

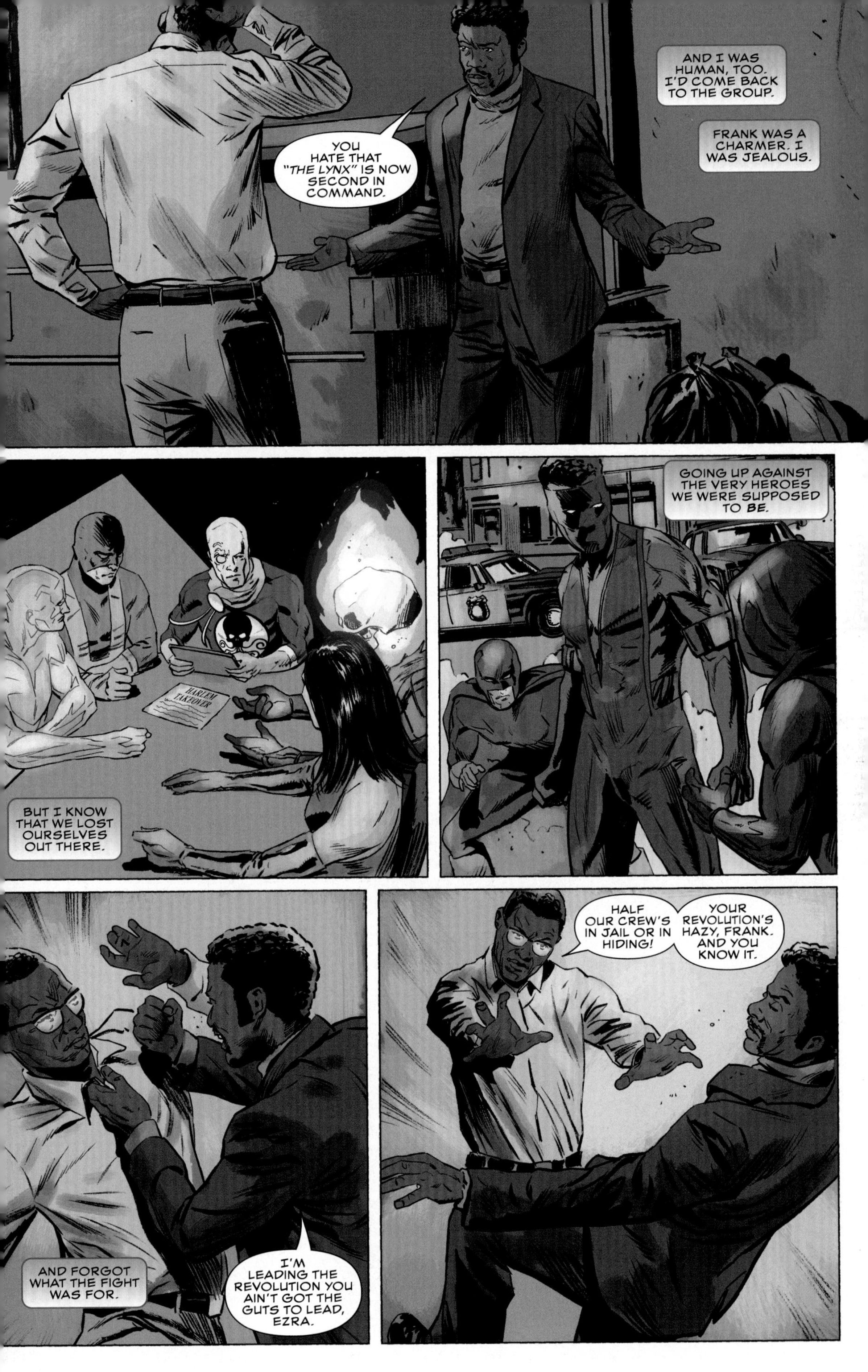
YOU HATE THAT "THE LYNX" IS NOW SECOND IN COMMAND.
AND I WAS HUMAN, TOO. I'D COME BACK TO THE GROUP.
FRANK WAS A CHARMER. I WAS JEALOUS.
HARLEM TAKEOVER
BUT I KNOW THAT WE LOST OURSELVES OUT THERE.
GOING UP AGAINST THE VERY HEROES WE WERE SUPPOSED TO BE.
AND FORGOT WHAT THE FIGHT WAS FOR.
I'M LEADING THE REVOLUTION YOU AIN'T GOT THE GUTS TO LEAD, EZRA.
HALF OUR CREW'S IN JAIL OR IN HIDING!
YOUR REVOLUTION'S HAZY, FRANK. AND YOU KNOW IT.

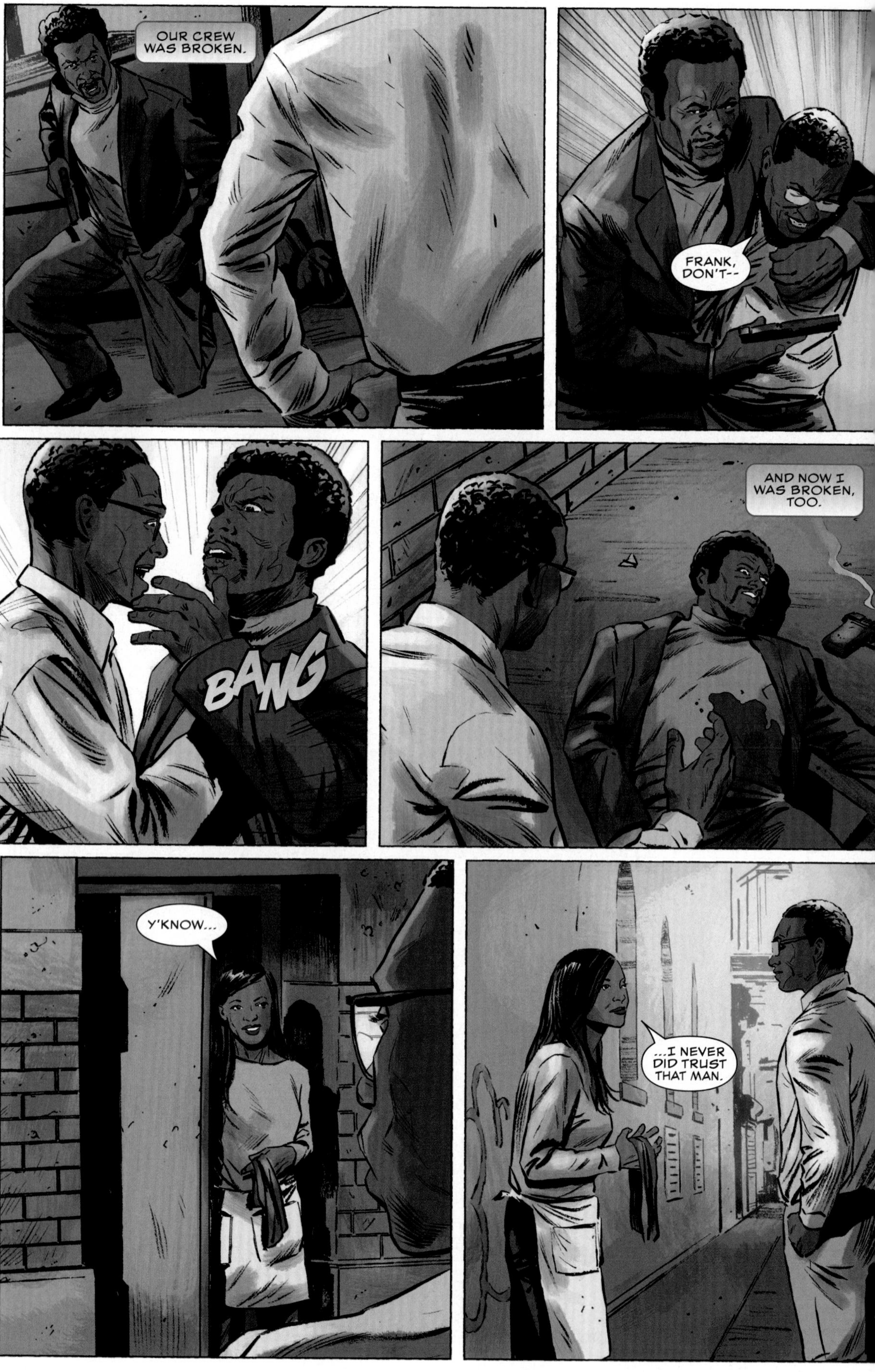
OUR CREW WAS BROKEN.
FRANK, DON'T--
BANG
AND NOW I WAS BROKEN, TOO.
Y'KNOW...
...I NEVER DID TRUST THAT MAN.

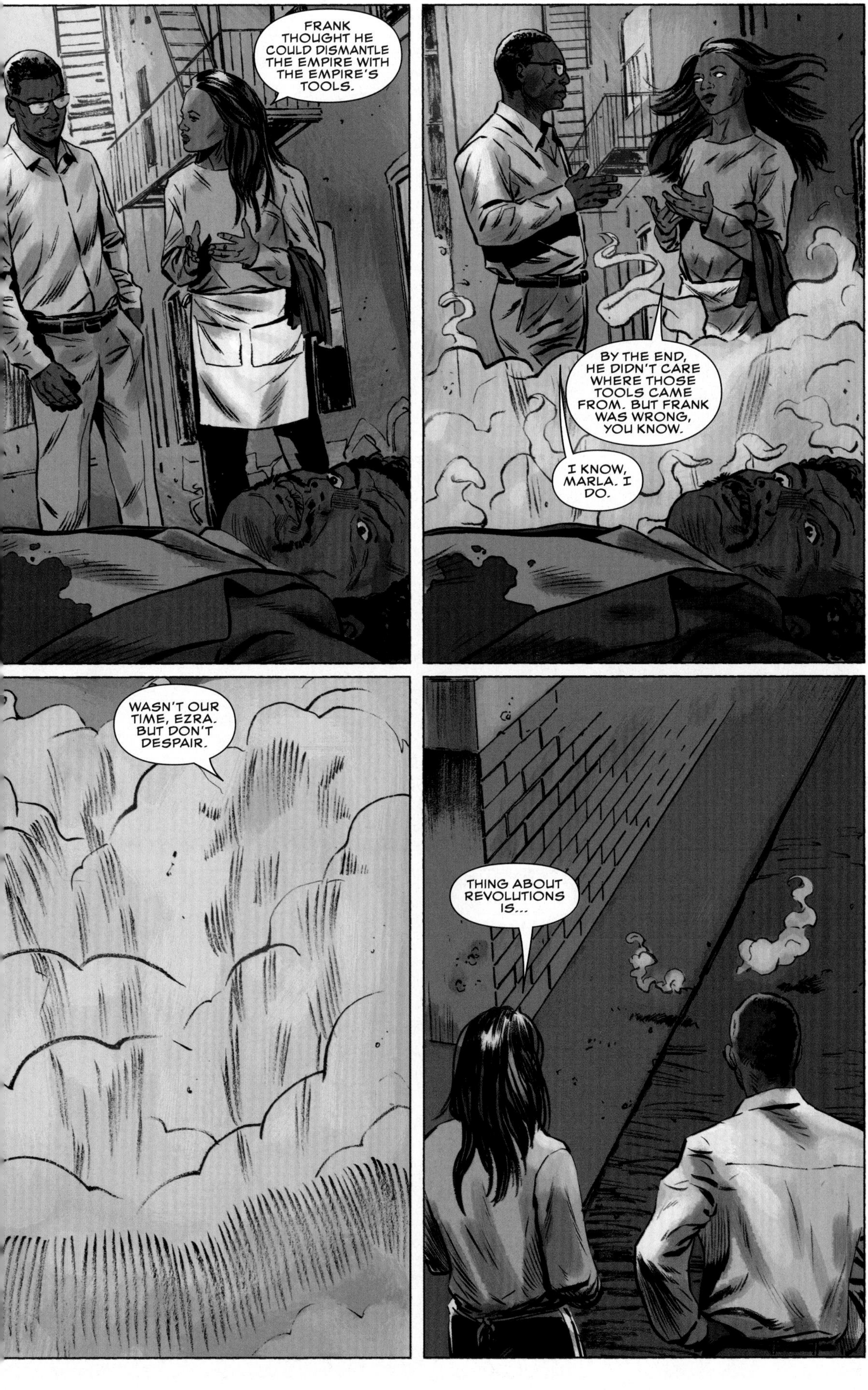
FRANK THOUGHT HE COULD DISMANTLE THE EMPIRE WITH THE EMPIRE'S TOOLS.
BY THE END, HE DIDN'T CARE WHERE THOSE TOOLS CAME FROM. BUT FRANK WAS WRONG, YOU KNOW.
I KNOW, MARLA. I DO.
WASN'T OUR TIME, EZRA. BUT DON'T DESPAIR.
THING ABOUT REVOLUTIONS IS...

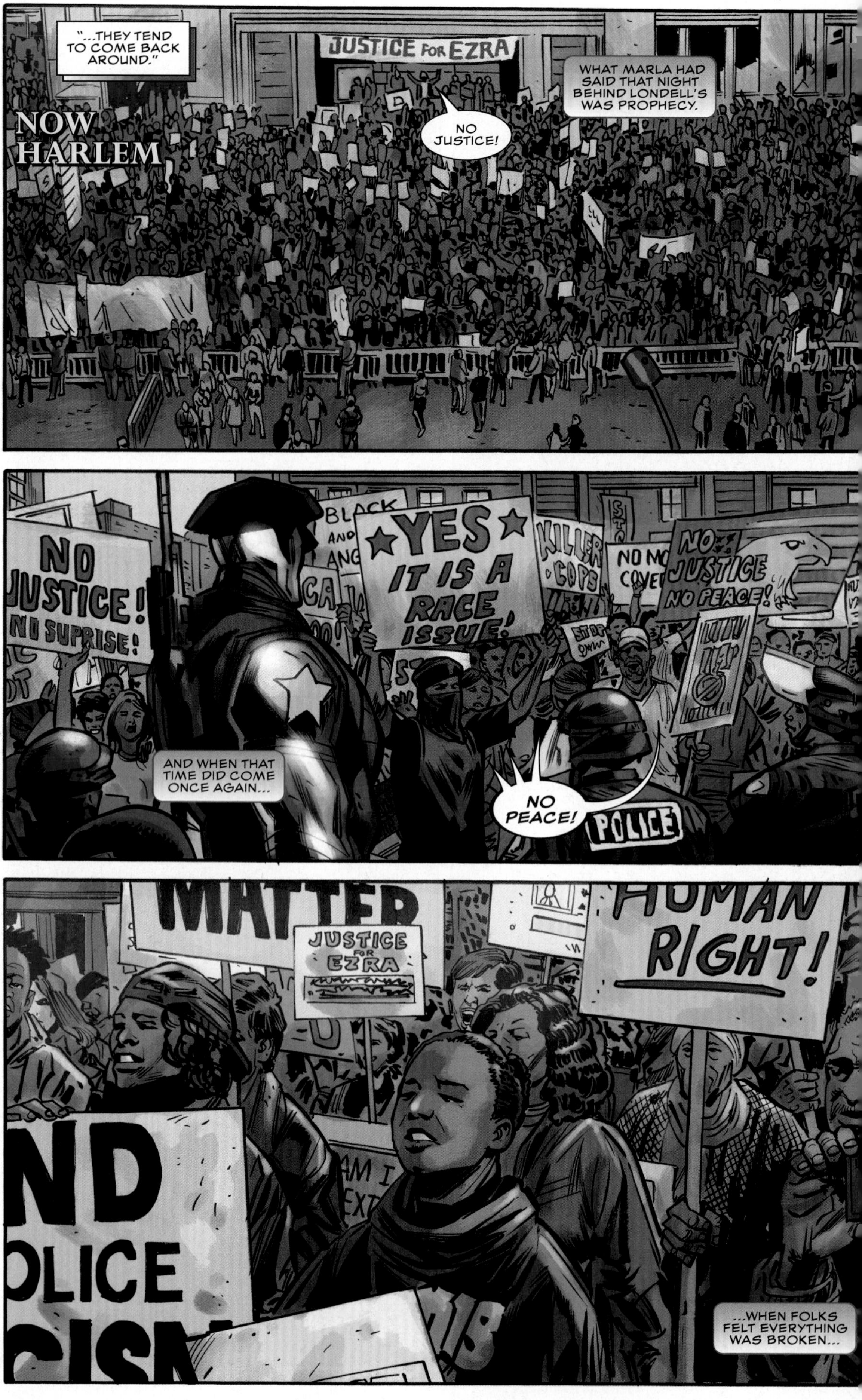
"...THEY TEND TO COME BACK AROUND."
NOW HARLEM
JUSTICE FOR EZRA
NO JUSTICE!
WHAT MARLA HAD SAID THAT NIGHT BEHIND LONDELL'S WAS PROPHECY.
NO JUSTICE! NO SUPRISE!
YES IT IS A RACE ISSUE!
KILLER COPS
NO JUSTICE NO PEACE!
AND WHEN THAT TIME DID COME ONCE AGAIN...
NO PEACE!
POLICE
MATTER
JUSTICE FOR EZRA
HUMAN RIGHT!
...WHEN FOLKS FELT EVERYTHING WAS BROKEN...

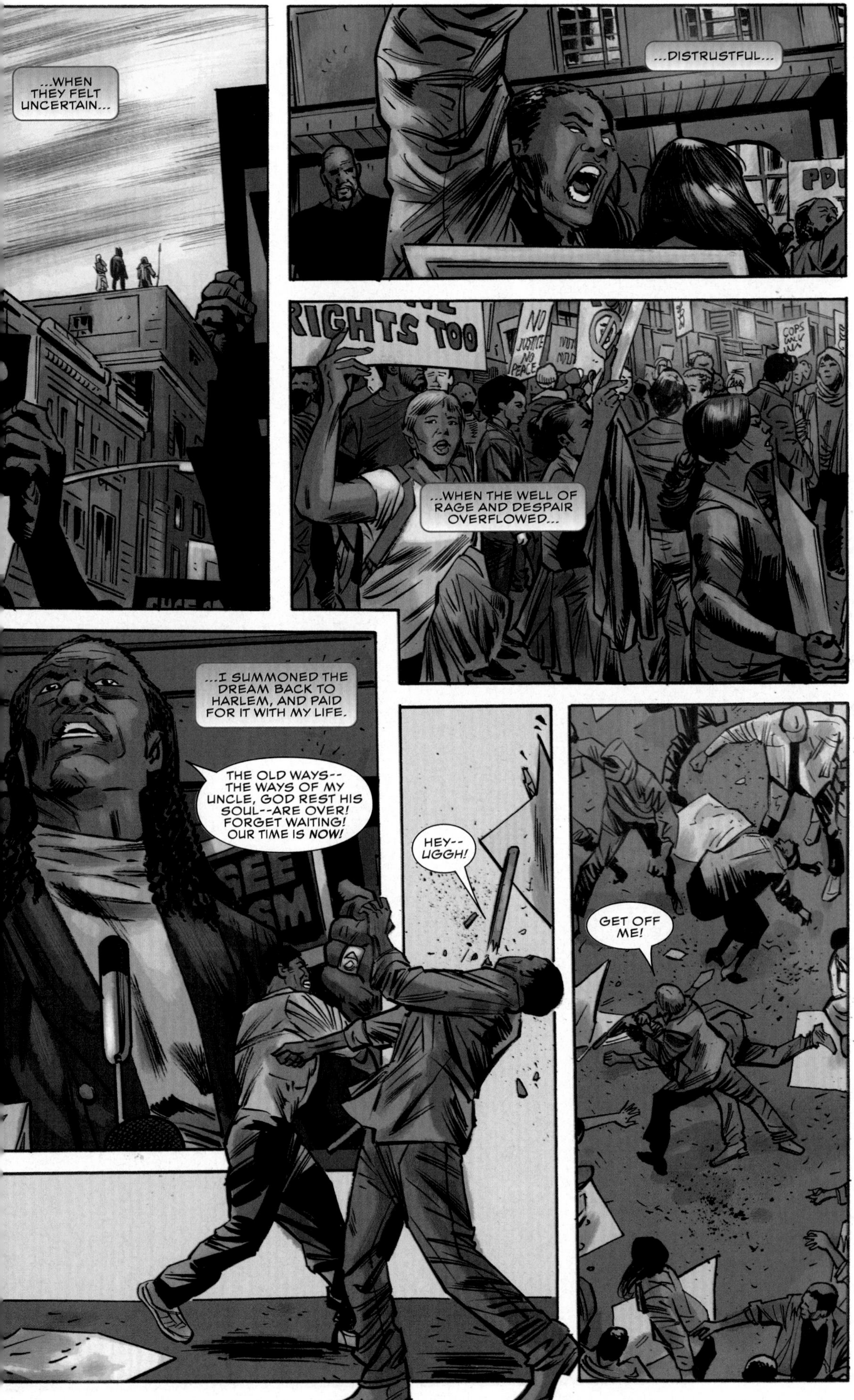
...WHEN THEY FELT UNCERTAIN...
...DISTRUSTFUL...
RIGHTS TOO
NO JUSTICE NO PEACE
...WHEN THE WELL OF RAGE AND DESPAIR OVERFLOWED...
...I SUMMONED THE DREAM BACK TO HARLEM, AND PAID FOR IT WITH MY LIFE.
THE OLD WAYS-- THE WAYS OF MY UNCLE, GOD REST HIS SOUL--ARE OVER! FORGET WAITING! OUR TIME IS NOW!
HEY-- UGGH!
GET OFF ME!

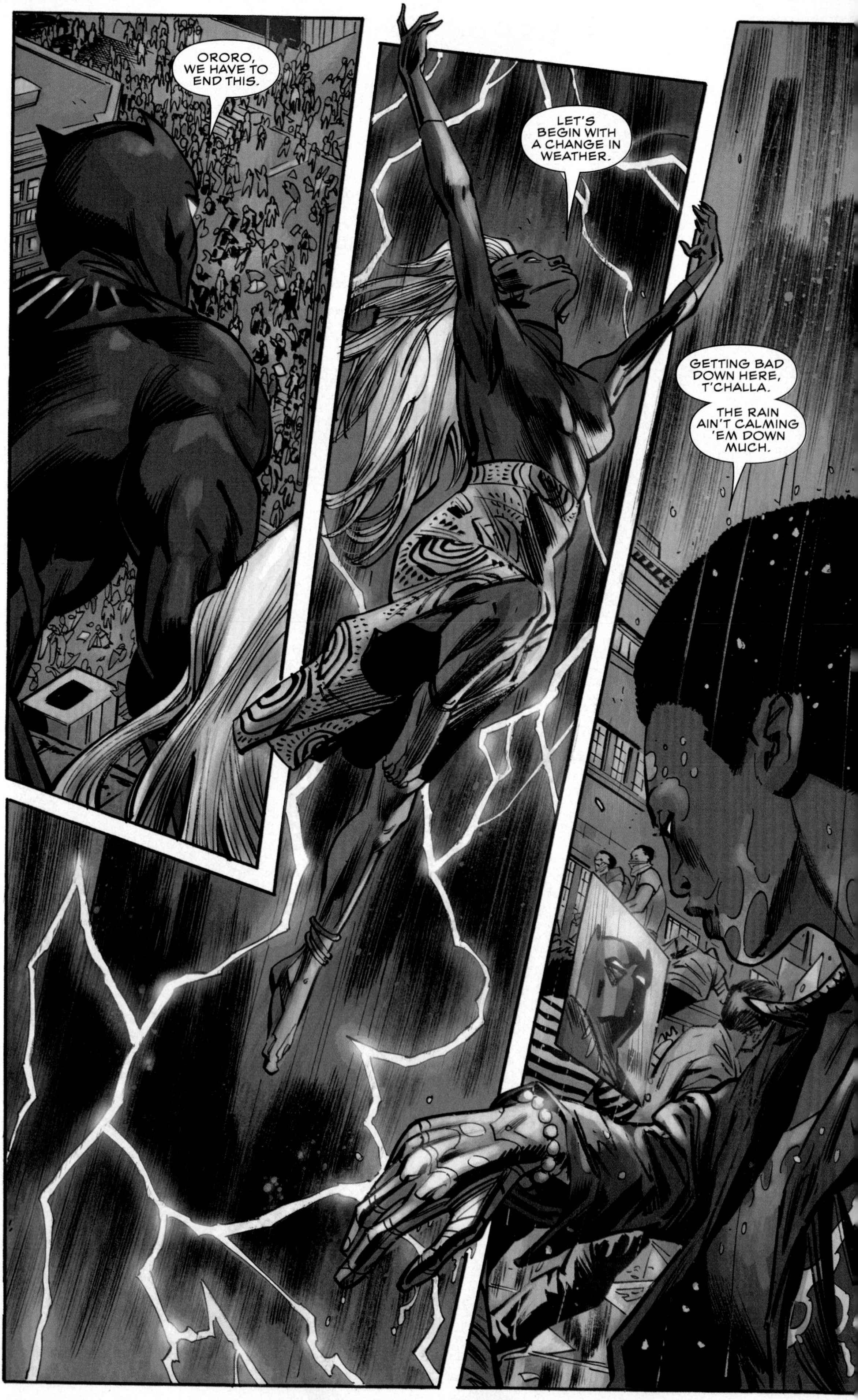
ORORO, WE HAVE TO END THIS.
LET'S BEGIN WITH A CHANGE IN WEATHER.
GETTING BAD DOWN HERE, T'CHALLA.
THE RAIN AIN'T CALMING 'EM DOWN MUCH.

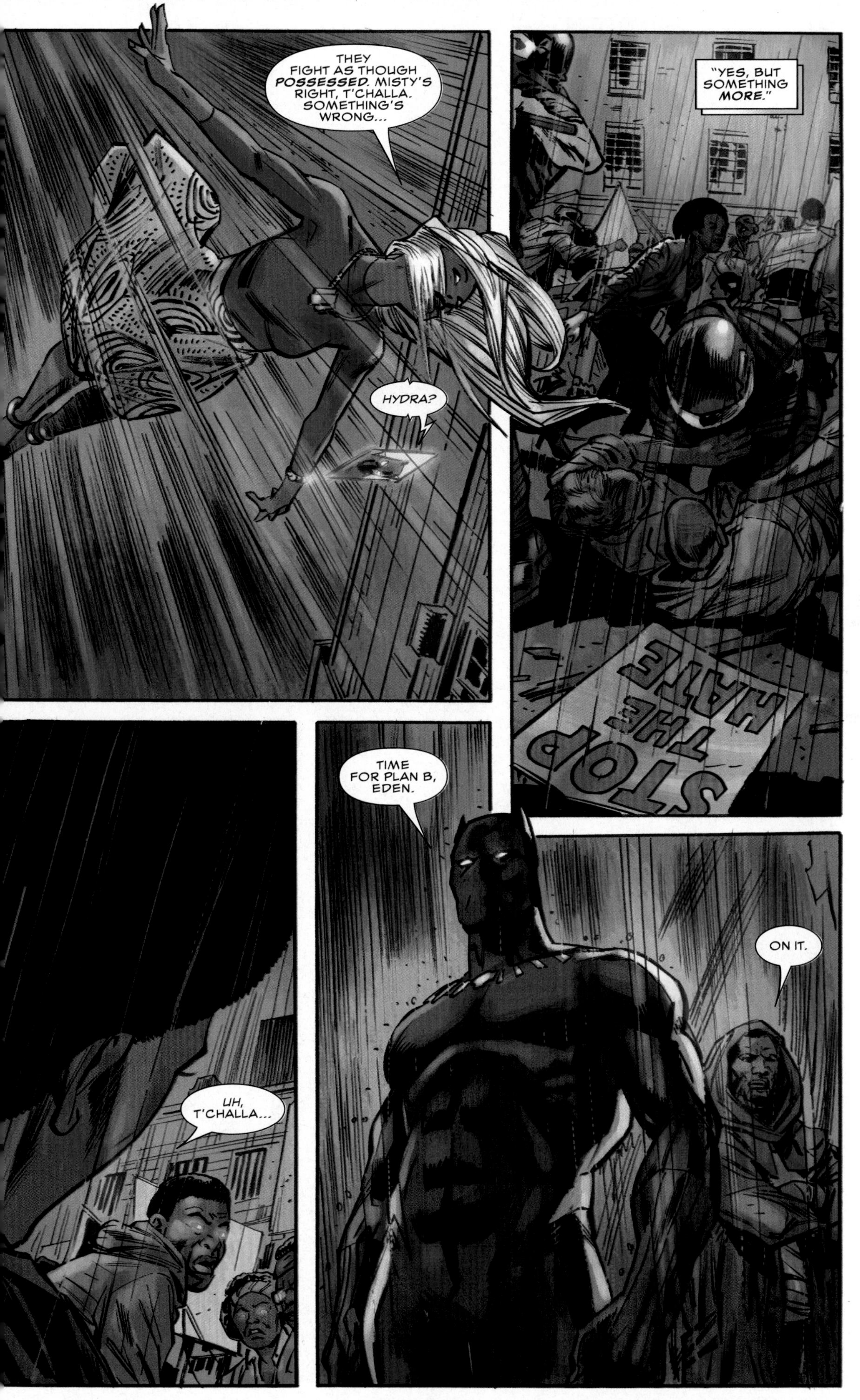
THEY FIGHT AS THOUGH POSSESSED. MISTY'S RIGHT, T'CHALLA. SOMETHING'S WRONG...
HYDRA?
"YES, BUT SOMETHING MORE."
STOP THE HATE
UH, T'CHALLA...
TIME FOR PLAN B, EDEN.
ON IT.

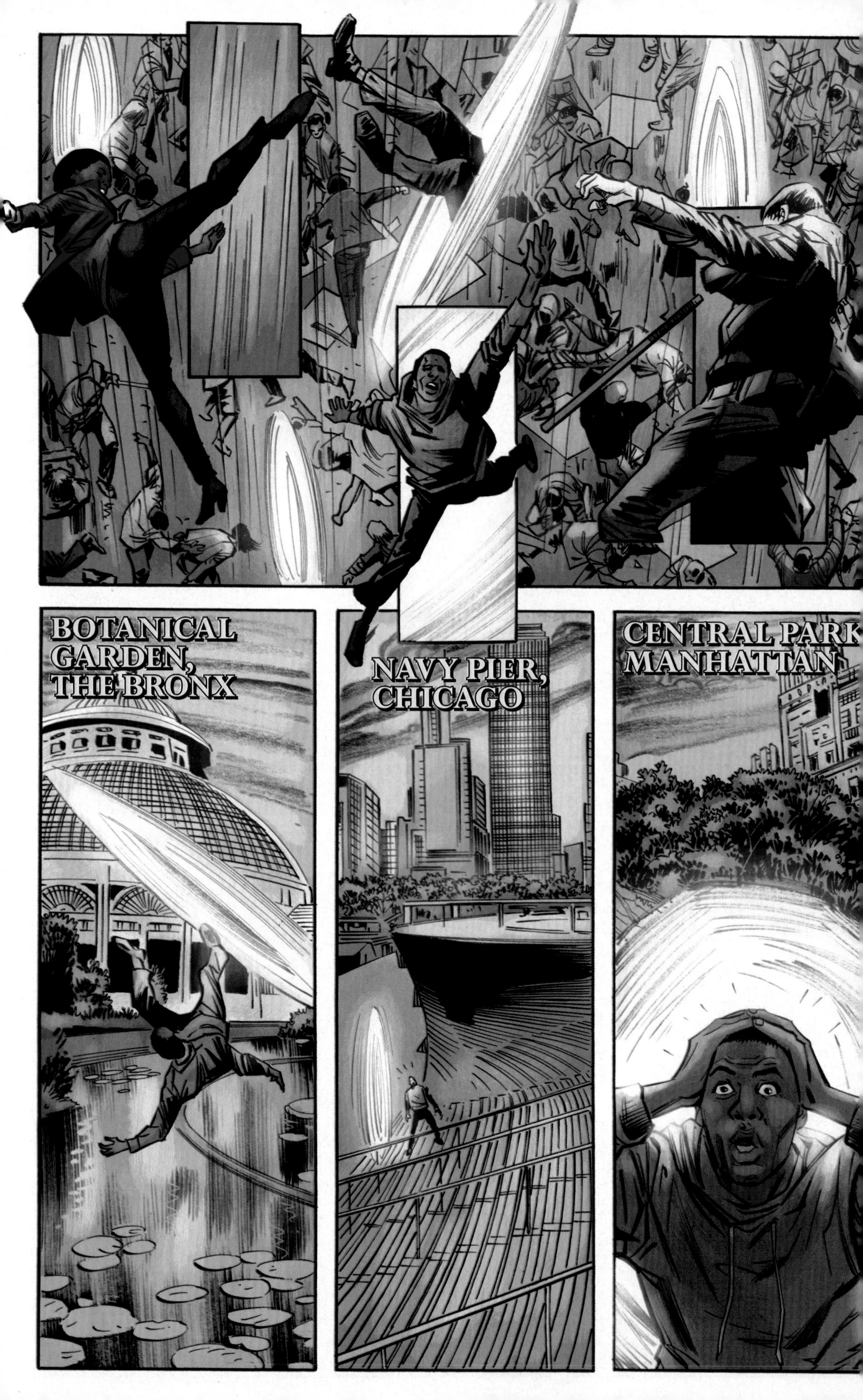
BOTANICAL GARDEN, THE BRONX
NAVY PIER, CHICAGO
CENTRAL PARK MANHATTAN

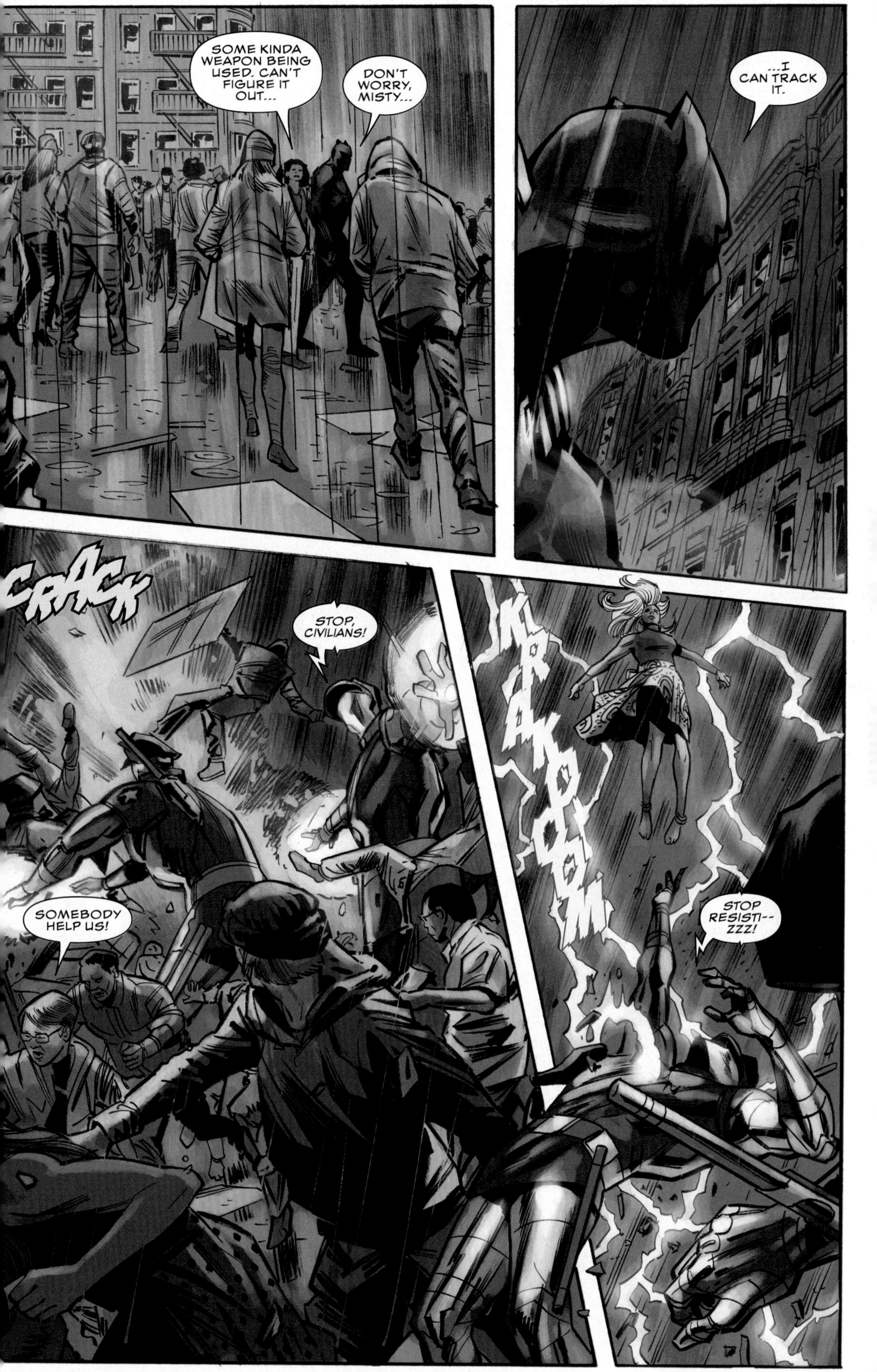
SOME KINDA WEAPON BEING USED. CAN'T FIGURE IT OUT...
DON'T WORRY, MISTY...
...I CAN TRACK IT.
CRACK
STOP, CIVILIANS!
SOMEBODY HELP US!
KRAKOOM
STOP RESISTI-- ZZZ!

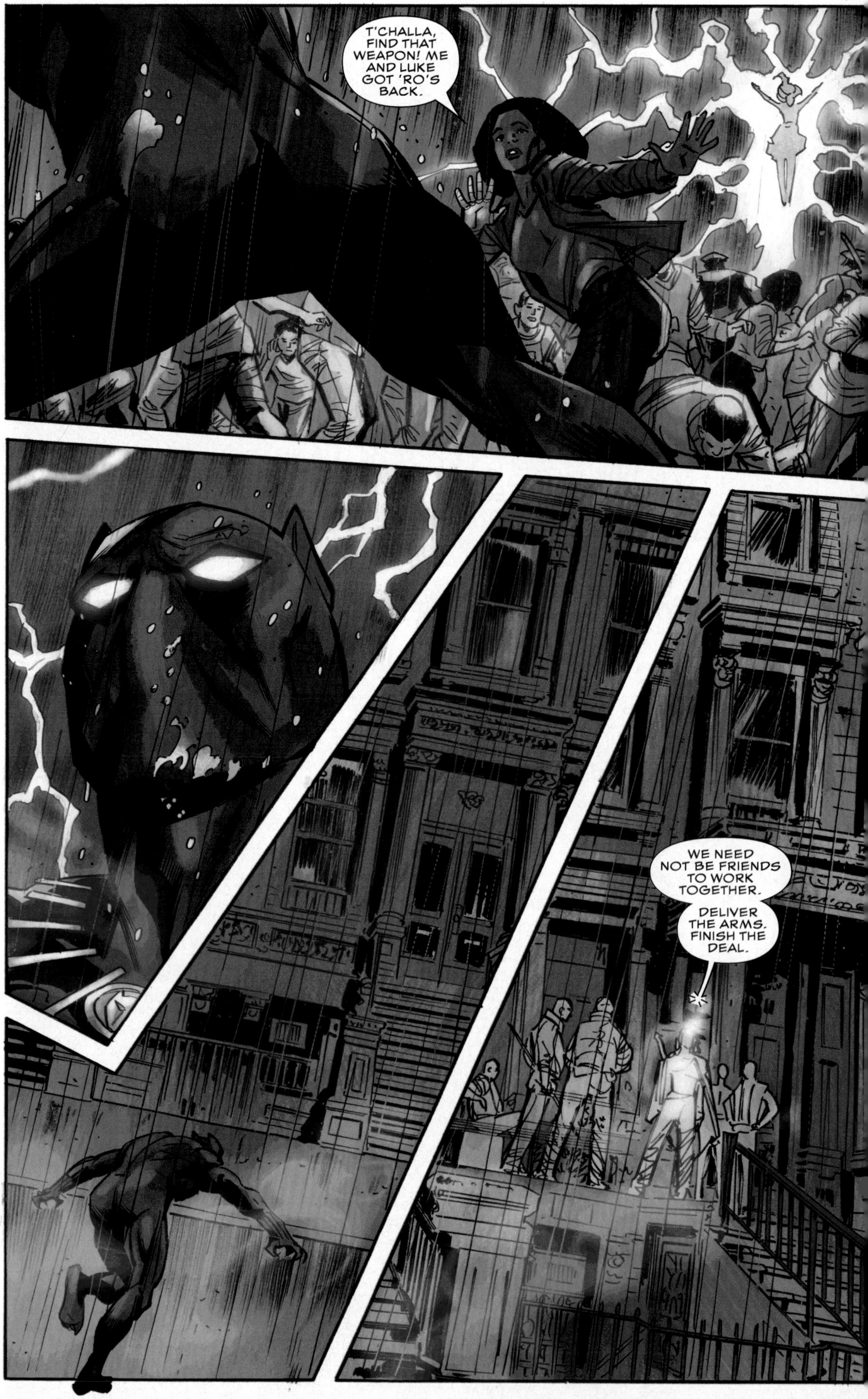
T'CHALLA, FIND THAT WEAPON! ME AND LUKE GOT 'RO'S BACK.
WE NEED NOT BE FRIENDS TO WORK TOGETHER.
DELIVER THE ARMS. FINISH THE DEAL.

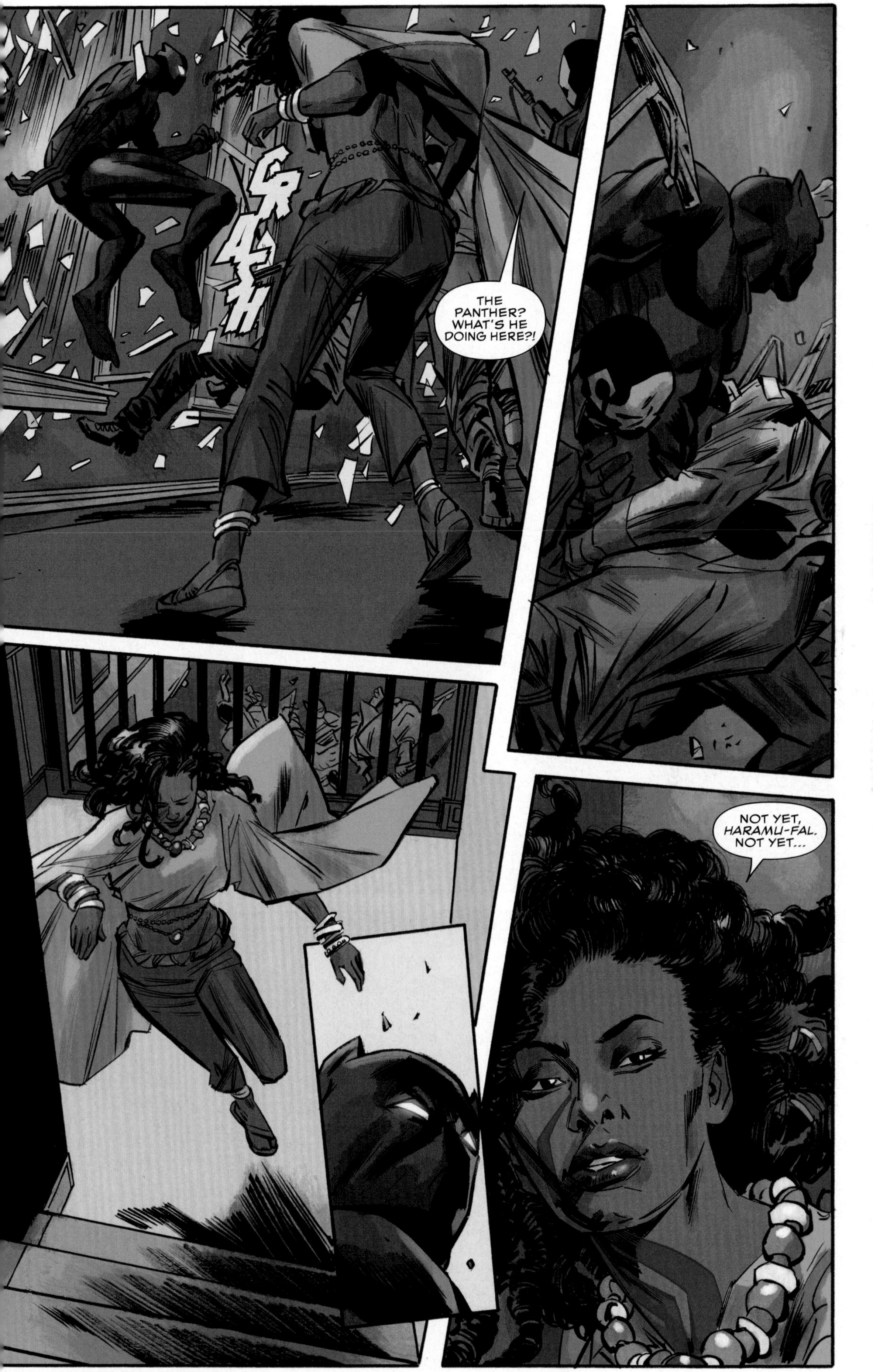
CRASH
THE PANTHER? WHAT'S HE DOING HERE?!
NOT YET, HARAMU-FAL. NOT YET...

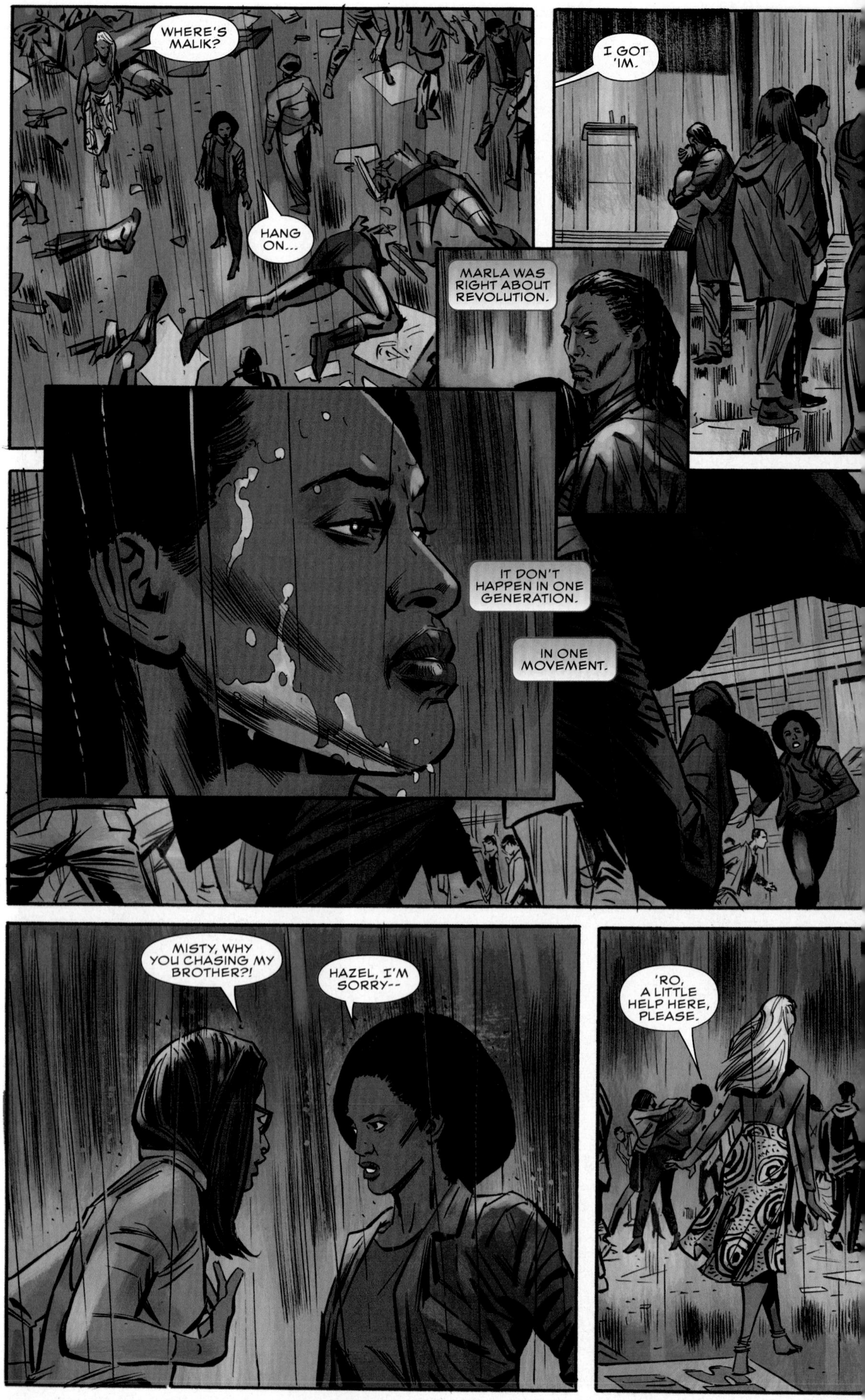
WHERE'S MALIK?
HANG ON...
I GOT 'IM.
MARLA WAS RIGHT ABOUT REVOLUTION.
IT DON'T HAPPEN IN ONE GENERATION.
IN ONE MOVEMENT.
MISTY, WHY YOU CHASING MY BROTHER?!
HAZEL, I'M SORRY--
'RO, A LITTLE HELP HERE, PLEASE.

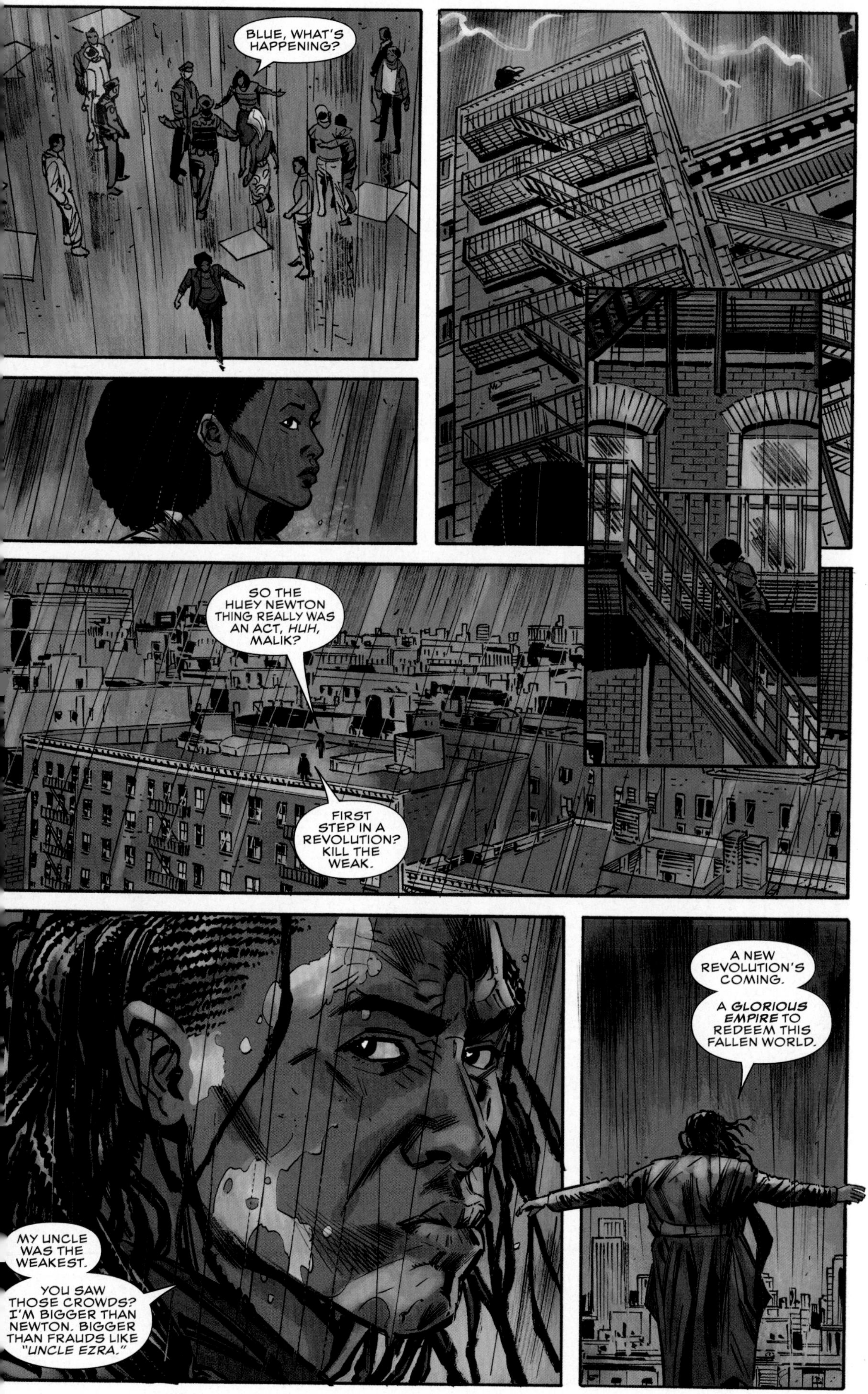
BLUE, WHAT'S HAPPENING?
SO THE HUEY NEWTON THING REALLY WAS AN ACT, *HUH*, MALIK?
FIRST STEP IN A REVOLUTION? KILL THE WEAK.
MY UNCLE WAS THE WEAKEST.
YOU SAW THOSE CROWDS? I'M BIGGER THAN NEWTON. BIGGER THAN FRAUDS LIKE "*UNCLE EZRA*."
A NEW REVOLUTION'S COMING.
A ***GLORIOUS EMPIRE*** TO REDEEM THIS FALLEN WORLD.

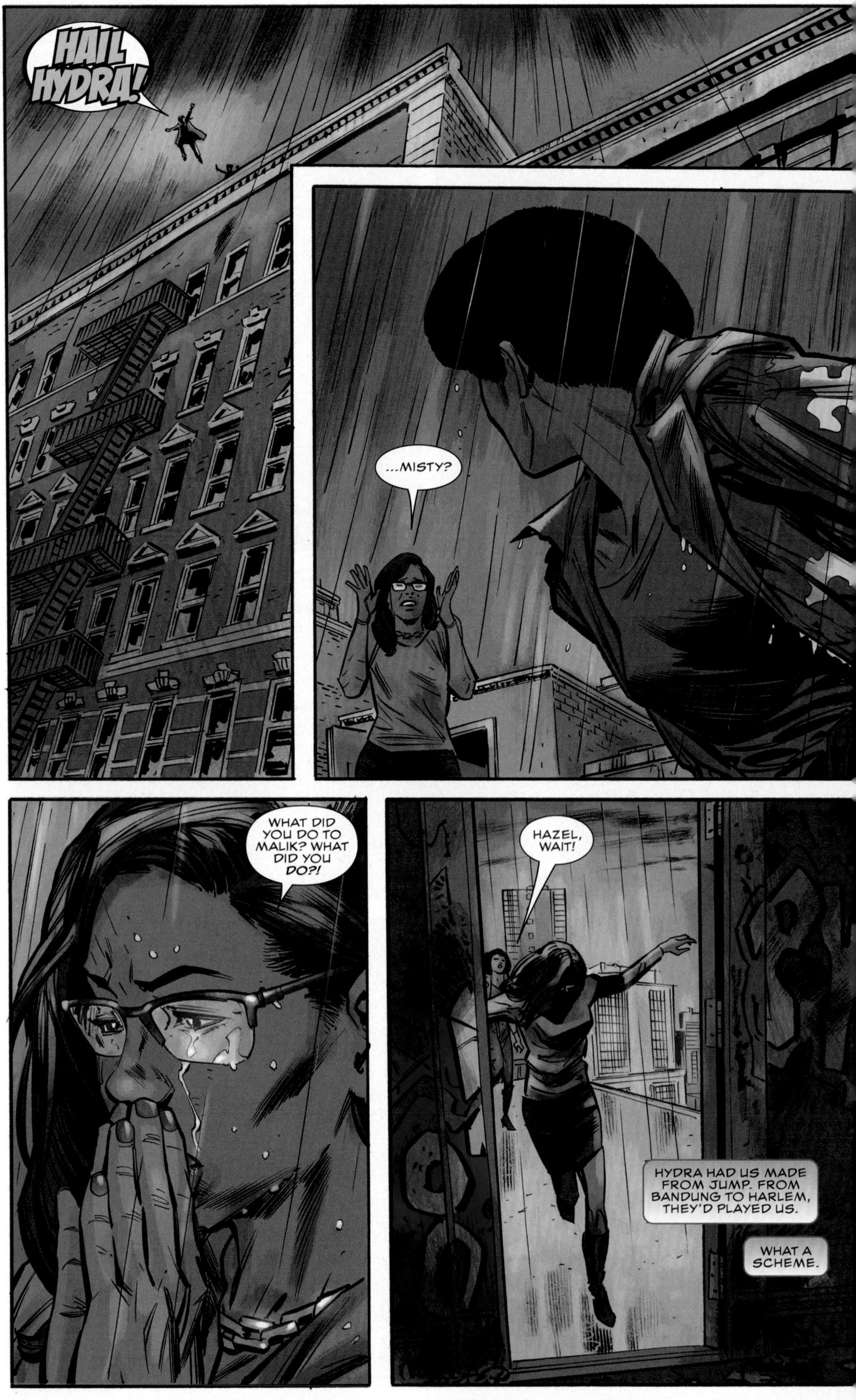
HAIL HYDRA!
...MISTY?
WHAT DID YOU DO TO MALIK? WHAT DID YOU DO?!
HAZEL, WAIT!
HYDRA HAD US MADE FROM JUMP. FROM BANDUNG TO HARLEM, THEY'D PLAYED US.
WHAT A SCHEME.

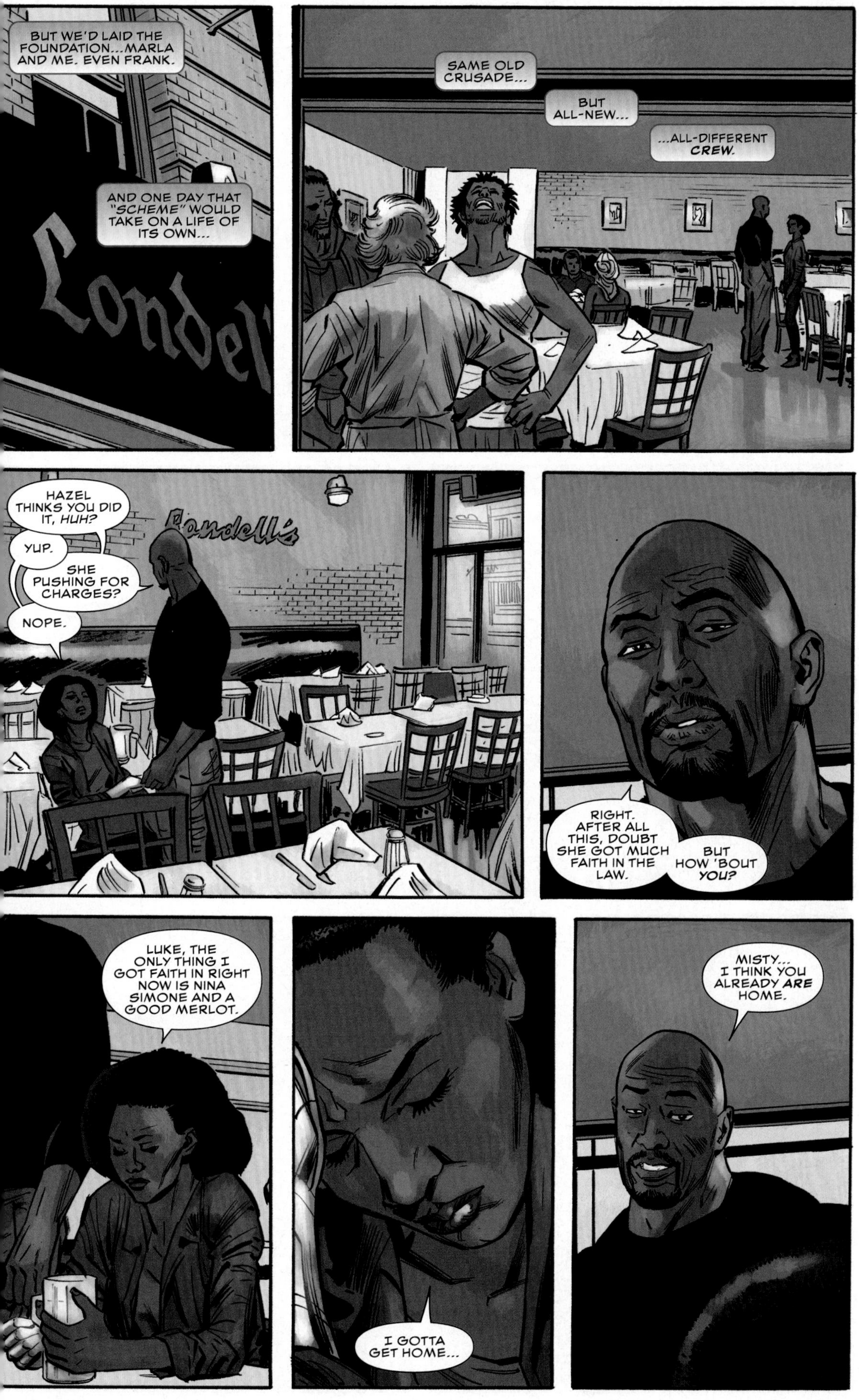
BUT WE'D LAID THE FOUNDATION...MARLA AND ME. EVEN FRANK.
AND ONE DAY THAT "SCHEME" WOULD TAKE ON A LIFE OF ITS OWN...
SAME OLD CRUSADE...
BUT ALL-NEW...
...ALL-DIFFERENT CREW.
HAZEL THINKS YOU DID IT, HUH?
YUP.
SHE PUSHING FOR CHARGES?
NOPE.
RIGHT. AFTER ALL THIS, DOUBT SHE GOT MUCH FAITH IN THE LAW.
BUT HOW 'BOUT YOU?
LUKE, THE ONLY THING I GOT FAITH IN RIGHT NOW IS NINA SIMONE AND A GOOD MERLOT.
I GOTTA GET HOME...
MISTY... I THINK YOU ALREADY ARE HOME.

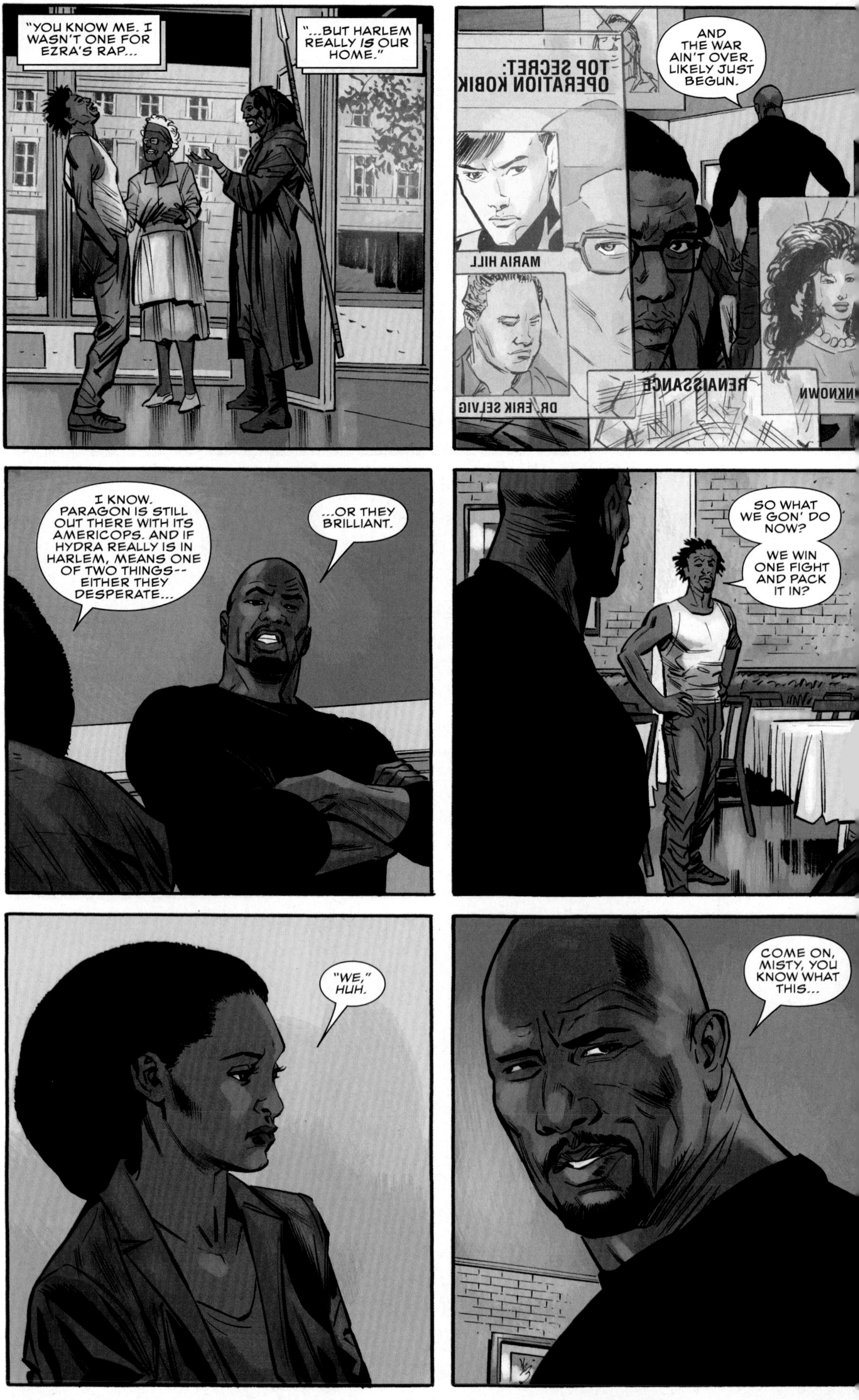
"YOU KNOW ME. I WASN'T ONE FOR EZRA'S RAP...
"...BUT HARLEM REALLY IS OUR HOME."
TOP SECRET: OPERATION KOBIK
MARIA HILL
DR. ERIK SELVIG
RENAISSANCE
AND THE WAR AIN'T OVER. LIKELY JUST BEGUN.
I KNOW. PARAGON IS STILL OUT THERE WITH ITS AMERICOPS. AND IF HYDRA REALLY IS IN HARLEM, MEANS ONE OF TWO THINGS-- EITHER THEY DESPERATE...
...OR THEY BRILLIANT.
SO WHAT WE GON' DO NOW?
WE WIN ONE FIGHT AND PACK IT IN?
"WE," HUH.
COME ON, MISTY, YOU KNOW WHAT THIS...

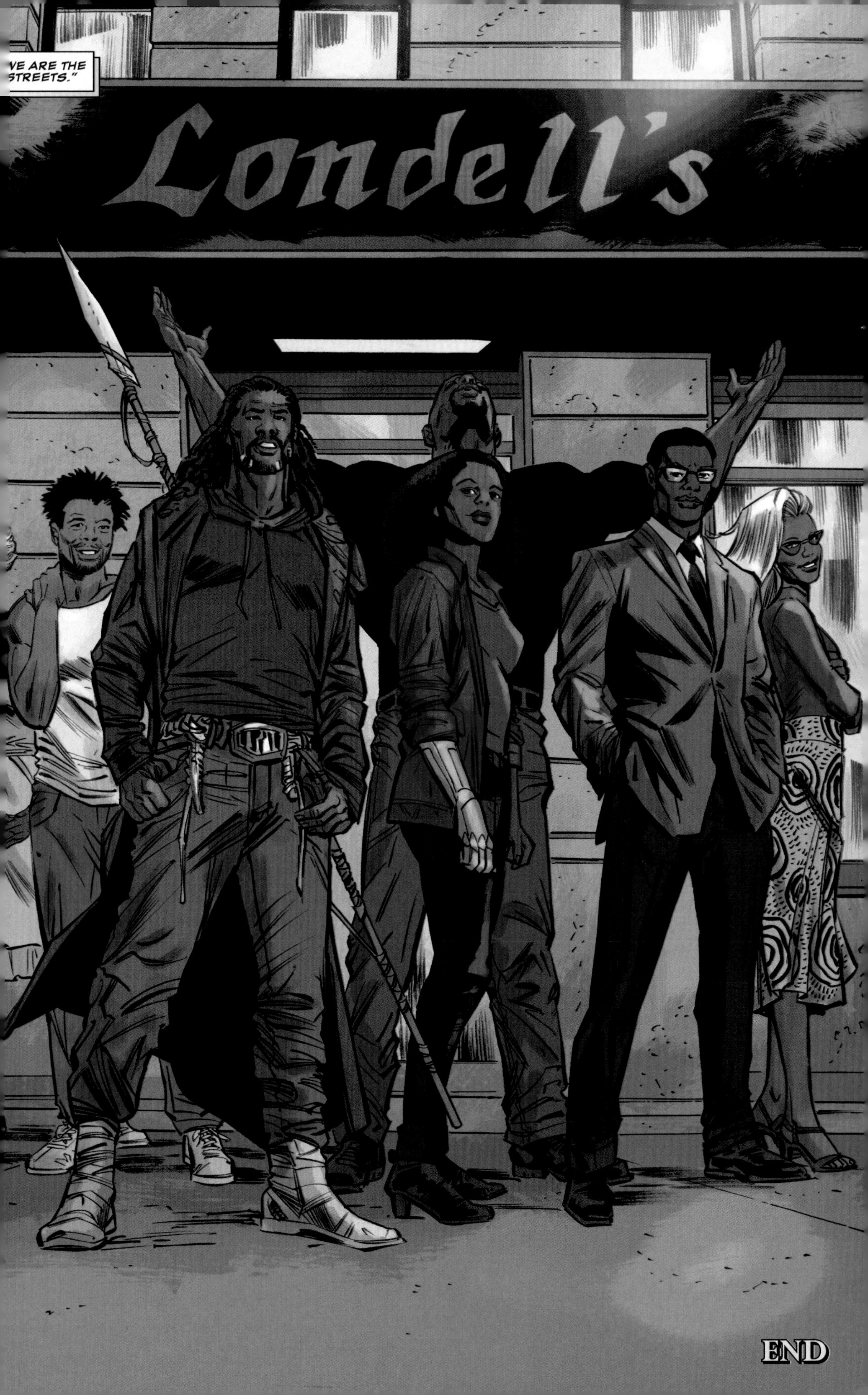

VE ARE THE STREETS."
Londell's
END

BUCKLER

#1 VARIANT
BY **RICH BUCKLER, TOM PALMER** & **RACHELLE ROSENBERG**

LENOX AVE
MALCOLM X BLVD

#1 VARIANT
BY **DAMION SCOTT** & **JOHN RAUCH**

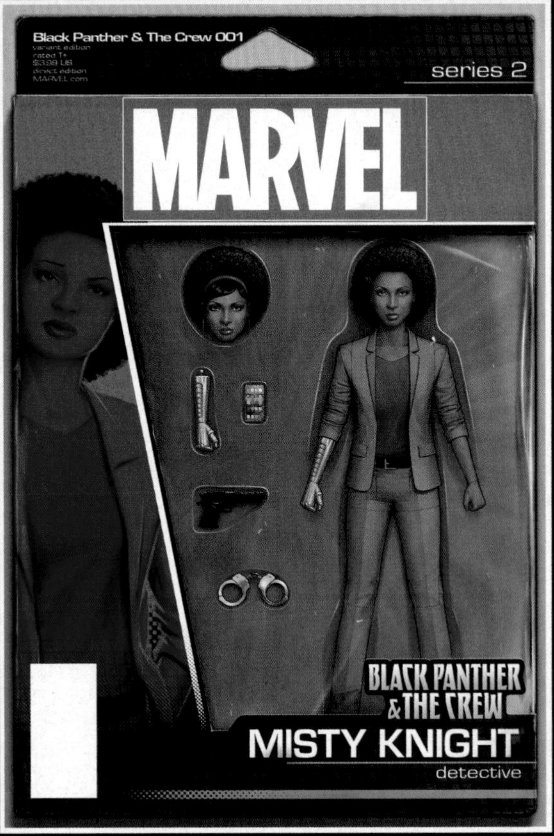
Black Panther & The Crew 001
series 2
MARVEL
BLACK PANTHER & THE CREW
MISTY KNIGHT
detective

#1 ACTION FIGURE VARIANT
BY **JOHN TYLER CHRSTOPHER**

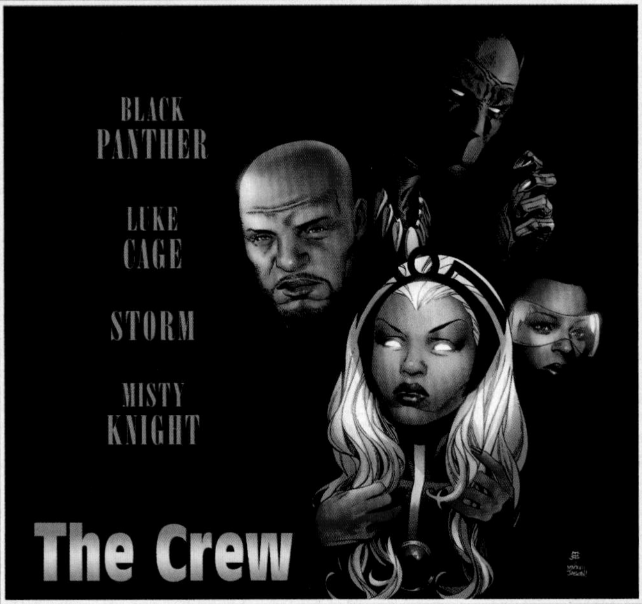
BLACK PANTHER
LUKE CAGE
STORM
MISTY KNIGHT
The Crew

#1 HIP-HOP VARIANT
BY **JIM CHEUNG** & **JASON KEITH**

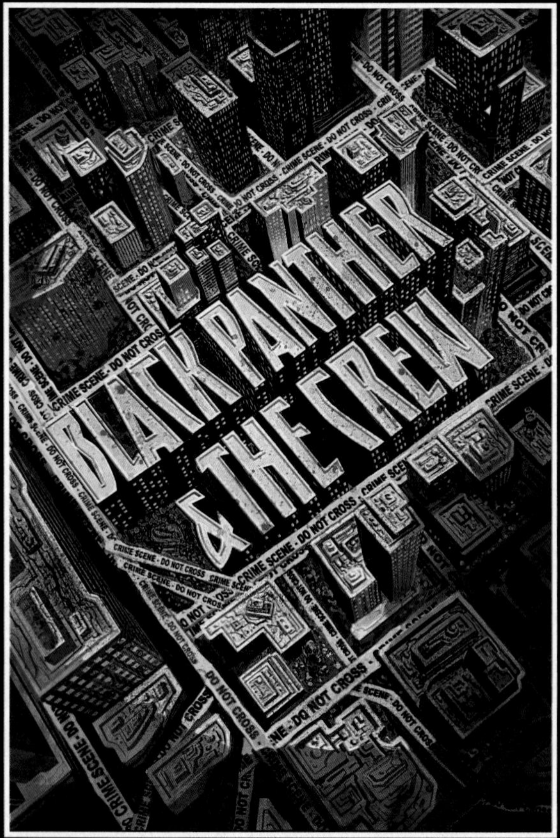
BLACK PANTHER
& THE CREW
CRIME SCENE - DO NOT CROSS

#2 VARIANT
BY **MIKE DEL MUNDO**

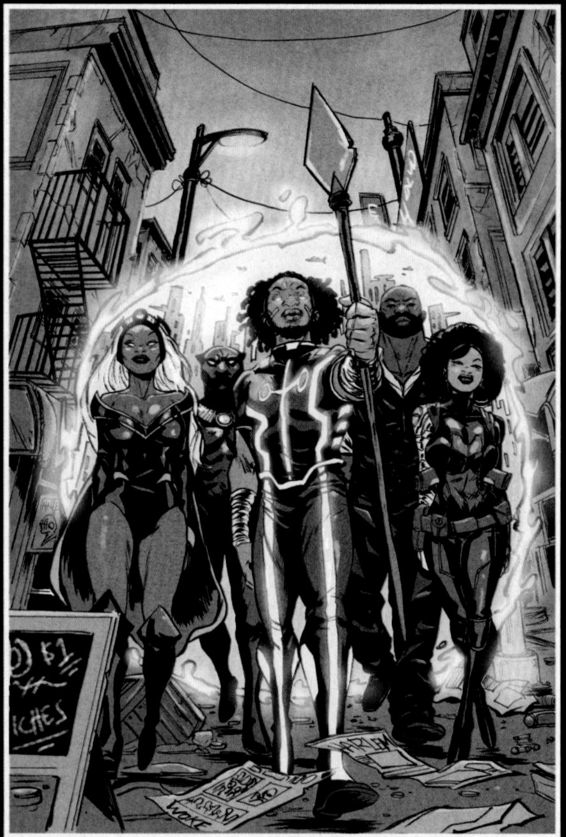
WOKE

#3 VARIANT
BY **SANFORD GREENE**

CHARACTER SKETCHES BY **BUTCH GUICE**

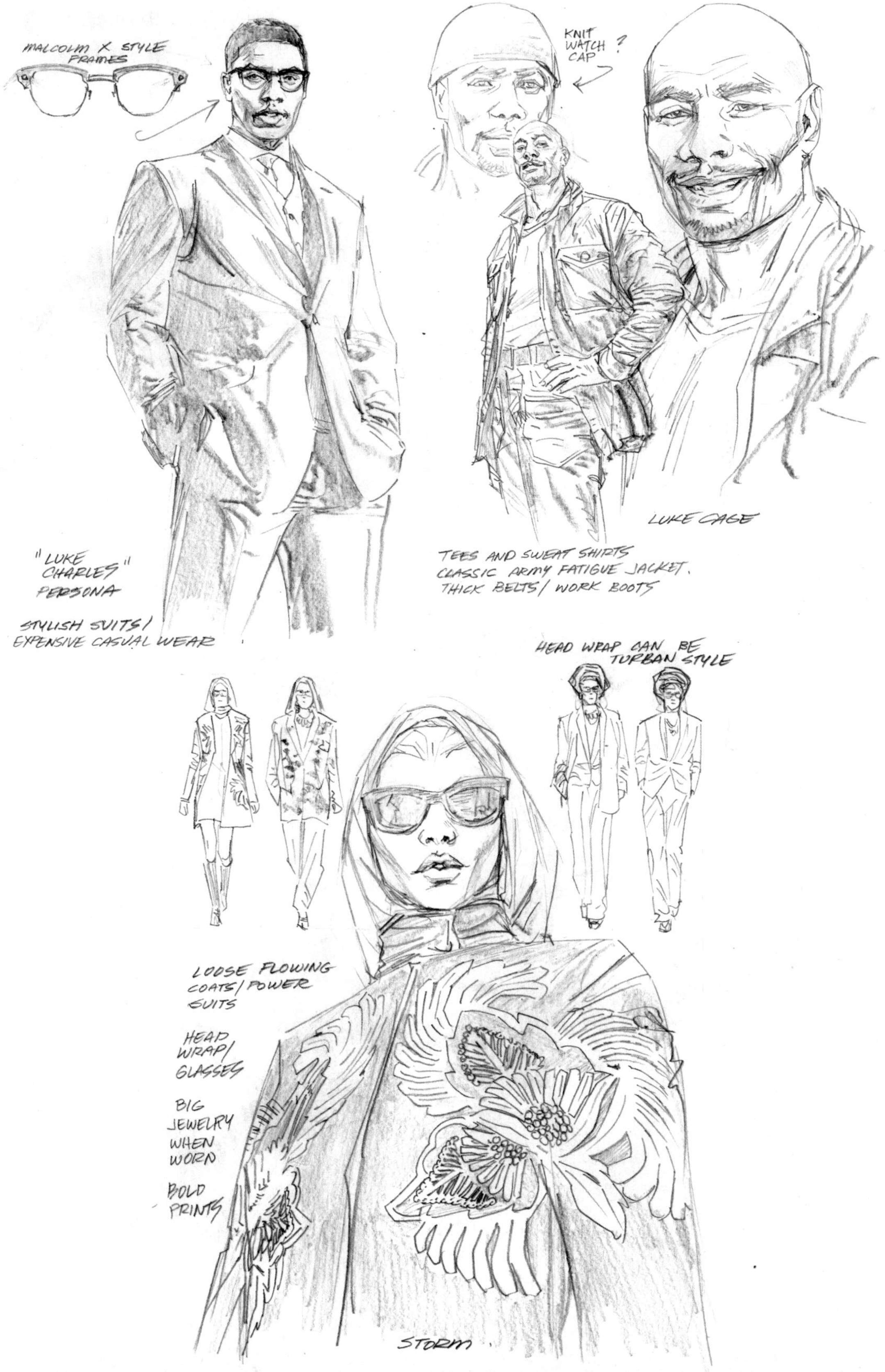

MALCOLM X STYLE FRAMES
KNIT WATCH CAP ?
LUKE CAGE
"LUKE CHARLES" PERSONA
STYLISH SUITS/ EXPENSIVE CASUAL WEAR
TEES AND SWEAT SHIRTS
CLASSIC ARMY FATIGUE JACKET.
THICK BELTS/ WORK BOOTS
HEAD WRAP CAN BE TURBAN STYLE
LOOSE FLOWING COATS/ POWER SUITS
HEAD WRAP/ GLASSES
BIG JEWELRY WHEN WORN
BOLD PRINTS
STORM

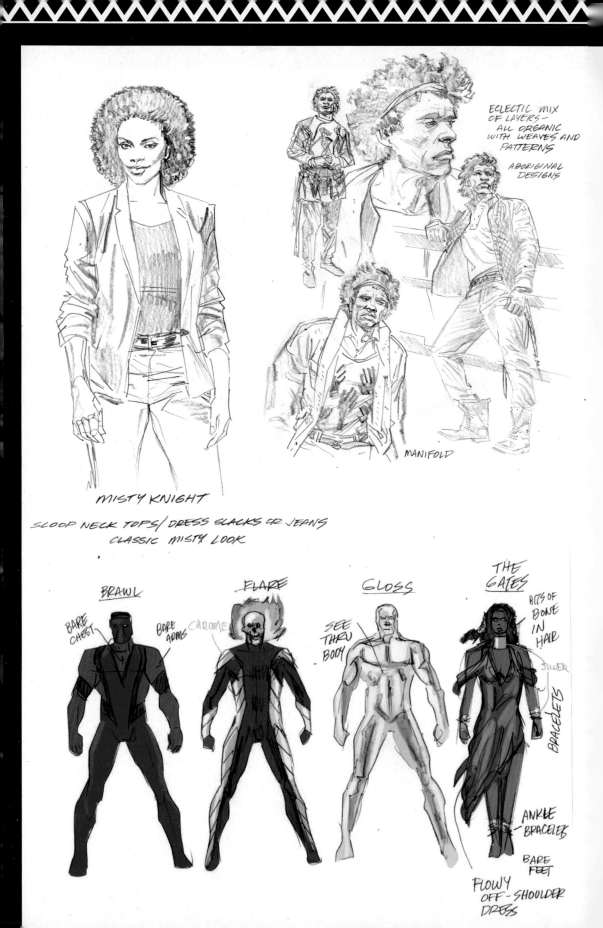

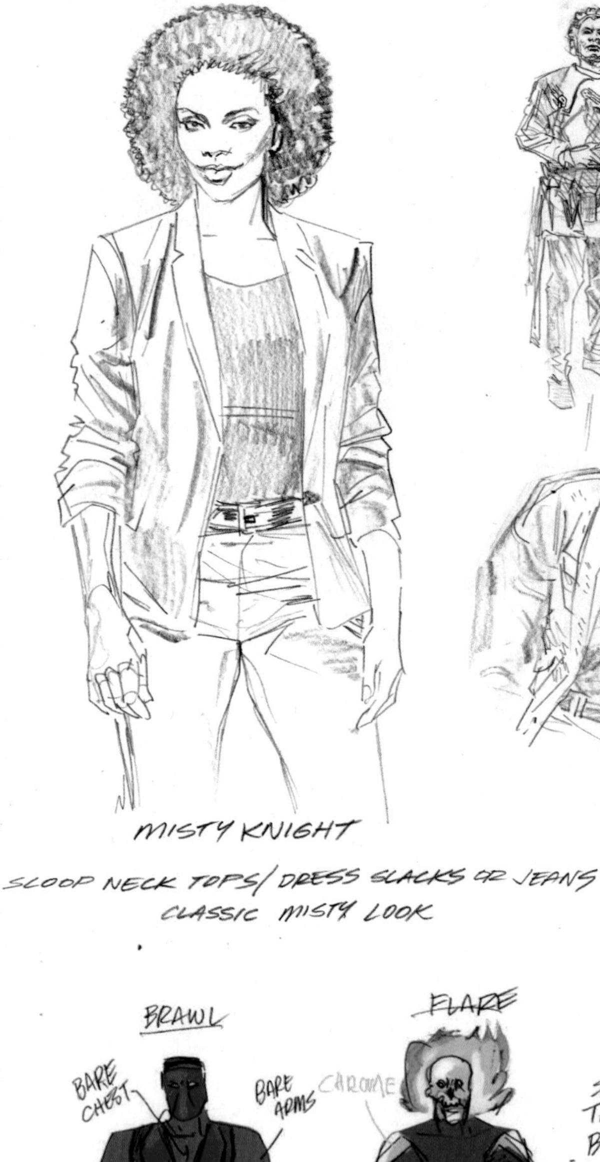
MISTY KNIGHT
SCOOP NECK TOPS/ DRESS SLACKS OR JEANS
CLASSIC MISTY LOOK

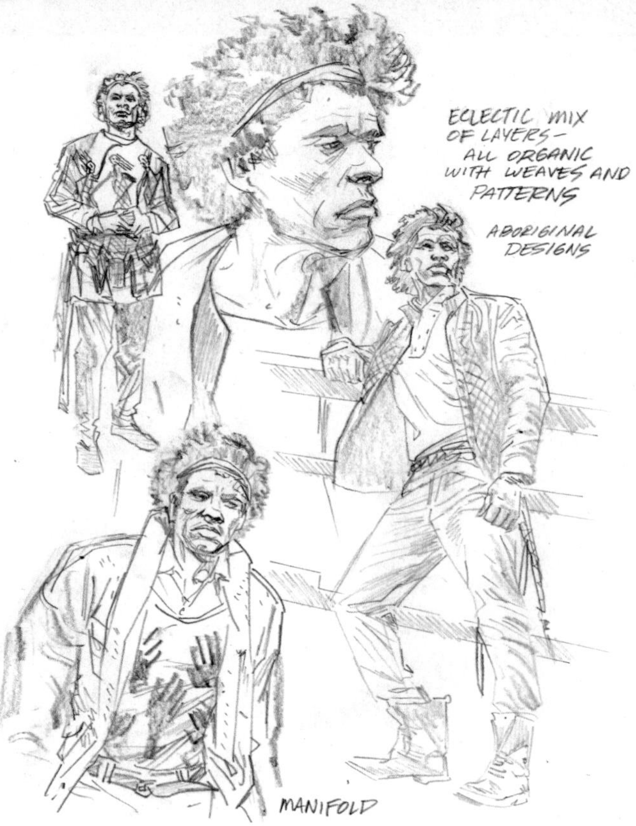
ECLECTIC MIX OF LAYERS— ALL ORGANIC WITH WEAVES AND PATTERNS
ABORIGINAL DESIGNS
MANIFOLD

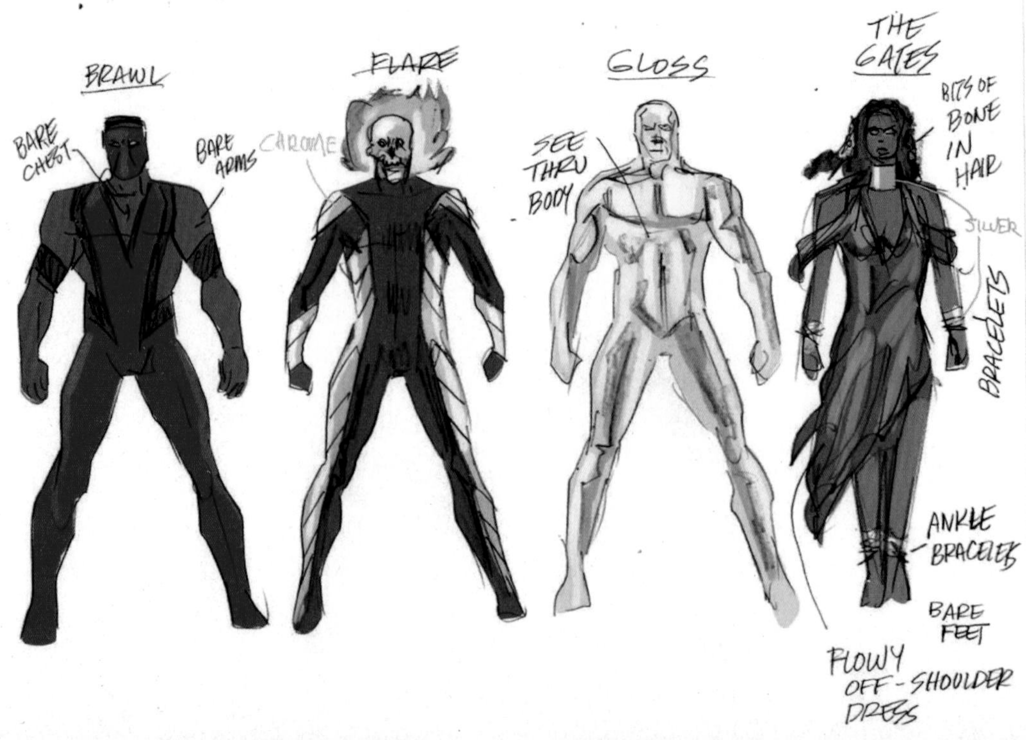
BRAWL
BARE CHEST
BARE ARMS
FLARE
CHROME
GLOSS
SEE THRU BODY
THE GATES
BITS OF BONE IN HAIR
SILVER
BRACELETS
ANKLE BRACELETS
BARE FEET
FLOWY OFF-SHOULDER DRESS